Frankston Library Service

Maconochie's Experiment

Alexander Maconochie, by Rippingville

Maconochie's Experiment

JOHN CLAY

JOHN MURRAY
Albemarle Street, London

By the same author

Culbertson: The Man Who Made Contract Bridge
John Masters: A Regimented Life
Men at Midlife
R. D. Laing: A Divided Self
Tales from the Bridge Table

Contents

Contents

Preface

I first came across Maconochie when I was working at Peper Harow in the 1970s. I had helped set up a residential therapeutic community there for disturbed adolescents, using milieu therapy to bring individuals out of their isolation and develop their unused potential. I had read about earlier penal reformers – John Howard in eighteenth-century England and Philippe Pinel in France in the early nineteenth century – and had also seen the name of Alexander Maconochie used intermittently. In his short time in charge of the convict settlement of Norfolk Island, 1,000 miles off the coast of New South Wales, Maconochie had fought valiantly against political indifference and bureaucratic hostility to rescue those in his care from the dehumanizing cycle of cruelty, despair and degradation that was the usual fate of those sentenced to transportation. References described him as 'ahead of his time'. Indeed Robert Hughes, in his *The Fatal Shore*, went so far as to describe him as 'the one and only inspired penal reformer to work in Australia throughout the whole history of transportation'.

This was quite a sweeping statement. I knew that Australia had been the receptacle for transported convicts, and that they were treated harshly and repressively there. How had Maconochie become involved? I discovered that he had arrived there not expecting to be drawn into the penal system. Shocked by what he saw on his arrival, he devised a new system of treatment, the mark system, a radical departure from existing methods that encouraged convicts to good behaviour as a way of shortening their sentences. As befitted Maconochie's era, the system combined punishment and reform and, with hindsight, came to be seen as the forerunner of twentieth-century methods, the aim being to break the cycle of repeated crime. Not everyone welcomed this new approach, for change, then as now, was viewed with mixed feelings, as this book goes to show.

AUSTRALIA

PACIFIC OCEAN

NORFOLK ISLAND

Sydney

VAN DIEMEN'S LAND

Launceston

Hobart

Mount Pitt 1,039ft

Cascade Bay

NORFOLK ISLAND

Longridge

Military Barracks

Landing place

Government House

Sydney Bay

Cemetery

Prisoners' Barracks

Nepean Island

PACIFIC OCEAN

N
W E
S

Philip Island

Landing place

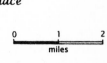

0   1   2
miles

For Harry

Voyage Out

ON 31ST AUGUST 1836 the *Eden*, 513 tons, left Portsmouth bound for Van Diemen's Land (modern Tasmania). On board were more than 250 convicts culled from the hulks in Woolwich and Portsmouth. The *Eden* had been built in London in 1826 and classed A1, and this was her second voyage as a convict ship. Most such vessels were British merchant ships converted to this new use. They were of small or moderate tonnage, usually under 600 tons and square-rigged. The government, as contractor, invariably tried to secure its ships at the lowest rate, while the ship-owners tendered their smaller vessels for two reasons: the voyage out to Australia was risky, and there was little chance of a return cargo.

The skippers were usually of the old type, short, hatchet-bearded men with broad shoulders, able to tell the weather from the ways of fish and birds, aware of the winds and currents of every ocean, standing for no nonsense. The ship's crew were mostly drawn from the lower reaches of society, and officers had often worked their way up from the fo'c'sle. They were hard-drinking, hard-swearing men, recruited mostly from waterside taverns by crimps and press-gangs. Indiscipline was rife and desertions frequent. Musters of convict ships show that many ships arrived two or three short of their full complement of crews. The average age of these tough, quarrelsome crew members was around twenty-five and officers were often no older; in some instances the second and third mates were young-sters of twenty-one.

The voyage out to Australia usually took four to five months. Convict ships sailed as soon as they were full, even in the depths of winter, so as to free space in the overcrowded gaols and hulks. They usually sailed badly and slowly, but speed was not as impor-tant as it was for an emigrant ship with paying passengers.

Four weeks after her departure, in mid-Atlantic, the *Eden* met the *Fairlie*, an emigrant passenger ship also bound for Australia. The two vessels approached within hailing distance and asked for each other's destination. The *Eden* was sailing direct to Van Diemen's Land and offered to wait for an hour to collect any messages from the *Fairlie*, due to stop at the Cape of Good Hope *en route*. A young passenger on board the *Fairlie*, William Henty, watched this mid-ocean encounter and noted in his diary: 'The *Eden* was an interesting object to us, lying so near. The convicts' heads shewed themselves by dozens peering at us, at every opening.' Soon both ships sailed on, but the peering eyes haunted Henty for the rest of his five-month voyage – a recurring image of the dark, unseen side of Australian life that he, like many of his contemporaries, knew so little about.

If life aboard convict ships such as the *Eden* was dark, hidden and confined, with convicts, as Henty's fleeting glimpse showed, being treated as cargo to be transported from one side of the world to the other, then life on the *Fairlie* was a different matter, above board, open and free. The two ships briefly meeting in mid-ocean represented parallel sides of Victorian life, and showed the gulf, so far as Australia was con-cerned, between the bond and the free, each with a prescribed place.

For the emigrant passengers aboard the *Fairlie* Australia repre-sented a land of opportunity where they could enrich, or even reinvent, themselves. At the very least, they could lead a life superior to that in Britain. 'Men that emigrate', wrote W.H. Leigh, a surgeon on a contemporary emigrant ship,

I should take to be divided into two classes: first, those that emigrate from a mature conviction that another land holds forth advantages which their own does not possess, and who are determined to 'rough it', come what may; and these are the people who will find emigration the answer. They will, with due exertion, meet with success, whether they be gentlemen with large families and small capital, labouring men, mechanics and tradesmen. The second class are those wild visionaries who court any new light, and snatch at any bubble which is more attractive than the last they followed. These restless and dissatisfied beings fancy every one is better off than themselves, and that every land enjoys advantages superior to their own.

The most eminent among the *Fairlie's* passengers was Sir John Franklin, the newly appointed Governor of Van Diemen's Land. With him was his private secretary, Alexander Maconochie. For both men, as for many on board the *Fairlie*, the voyage to Australia represented a definite turning-point in their lives. Franklin was a Lincolnshire man, born in 1786, the ninth child of a large middle-class family. Passionate about the sea, he joined the Royal Navy at the age of fourteen and first saw Australia when he accompanied his uncle-by-marriage Captain Matthew Flinders on his famous Australian surveying trip on the *Investigator* in the early 1800s. It was then that he first 'imbibed that zeal for discovery ... which in fact determined the whole character of my life'. Back in the navy in England, Franklin took part in the Battle of Trafalgar aboard the *Bellerophon*, where his 'very conspicuous zeal and activity' were noted. After the Napoleonic Wars Franklin, like many ex-naval captains ashore on half pay, decided to seek fame and glory by becoming an explorer. His quest was to find the North-West Passage, the as yet uncharted Arctic route from the North Atlantic to the Pacific. His first expedition was blocked by ice, and his second in 1819 was halted by bad weather and unhelpful native traders and trading companies. Half of his party of ten had to turn back, while Franklin himself and four others struggled to reach the Arctic. Extreme hunger forced them to eat their boots, having boiled them first.

John Franklin

Franklin survived, but only just. One member of the party went delirious through starvation, and murdered and ate a fellow expedition member.

After a brief marriage to Eleanor Anne Porden, a lively young poet who soon died of tuberculosis, leaving a young daughter, Eleanor, Sir John married again. His second wife was another forthright, intelligent woman, Jane Griffin, the daughter of a wealthy London silk merchant. Eight years into their marriage Franklin was offered the post of Governor of Van Diemen's Land, at a salary of £2,500 a year. Lord Glenelg, the Secretary of State for the Colonies, wrote to him, 'I shall be very happy if you feel yourself enabled to accept this important and interesting station. I beg you will take time to consider the matter and consult with your friends – but it would be desirable if you could with perfect convenience let me know your decision by the end of next week.' Franklin accepted, but, not wanting to jeopardize his naval career, insisted on an assurance from the Admiralty that it would not 'militate against my future employment in the active line of my profession, to which I am devoted'.

Alexander Maconochie, Franklin's private secretary, was born in 1787 in Edinburgh, where his father took over the post of customs commissioner from the economist Adam Smith. However, when the boy was just nine years old his father died and the young Alexander was sent to live with his paternal uncle Allan Maconochie, a prominent Edinburgh lawyer (later to become Lord Meadowbank). The uncle wanted to make his young ward a lawyer too, but Alexander had other ideas. He was thrusting, ambitious, personable and, possibly because of this chequered past, a bit chippy. His restlessness got the better of him and he went off to sea, enlisting as a first-class volunteer in August 1803 at the age of fifteen. It undoubtedly hurt his family. When he looked back later in life, Maconochie reflected: 'I was about fifteen before I was enabled, with much difficulty, to break away to sea.' The addition of 'with much difficulty' indicates the family resistance, but also shows the young Maconochie's determination.

Family connections mattered in those days, and Maconochie's uncle had him placed 'under the special care' of the Hon. Sir Alexander Inglis Cochrane, captain of the *Northumberland*, a 74-gun ship of the line, now on the Mediterranean station. Maconochie enjoyed shipboard life, its routines, sudden spurts of activity and chance encounters with enemy ships. While off the coast of Spain, he took up learning Spanish, aided by trips ashore. Indeed he became so keen on his studies that it soon earned him the *sobriquet* of 'Our Colleges' from his fellow midshipmen, a slightly mocking term that hinted at an excess of enthusiasm. The *Northumberland* went to the West Indies in pursuit of the French squadron and on the journey Maconochie followed 'the earnest exhortations of the admiral' to continue his studies, 'especially in modern languages and mathematics'. It seemed to work, as it 'procured' him notice from the superior officers of the fleet. There was a particular moment when he got close to the seat of power.

In the West Indies commenced my chief fighting experience, and here I, for the first and only time in my life, saw, and was even in a sort brought into contact with, Nelson. It was on the occasion of his rapid chase of the French fleet to the West Indies, some months before Trafalgar. He first touched at Antigua, thence passed by some of the other islands to Trinidad, receiving some slight reinforcements, among which was our ship, the *Northumberland*, 74, and finally hove to off Port d'Espagne, in the Gulf of Paria, when he was waited on by the admiral and captains present, and received the latest information. I was midshipman in the boat with Sir Alexander Cochrane, and was then for about an hour alongside and aboard the *Victory*. I was standing on her quarter-deck, when Lord Nelson came out of the cabin, with a large glass under his arm, and crossing to where I stood on the lee side, he said to me, 'Youngster, give me a shoulder,' and made a motion so to employ me; but, changing his mind, he turned up the poop ladder, and I never saw him afterwards. He looked heated and impatient, and finding the French fleet had sailed, in about an hour followed, and again made sail for England.

Proximity to the great spurred Maconochie on. He was transferred to the *Belle Isle* (74 guns), which helped defeat the French at the Battle of Santo Domingo and laid siege to various French, Spanish, Danish and Swedish islands in the West Indies. Maconochie was twice wounded in these skirmishes, as well as catching yellow fever. But his ascent continued and he was made lieutenant aboard Captain Thomas Cochrane's ship, the frigate *Ethalion*. Cochrane, the son of Sir Alexander, was a buccaneering figure and involved Maconochie in a full-blooded seafaring existence. Once the *Ethalion* was in home waters, Maconochie transferred to the *Grasshopper*, an 18-gun brig now on the Baltic station. In December 1811 the Baltic fleet of over 200 vessels was on its way back to Britain for Christmas when they encountered one of the worst storms in British naval history. Maconochie, on board the *Grasshopper*, was in charge of the middle watch from midnight to 4 a.m. By now the wind had increased to gale force and it was bitterly cold. At about 3 a.m. he suddenly saw the *Hero* (74 guns) veer across his bow as if sounding. He instantly eased his own helm over and passed behind her stern. It was a fortunate decision, for, just as he did so, the *Hero* foundered and struck fast on the sandy bottom close to the Dutch shore. Maconochie's ship also went aground momentarily. Captain Fanshawe, the officers and crew of the *Grasshopper* all hurried up on deck.

The official report went on:

At half-past three the hands were turned up, the ship being in broken water, we found we were on a sandbank, the pilots imagining it to be Smith's Knoll [off Winterton]. The captain instantly ordered the brig to be steered SSE, thinking to get out to sea, but she continued striking so hard for a length of time that we had almost given her up for lost, when suddenly and very fortunately, we fell into three fathoms water, upon which the captain caused an anchor to be let go. We again perceived the *Hero* (as we then thought) also at an anchor, though she fired guns and burnt blue lights; but, when day broke, we had the mortification of witnessing a most horrific scene; the *Hero* was totally dismasted; and on her larboard beam ends, with her head to the NE about a mile from us, upon the Haek's [Haake] Sand, as we then found we were inside of it, off the Texel Island: the ship's company were all crowded together on the poop and forecastle. As soon as the daylight had well appeared she hoisted a flag of truce and fired a gun, which we repeated, and very shortly after saw a lugger, two brigs, and several small vessels, plying out of the Texel to our assistance; but owing to the flood tide having made, and the wind blowing a perfect gale at NNW the lugger was only able to come within two or three miles of us by two o'clock in the afternoon. In the meantime we hoisted out our boats, and made an attempt to get near the *Hero*, but the surf was so high that it was all ineffectual, and we were under the cruel necessity of seeing so many of our brave countrymen perishing, without being able to render them any assistance. The *Grasshopper* at the same time was constantly striking very hard, though everything had been thrown overboard to lighten her, except the guns, upon which it was feared she would have bilged. The master was then sent to sound in every direction, for a passage to make our escape by (though I have since found out, that an escape was totally impossible); but quarter less three, and two fathoms and a half were the only soundings he could meet with. The captain, therefore, with the opinion of the officers, agreed, that we had no chance of saving ourselves, but by surrendering to the enemy, who were at this time, as I have before mentioned, coming to our assistance, and that of the *Hero*, from whose wreck, I am sorry to say, not one soul has been saved. At close of day, finding the weather threatening to be worse, and the brig striking so repeatedly, we cut the cable and ran for the port in view; when we approached the lugger, which was at this time anchored, she sent a pilot to us, who took us into the Texel (Niewe Diep), where we surrendered to the Dutch squadron, under the command of Admiral de Winter, who, I must in justice say, has behaved to us in the most humane and attentive manner. They also used every means in their power to save the crew of the *Hero*; but the badness of the weather rendered it totally impossible. We lost only one man, Mr King the pilot, who was killed by a capstern bar, which flew out as we were heaving in cable to put service in the hawse.

The *Hero* lost 600 men, with no survivors. In all, some 2,000 men and nearly 200 vessels were lost that night, including the *Hero*, the *St George* (98 guns), the flagship of Admiral Reynolds, and the *Defence* (74 guns). The Dutch coast was strewn for miles around with ships' fragments and bodies.

Maconochie, looking back on this incident, viewed his instinctive reaction as lucky. 'Had I not, by an apparent accident, and, in fact, under the influence of a mistake, altered the ship's course, we should have taken the ground on our broadside; in five minutes we should have been turned over, and have perished to a man.' He added a detail that seemed significant to him at the time and later: 'In the midst of our danger, an incident almost ludicrous occurred, which I well remember as if yesterday. A small scamp of a boy rushed up in the confusion to ask what we were about, and an old boatswain's mate, named Cossie, called out with his rough, good-humoured voice, "Take care of that boy, he is my only hope now," intimating, even at the time, to the infinite amusement of the rest of the crew, that he was surely not born to be drowned.' Maconochie said he often thought of this afterwards, as a sign, too, that he was fated to survive and eventually to find his own destiny later on in life.

The officers and crew of *Grasshopper* were handed over by the Dutch to the French as prisoners of war and marched across country to Sedan in northern France, 400 miles away. From Sedan they were sent on to the fortress at Verdun. It was now February 1812, and Maconochie's spirits sank. 'We had nothing to look forward to but a protracted and harsh confinement.' In prison with him were an English lawyer and his wife, unluckily detained while on honeymoon in France when war broke out. At the husband's instigation Maconochie took up studying law again, and even thought of changing his profession back to it. He now spent two and a half years in captivity, an experience that gave him firsthand experience of a confined, often despairing, existence far away from home. This was to be crucial later on.

After Napoleon's defeat and exile to Elba in 1814, Maconochie was freed and rejoined the navy, again under Cochrane's command. Cochrane was now commander-in-chief of the British fleet on the American coast and as adventurous as ever: 'he kept the whole of the sea coast in a continual state of alarm.' They sailed up the Potomac to launch a successful attack on Washington but were later defeated at New Orleans. Maconochie soon had his first command as captain of the *Trave*, and afterwards of the *Calliope*, a 'very clever, handy' 10-gun brig. On the *Calliope* he was sent to Quebec to collect some of the British army and transport them back home in the run-up to Waterloo. Another incident of future use took place.

At Quebec, the idea first occurred to me of a principle in discipline which I afterwards carried into effect ... It was that of mutual responsibility among my men. Peace having just been concluded in

America, and preparations for hostilities, consequent upon the escape of Buonaparte from Elba, having commenced in England, desertion from our shipping of men anxious to hasten to the seat of war was almost universal. To check it, it became common in our fleet to grant no leave of absence. I had previously given this liberally, and was unwilling to stop it at once. It occurred to me to grant it on a system requiring those who obtained it to return on board before their companions in the watch or boat to which they belonged could receive the same favour; and, without saying that no one every broke this compact, I may assert that such a breach of faith very seldom occurred. Return from leave became the rule, instead of the rare exception.

He was making each member of his crew responsible for the others, an early experiment in group pressure, and an indication too of his willingness to adapt to circumstances, to improvise. He was relying on his intuition or instinct, and it reinforced his belief in the essential co-operativeness of man, his mutuality.

On the way home from Quebec another chance to show initiative arose.

After six weeks' detention at Quebec, the troops were ready to embark, and I was selected to hasten before and announce their approaching departure. My only orders were to lose no time by the way, and I thus was led to make another experiment, which gave me at the time great anxiety, but proved eventually most successful. We had a fair and even fresh wind all the way home, but one of the thickest and most continuous fogs I almost ever saw. With the fleet behind us we could not afford to be cautious, so I had a bucket of water drawn almost every ten minutes during the voyage, and a thermometer plunged into it, concluding that on approaching an iceberg the temperature would fall. I was a young captain then, and, with my first lieutenant and master, kept on deck day and night, watching the glass incessantly. As it happened, the temperature did not vary materially throughout, but the freedom with which we were enabled thus to run gave us an extremely short-passage, I think nineteen days from land to land, while the fleet behind us was not less than thirty days, to our infinite gratification.

After Waterloo, Maconochie, like so many other naval captains, was retired ashore on half pay. He returned to live with his mother in Warriston Crescent, to the east of his native Edinburgh. Now aged twenty-eight, he was uncertain what to do next, but mindful of his seafaring experience, he wrote his first pamphlet, *Considerations on the propriety of establishing a colony in one of the Sandwich Islands. Being the substance of a memoir submitted to . . . the Secretary of State for War and Colonies*, and sent it off to the Colonial Office in 1816, presumably hoping for a posting. The Sandwich Islands were in the Pacific, and Maconochie's line was that they could become naval and commercial outposts like Malta or Gibraltar, to be used by whalers or as revictualling harbours for naval and deep-sea ships. Strategically they would be able to monitor Russia's presence in the Pacific, since Russia was always seen as a threat. His proposals were to the point, as not long afterwards Stamford Raffles set up just such a commercial and naval outpost in Singapore. In his pamphlet Maconochie argued that, unless action was taken quickly, the Sandwich Islands would fall into the hands of Russia or the United States of America. His prediction came true, as they were soon annexed by the United States and renamed Hawaii.

Two years later Maconochie wrote a longer publication, still on the Pacific. This was *A Summary View of the Statistics and Existing Commerce of the Principal Shores of the Pacific Ocean. With a Sketch of the Advantages, political and commercial, which would result from the establishment of a Central Free Port within its Limits; and also of one in the Southern Atlantic viz. within the territory of the Cape of Good Hope, conferring on this latter, in particular, the same privilege of direct trade with India and the northern Atlantic, bestowed lately on Malta and Gibraltar.* It covered much the same ground, stressing Britain's underappreciation of the importance, commercial or otherwise, of the Pacific. It received favourable reviews, notably in *Blackwood's Magazine*: 'this very interesting and entertaining little volume has been illustrated with considerable variety of historical anecdote and allusion, and ... heightened by an exceedingly precise and perspicuous general arrangement.' New

South Wales was briefly mentioned: 'the most important object [of a convict colony] is the reform of convicts, not their punishment only, and still less their exile', he wrote, and 'prisoners' liberation ought to depend upon their own exertion, not solely upon the lapse of time' – ideas that were to resurface later.

In 1821 his mother died and the next year, now aged thirty-five, Maconochie married Mary Hutton Browne, an army officer's daughter from Bamburgh, Northumberland. She was eight years younger than him. Their first child, Mary Ann, was born ten months later, in 1823, and they then moved to a larger house, Northcliff, at North Queensferry, just across the Firth of Forth to the west of the Forth Bridge. It had a farm attached and the aim was to become self-sufficient. Two more children Catherine and Alexander, were soon born. As there was no school at North Queensferry, Maconochie enterprisingly built and started one up himself. He took a close interest in local affairs, challenging the local ferry company to improve its services with another pamphlet, entitled *Principles of Ferrying: A Memorial on the Present State and Capabilities of the Queen's Ferry Passage.*

Farming proved unprofitable, and in 1828, with a growing family (he was to have six children in all – two girls and four boys), Maconochie moved south with his family to London. They lived first in Bloomsbury, at 15 Great Russell Street, next door to the British Museum, where he continued his writing career with tracts on *Steam Navigation* and *Thoughts on the present state and future commercial policy of the country; with a plan of a periodical work to be confined exclusively to commercial subjects.* In London he recontacted former naval acquaintances such as the Arctic explorer George Back, Sir John Barrow (then Second Secretary at the Admiralty), Captain (later Admiral) Francis Beaufort (inventor of the Beaufort scale) and another old naval friend, Franklin. Some of these were members of an exclusive dining club, the Raleigh Club, at whose fortnightly dinners a menu made up of specialities chosen by a particular member from an unusual part of the world he knew, or had been travelling in, was served. The menu for their inaugural dinner was reindeer from

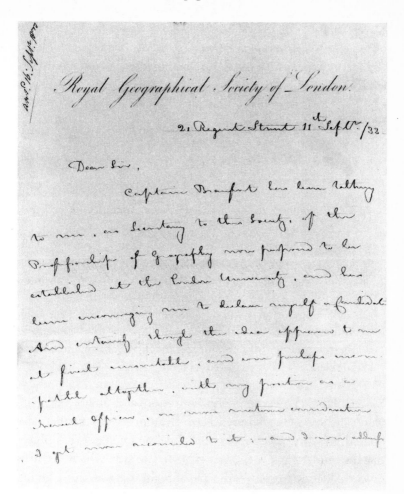

Maconochie's letter of application for the post of Professor of
Geography at London University, 1833

Spitsbergen and crystallized berries from Lapland. The Raleigh
Club led to the formation of the Geographical Society (the royal
charter was granted when William IV became patron).
Maconochie was appointed its first secretary on 16th July 1830,
his candidature supported by Barrow, among others. As secretary,
Maconochie's tasks were to arrange lectures, records the minutes
of society meetings, edit the society's journal (and negotiate with

Mr Murray of Albemarle Street to have it published), purchase books and maps, and generally take care of finances.

Maconochie was clearly a competent secretary, and this in part led to his second appointment as first Professor of Geography at London University. His candidature was seconded this time by Beaufort:

> I cannot but think that the character he has established and the talents he has displayed as Secretary to the Royal Geographical Society must render any individual recommendation superfluous. I shall confine myself to the knowledge he possesses and his power of imparting it to his pupils. With respect to the first, I am not acquainted with any person who has acquired a greater stock of accurate geographic information – or who has larger and sounder views on that widely comprehensive subject – or who can more clearly convey that information, or illustrate those views by apposite and interesting facts. But the second point – the power and habit of communication – is a far more essential quality in a lecturer, and it is on this ground that I consider him to be peculiarly suited to the vacant chair.

Maconochie's power of communication and ability to relate were already being stressed, but Beaufort went further and praised 'the unwearied zeal with which he pursues every object that he undertakes – the benevolent warmth which he feels towards young people – the pleasure he derives from giving instruction, joined to the experience he has had in education – and the fluency with which he can vary his explanations so as to adapt them to the different capacities of the class', adding 'all these appear to me to constitute the true characteristics of a public teacher.' Maconochie's inaugural lectures as Professor of Geography attracted large, distinguished audiences. *The Times* commented on the 'luminous view' he gave of the adventures of Captain Ross in the Arctic and Captain Burnes in Afghanistan and noted his first lecture was attended by over 350 people, which 'showed how well he is qualified in his office'.

In 1836, three years later, Maconochie's friend Franklin suddenly invited him to be his private secretary in Van Diemen's Land. Franklin had just been appointed Governor there, his first civil appointment, and he wanted an old and trusted friend to be at his side. Maconochie's immediate response was to hesitate; after all he was now becoming well established, with an important position in London life. But his old restlessness and adventurous spirit came to the fore, and the far Pacific had always been one of his interests. In addition, Franklin offered to help him find something better and more remunerative once they were in Australia. Maconochie agreed to take up Franklin's offer and resigned his posts at the Royal Geographical Society and at the University of London, although his family, understandably enough, was less keen to go.

By the time of his departure on the *Fairlie*, Maconochie had already been approached with regard to other projects he might undertake in Van Diemen's Land. This was common practice at the time: many a traveller to a distant land was asked by a London-based philanthropic society to perform some such useful task on its behalf once he had arrived at his far-off destination. Maconochie's first commission was from the Society for the Diffusion of Useful Knowledge, which asked him to take suitable books out with him to Van Diemen's Land as a means of 'informing and benefiting the convict population there', though the real aim of this exercise was to 'polish and enlarge the minds of their Masters'. Maconochie agreed and busied himself with this before he left, obtaining grants towards it of £20 each from the Religious Tract Society and the Religious Reform Society.

More importantly, however, Maconochie agreed to undertake a commission from the Society for the Improvement of Prison Discipline. The society, founded in 1816, had by now become the foremost pressure group outside parliament for penal reform. It published detailed, closely argued reports from its findings, and its influence was considerable as its trustees included dukes, bishops, MPs and luminaries such as Thomas Fowell Buxton and William Wilberforce. It asked Maconochie to answer a list of sixty-seven questions on the methods of convict management in

Van Diemen's Land. Maconochie immediately recognized the significance and sensitivity of this and wisely showed the survey to Sir George Grey, then Under-Secretary to Lord Glenelg at the Colonial Office, before he left Britain. Grey had approved of the project, but asked Maconochie to send his answers to the questions back first to him at the Colonial Office before being sent on to the Society for the Improvement of Prison Discipline. Grey put it thus: 'We desire no concealments whatsoever, our object is truth, the whole truth, but we must require it to come *first* to us, the inconvenience is very great of statements from authority first meeting us outside.' Distances at that time being so enormous and communications so lengthy – a letter took at least four months to reach Australia, and the reply would take just as long – the British government always exercised caution over unofficial reports arriving home from distant lands and wanted to have a good look at them first. Maconochie agreed to follow this procedure.

The first question the society wanted Maconochie to answer was: 'On landing in the colony, under whose care and superintendence are the convicts placed?' Most of the questions that followed were similarly factual. The final one, however, gave him a wide-ranging brief: 'Make such general remarks as occur on the whole convict system of the colony, and its effects on the moral and social state of the community: also remark on the effect of the latter, and enter on the subject largely, making any observation which may be useful in regard thereto.' Maconochie's reply to this question was to have momentous consequences.

Transportation

BY THE TIME transportation to Australia was finally abandoned in 1868, 161,021 men and 24,900 women had been sent there. Most were sent either to New South Wales or Van Diemen's Land, but a few were also sent in the later stages to Western Australia. There were only three terms of sentence: about half of those transported were sent out for seven years, a quarter were sent for fourteen years and a quarter were transported for life. Their average age was twenty-six, three-quarters were single, and most were from the working classes. Two thirds were Protestant, and one third Catholic, and men outnumbered women by six to one.

Transportation began in the first Elizabethan era. A Vagrancy Act of 1597 allowed for 'Rogues, Vagabonds and Sturdy Beggars' to be banished from the realm and 'conveyed to such parts beyond the seas' as could receive them. Transportation grew rapidly when the American colonies were founded at the start of the seventeenth century. Criminals sentenced to death in Britain had their sentences commuted and were sent out as labour to work on the new tobacco and cotton plantations in Virginia and Maryland. Sir Thomas Dale, Marshal of Virginia, took with him 300 'disorderly persons' in 1611 but these proved to be so 'profane and mutinous ... diseased and crazed' that 'not sixty of them may be employed'. Yet the policy was continued. New settlements in America needed more labour, and convicts, including some political prisoners such as those captured by Cromwell in the early 1650s, continued to be sent there.

Up to the time of the American War of Independence some 40,000 convicts were sent out from Britain in this way, a quarter of them Irish. When the American colonies inconveniently rebelled in 1775, no more could be sent, but by now America had its own resident work-force, with black West African slaves arriving in increasing numbers. Having lost this favoured outlet, British prisons soon filled up again. Something had to be done. With typical arrogance, Britain assumed it would be able to continue to send convicts out to America once the 'troubles' there had been sorted out. George III wrote to Lord North accordingly: 'Undoubtedly the Americans cannot expect nor ever will receive any favour from Me, but the permitting them to obtain Men unworthy to remain in this Island I shall certainly consent to.'

A stopgap measure was needed which, as often happens in British institutional life, became a permanent solution. The naval transports which had formerly carried transported convicts across the Atlantic were now pressed into service as hulks, stationary prisons in harbours such as Plymouth and Portsmouth or the Thames estuary, housing between 400 and 500 men. Former men-of-war, many of them lying abandoned in southern naval ports, their masts and rigging rotten, were also used. The *Bellerophon* (old '*Billy Ruffian*' as she was known), on which Sir John Franklin served at Trafalgar, was one such vessel. But so crowded did these hulks become that disease was rife and typhus endemic. Healthy citizens feared to go on board.

While hulks were being set up as overflow prisons, a longer-term solution was being sought. Transportation had solved the prison crisis before, so why not try it again? Gibraltar and West Africa were considered as possible outlets. Australia was then an unknown continent and had only recently been discovered by Captain Cook in 1770. In 1779 the government committee looking into transportation summoned the botanist Sir Joseph Banks to their meeting as he had accompanied Cook on his first expedition. Banks spoke of Botany Bay, so named by him because of the variety of plants growing there. It sounded suitable. A strategic outlet such as Australia would benefit as it could oversee Far Eastern trade routes, so vital to British prosperity at that time, and deny France power in the East. Cook's second voyage there, on the *Resolution*, in 1774, had yielded another reason in favour of Australia. He had discovered Norfolk Island, a remote spot a thousand miles off the coast of Australia in the western Pacific. On landing he noticed it was stocked with tall pine trees and wild flax. In the eighteenth century pine trees and flax had considerable importance for the navy. Ships' masts were made of pine, and flax was used for their sailcloth. Pine trees had a natural straightness and their resin lubricated the friction between the fibres in their grain, giving much needed suppleness in heavy seas. A full ship-of-the-line needed a main mast at least 3 feet thick and over 100 feet high. At the time most mast timbers came from Riga in the Russian Baltic, but bringing them back by ship to Britain was a hazardous journey through

A hulk off Woolwich, with a convict ship alongside

enemy Dutch and French fleets. When the government committee heard of Norfolk Island pines waiting to provide mast timbers and of the island's indigenous flax plant *phornium tenax* ready to be reaped, its choice of Botany Bay as the next destination for renewed transportation was settled. The First Fleet, comprising six convict ships transporting 558 male and 192 female convicts, sailed from Spithead in May 1787 under Captain Arthur Phillip and arrived in Botany Bay in January 1788.

In eighteenth-century England more than 200 crimes were punishable by death. In the 1820s this number was reduced by Peel to about 100, divided into three classes: first, murder and those offences likely to lead to murder, for which people were always hanged; second, arson, highway robbery and piracy, for which execution was very frequent; and third, those offences, mostly fraud, where the punishment of death was pronounced but never executed. Most of the latter were commuted to transportation. L.L. Robson, in his book *The Convict Settlers of Australia*, carried out a comprehensive survey of male convicts transported. Four-fifths, he calculated, were transported for 'offences against property'. Of these, 34 per cent were for unspecified larcenies; 15 per cent for particular offences such as burglary (including housebreaking); 13 per cent for stealing domestic or farm animals (poaching, in fact, accounted for less than 0.3 per cent); and 6 per cent for 'theft of wearing apparel', a revealing statistic since it shows how ill clothed the poor then were. A further 3 per cent were for 'offences against the person', which included assault, rape, kidnapping, sodomy, manslaughter and murder. About 4 per cent were sent for 'offences of a public nature', which included 'coining' bad money, treason, conspiracy to riot, or being a member of a trade union or of an Irish secret society such as the Ribbonmen or Whiteboys. A tiny percentage had committed bigamy, while even fewer were transported for smuggling or for perjury.

The law on thieving was very complicated, since many types of larceny still merited capital punishment. Much depended on the value of the goods stolen and on the method used, namely whether the theft was from a person in the street, or by house-breaking, or by 'putting in fear' the victim. It was a capital offence, for example, to steal goods to the value of more than 5s. if this was from a shop, more than 1s. from housebreaking, or more than 40s. from a common dwelling-house. Prosecutors and juries often deliberately undervalued stolen property to ensure the death sentence was not pronounced, which explains why cases can be found where the value of goods stolen was written down as worth exactly 10d. or 39s. This deflating of value also helps to explain why many convicts were transported for seemingly less serious crimes than was actually the case. Judges and magistrates could use their discretion in deciding who was to be transported, taking into account a man's past record, his previous convictions and his character and reputation in his neighbourhood, though this reliance on local hearsay led to many unsafe convictions.

Most were urban, rather than rural, offenders, tried at assizes and quarter sessions in London and the six chief counties: Lancashire, Yorkshire, Warwickshire, Surrey, Gloucestershire and Kent. About one transported convict in three was tried in Ireland, most of them in Dublin. Once sentenced to conviction, convicts were sent to English gaols – in London it was usually Millbank penitentiary, on the site of the present Tate Gallery – or to hulks until their contract for transportation, generally comprising a shipload of between 200 and 250 convicts, was made up. The pain felt by families on conviction for transportation never diminished. Mary Carpenter, the nineteenth-century social reformer, witnessed a mother who had used her little girl for shoplifting being sent for transportation at Liverpool assizes. When the mother was sentenced, Carpenter saw the 'agony of the parent and child, their agonizing grief when they were removed from the dock ... and the child torn from the mother whose guilt she cannot comprehend'. Earlier she had visited Liverpool Borough Gaol and had followed the warder's jangling keys to see prisoners sitting blankly in the special red canvas prison uniform that meant transportation. She commented,

A hulk at Deptford

'they must be brooding over bad thoughts, hopeless of the future, in a sort of living death.' She saw over a hundred child prisoners there – the youngest aged seven and a half and sent to trial for stealing 2½d. 'When a boy once comes in', the warder told her, 'he is almost certain to come again until he is transported.'

At the beginning, convict ships followed the same roundabout route to Australia, via the Canary Islands, Rio de Janeiro and the Cape of Good Hope, to make fullest use of the prevailing winds and currents: first the Canary Current, then the north-east and south-east trade winds before reaching Rio, where they restocked and took on fresh water. The Thames river water which they had taken on board at the start had usually soured two or three times by then. Thames water was meant to be properly filtered and only to be drawn at certain stages of the tide, but convict ships had to take it whenever they could, and this meant it often went bad and had a noticeable sour and rotten taste, with a dark, peat-like sediment at the bottom of the cask. From Rio the ship followed the westerlies down to the Cape of Good Hope, where more fresh water, fresh meat and vegetables, plants and even livestock would be taken on board. Fresh meat and vegetables were a necessary precaution against scurvy.

For convicts the start of the voyage was a desperate moment. Painful farewells took place as family, friends and relatives were allowed on board to participate in this final goodbye, many fearing, not without reason, they would never see their relations or loved ones again. The noise and bustle of activity on board ship before departure were in sharp contrast to the gloom and silence of hulks or prison. This unsettled many and the shock was sometimes so great that they had hysterical, or epileptic, fits, and fell into states of insensibility, lasting from ten to thirty minutes, resembling a deep sleep.

Before being put on board, prisoners were spruced up, washed and issued with new regulation clothing, which they changed weekly. Men were given blue cloth jackets and waistcoats, coarse linen shirts, duck trousers, yarn stockings and woollen caps – garments suitable for a summer voyage, but offering little protection in winter. Woollen garments were not allowed for fear of harbouring bugs and disease. Bed-clothing consisted of a single blanket in summer or winter. Strong gales, with high seas and heavy rain, often made the drying of laundry and of sodden garments almost impossible.

Once on board, the convicts were placed in the charge of the surgeon-superintendent, who became responsible for their delivery in good order and in good health to the penal colony. A detachment of soldiers accompanied each shipload to keep convicts under control. Each prisoner was given a number, his bedding, pillow and blanket, and put in a shared mess of six persons. His eating utensils were two wooden bowls with a wooden spoon and, for drinking, he had to share a horn tumbler used with the communal keg of water. In female transports, as an extra concession, a kettle was provided for making tea. Each day began with the convict rolling up his bedding at about 4.30 a.m. and securing it with two pieces of twine before storing it on deck during daytime. Once the sun was up, the prison doors were opened. Baths were taken in tubs placed on deck, with buckets of water being thrown over each prisoner. Throughout the day prisoners helped with the running of the ship. The more responsible were known as 'captains of the deck': four officiated inside the prison and two upon deck, responsible for keeping the place tidy, sorting out the rations and supervising the orderly demeanour of the other five mess members. Other duties were to fill the communal cistern of water every day, take charge of the hospital and ensure others attended school. Public notices put up on deck listed the times of divine service, when and how to clean the deck, washing days, times of musters, of schools, and lastly a version of criminal code, 'plainly expressing' offences that, if committed on board, would be punished as described.

Throughout the morning the upper and lower decks were swabbed, cleaned, scrubbed, scraped and 'dry holystoned', or scoured. All prisoners were kept on deck until the prison quarters below were thoroughly dry. Schooling took place during the morning; those not enrolled at the school picked oakum or worked at learning trades. In female ships needlework was permitted. Lime juice – to prevent scurvy – was served just before the noon meal, mixed with sugar and water to make a half pint of what was called sherbert. Education began again in the afternoon and supper was usually served at four o'clock. Games such as leapfrog and singing might take place in the afternoon.

In the evening the convicts were mustered in the prison, with their shoes and stockings off and trousers rolled above their knees, as they were checked for cleanliness, since many of them would not wash during the voyage unless compelled to do so. Beds were taken below after supper, and at sunset all were mustered below and the prison locked. A sentry with a drawn cutlass stood guarding the prison doors at all times. Convict ships had about thirty soldiers on board, who composed the guard, under the command of a commissioned officer. On Sundays when convicts were all gathered on the quarter-deck to hear the church service, the guard was still kept under arms during the period of the service.

The post of surgeon-superintendent, the convicts' closest ally,

On board a hulk

had been created largely as a result of the efforts of a former
transported convict, William Redfern, who qualified as a Royal
Navy surgeon in 1797 and was then posted to a ship in
Portsmouth that became involved in the mutiny at the Nore that

same year. Redfern was alleged to have advised the mutineers 'to be more united among themselves' and was transported. After his sentence he practiced as a doctor in Sydney. In 1814 he was asked to investigate the heavy mortality on board three recently arrived convict ships, the *Surry*, *General Hewitt* and *Three Bees*. His report recommended better ventilation, an improved diet and clothing for prisoners, and an 'approved and skilful' surgeon on board each convict ship. After the Napoleonic Wars trained naval surgeons were plentiful and from then on a qualified surgeon-superintendent was put on board all convict ships. The surgeon-superintendent kept a log of the voyage, in which he recorded the daily routines of shipboard life – illnesses and deaths, cleaning and scraping, lancing abscesses, treating blankets that had become lousy by soaking them all night in urine-tubs to kill insects, accounts of prisoners squabbling and of soldiers and women convicts fighting, of whispers of mutiny and other misdemeanours. The surgeon dispensed advice, purges and blisters, and buried the dead. At the end of the voyage an official from the Colonial Secretary's office arrived on board and would always ask the same question of the mustered prisoners: 'Is there any complaint about the Surgeon?' 'No, no, God bless him', was the invariable answer.

Peter Cunningham, a surgeon-superintendent in the 1820s, deliberately appointed as his captains of the deck thieves of the 'highest repute' as these would be certain to keep the others in order. Cunningham noticed how, with prisoners, informing, or 'nosing', was seen as the worst possible offence, and the culprit would be singled out by 'spitting when passing to windward of him; taking advantage of a roll of the ship to stamp, as if by accident, upon his feet; or tumbling against him, to give him a break-neck fall upon deck: and if all these be not deemed sufficient, muffling him at night in a blanket while beating him'.

Cunningham kept a lamp burning in the prison during the night and used ex-soldiers, court-martialled and sentenced to transportation (some were deserters, with a D branded on their left arm), as convict sentries then. He noticed these military convicts liked to boast of their floggings and of the scars of the cat-o'-nine tails upon their backs 'with the same sort of pride that an old campaigner will display when pointing to his Waterloo medal'. It became their jackdaw plumage.

The ship's prison, where prisoners spent most of their journey, was situated in the 'tween decks. Cunningham described it thus: 'Two rows of sleeping-berths, one above the other extend on each side of the between decks, each berth being 6 feet square, and calculated to hold four convicts, every one thus possessing 18 inches space to sleep in – and ample space, too.' A strong grated barricade, spiked with iron, was built across the ship at the steerage bulkhead so that officers could get a free view of the prisoners. Light and air were admitted through forward hatches, which were strongly grated and usually shut at night. Only one set of keys to the prison doors was normally kept on board. In the *Eliza* in 1822 the second mate, having just locked up the prison for the night, was unexpectedly swept overboard with the keys. The only way to unlock the prison the next morning was to get one of the convicts to pick its lock.

Inside the prison quarters the air was often foul. The heat at night in the tropics rose to a temperature of between 90° and 100° and surgeons sometimes allowed prisoners to sleep on deck, sixty at a time, changing them round every four hours. In stormy weather the air scuttles had to be kept shut to stop water getting in, but they were also sometimes shut in good weather, as many ships laboured and pitched a good deal. The stench of perspiring, closely packed human beings became overwhelming. As the heat increased, so did the humidity, and vermin crept out of the woodwork: bedbugs, lice, cockroaches and fleas.

Punishment on board was usually the lash. Shipboard floggings in the first years of transportation were brutal and excessive, as timid masters resorted to the lash at the first sign of dissent. A prisoner about to be flogged stood tied to a grating by the deck gangway and the flogging was done with a cat-o'-nine-tails, watched by all the prisoners and the ship's company. Next to flogging, the most common punishment was 'ironing'.

Prisoners were placed in single or double irons, secured by a ringbolt at either end, generally for twenty-four or forty-eight hours, but in some cases for several days or even (in the case of suspected mutineers) for the entire duration of the voyage. Eventually, like flogging, ironing was laid aside. Instead, offenders were sometimes made to stand erect in a narrow box on deck, a form of solitary confinement more effective with male prisoners than with women, who used to wail so loudly that a cistern of water was placed on top of the box to be turned over upon those who 'persisted in using their tongues'.

Women prisoners were also occasionally flogged or caned. In the *Elizabeth* in 1836 the master, Robert Espie, had women whipped over their arms, legs and backs with a stout piece of rope. On other ships women prisoners might have their heads shaved. The surgeon of the *Diana* in 1833 thought this the only punishment that the women really dreaded, though it only 'renders them still more incorrigible, fancying, as they do, that they have suffered the last and worst degradation'. Sometimes women were made to wear a scold's bridle or to parade the deck in a tub; indeed, women convicts were often thought to be more troublesome and difficult to manage than men. 'If there ever was a hell afloat', wrote T. Clarke, surgeon of the *Kains* in 1830, 'it must have been in the shape of a female convict ship – quarrelling, fighting, thieving, destroying in private each other's property from a mere spirit of devilishness, conversation with each other most abandoned, without feeling or shame.' In female convict ships prostitution with the military and crew always went on and efforts to stamp it out were seldom successful. Some women had to bring their babies with them and many died as a result since they lacked proper infant food. Older children too suffered on these voyages, as they were not given any special clothing to start off with and often came aboard in rags with their mothers. Kindly surgeons usually improvised clothing for them by cutting up sheets and blankets to make shirts and trousers. To begin with, juveniles were transported on the same ships as their elders and frequently corrupted by them on board. On some ships they slept in a separate apartment but mingled with the older prisoners on deck. Between 1812 and 1817 a total of 1,117 convicts under the age of twenty-one were sent out, including five boys aged eleven and six boys and one girl aged twelve.

Since voyages to Australia were long and tedious, ways had to be found of keeping prisoners busy. Endlessly scrubbing, scraping, swabbing and dry holystoning, the decks was one way of doing it, as were picking oakum and sewing trousers and jackets, or knitting socks. Some convicts carved scrimshaw, or manufactured toothpicks, tobacco-stoppers and other ornaments out of whale bones. Exercise filled up the time and took place on deck.

Cunningham was a realist. 'All you ought attempt, under such circumstances, is to bring about regularity and decency of conduct. If you aim at more, you only make hypocrites, which is ten times worse than permitting them to remain (as you found them) open downright knaves.' Cunningham understood that reform was only possible if the setting was right and, on a crowded ship with a particular culture, this was impossible. He noticed how prisoners loved gambling, dice, cards, pitch and toss and 'various other speculations'. Convicts gambled for anything from tobacco to clothes, and, if no cards were available, they dismembered Bibles and prayer books to make them.

Cunningham encouraged his convicts to put on plays. A favourite performance, appropriately, was 'Forty Thieves', with no shortage of volunteer actors. Another was a mock-heroic Old Bailey trial where the Chief Justice of England sat perched upon a three-legged stool, with bedding under him for a cushion, a patchwork quilt for his robe of office and a huge swab combed over his head and shoulders in lieu of a wig. Barristers, with blankets round them for gowns, pleaded eloquently, browbeating and cross-questioning the witnesses according to the best-laid-down rules and 'chicanery' of law, while the culprit stood quaking in the dock, 'awed by the terrific frowns which the indignant judge every now and then cast upon him'.

Education was part of the daily routine and many convicts first learnt how to read or write on the voyage, a beneficial side product of transportation. Surgeon-superintendents were in charge of this schooling, and of convicts' moral instruction. The degree of attention varied. Cunningham, on his first appointment, had tried exhorting prisoners to mend their ways, promising to report those whose behaviour had changed for the better to the authorities once they arrived, especially those who had made a 'good use of the religious books placed in their hands.' His advice was 'in all appearance, strictly attended to', as a very considerable number appeared to become 'grave and devout' whom he had before noticed as among the worst in the ship, 'while Scripture readers and readers of religious tracts multiplied around me on all hands'. One old 'fence' was at the head of this devout party. Cunningham was pleased to observe him setting a good example to his juniors as they carried out their devotions next to the hospital where Cunningham saw them on every sick visit he made. 'I deemed that their fixing upon this conspicuous place, as well as their invariably meeting at the morning and evening hours when I visited the sick, might arise from their anxiety to demonstrate that my advice had not been thrown away.' Their meetings continued for about a fortnight. Then a 'shrewd clever Yorkshireman' told Cunningham with a knowing smile, 'It is out of no disrespect to you, sir, but the praying party care not a straw about religion, but expect you to do something for them when they land: now, if you will just walk into the hospital by the other door, you will see how quickly they will drop away, – for indeed some are tired of it already!' Cunningham followed his advice and, true enough, the party gradually dropped away until only the old 'fence' remained, who continued Bible-reading to the end of the voyage, drawling out the words of scripture in a deep voice, 'and casting at me ever and anon that sort of significant glance which seemed to whisper, "Don't you see how religious I am!"'

Cunningham found that Irish Catholics seemed genuinely devout, counting their beads and fervently crossing themselves and repeating their prayers from the book. 'There was no ostentation in this, because I often saw them do so when they could have no idea I was near; but indeed a great portion of them were poor simple peasantry, transported for very trumpery offences.'

Cunningham had to read all their letters home and many thought up ingenious excuses to account for their sudden departure from the country. Cunningham's hospital man, for instance, wrote to his mother: 'You will be rejoiced to hear that I am in a good situation at last, after all the pain my misconduct has given you which shall never be the case again. I have been appointed to the lucrative situation of doctor's mate of the *Recovery* East Indiaman, now bound on a voyage to that country; and as it is my intention to settle in one of the distant colonies, you need not expect me in England for many years to come.'

In their letters home, Irish convicts never failed to give 'a most circumstantial account of what the breakfast, dinner, and supper, consisted of; a minute list of the clothes supplied, and generally laying particular emphasis on the important fact of having a blanket and bed to "my own self entirely," which seemed to be somewhat of a novelty by their many circumlocutions about it.' Cunningham compared Irish and English convicts:

'If you desire an English convict to do any particular thing, unless you either order him by name, or touch him, so as to point out the identical person you mean, seldom a man will stir; while in an Irish convict-ship, on the contrary, if you merely chance to look round as if you wanted something, half-a-dozen will start up, to anticipate your wishes. I have been at times most bitterly provoked by the conduct of some of these saturnine-faced English knaves – the very man I was looking steadfastly at while desiring him to do some petty thing for me often staring first at me and then at his comrades, with a sort of inquisitive wondering look, as if to make it appear he did not conceive I was addressing him. This does not arise so much from stubborn churlishness of mood, as form a general maxim among English thieves to consider everything in shape of work as a degradation.

The English divided themselves into city folk, 'Tommies' and 'yokels', the Irish into the 'Cork boys' the 'Dublin boys' and the

'North boys'. Tribal conflicts, then as now, ensued and 'so zealous were they in upholding their respective tribes that when two individuals of different classes quarrelled, there was no possibility of arriving at the truth, since a dozen of each class will rush forward, and bawl out at once, in favour of their respective comrades, evidence of the most conflicting, contradictory nature.'

Food for convicts was of surprisingly good quality, with convicts receiving two-thirds of the Royal Navy ration. The staple diet was salt or brined beef, known as 'salt horses', as no doubt some of it was. In Cunningham's time a typical week's menu was: 'Sunday, plum pudding with suet in it, about a pound to each man, likewise a pound of beef; Monday, pork (a pound with peas in it); Tuesday, beef and rice; Wednesday, same as Sunday; Thursday, same as Monday; Friday, beef and rice and pudding; Saturday, pork only.' Dishonest masters, however, sometimes cheated their convicts by using false weights and measures for the rations. One convict ship's captain was alleged to have sold off his surplus rations on the Sydney quayside soon after arrival.

3

Convict Life

WHEN THE SHIP arrived at the end of the journey, the port health officer came on board to issue a clean bill of health, unless there had been disease aboard and quarantine was needed. Then the naval officer inspected the ship, heard any complaints and reported back to the colonial governor. The Principal Superintendent of Convicts came next to gather information about the convicts, each of whom he examined individually, relying more on his own shrewd questioning skills than on the indent papers forwarded by the British authorities, which were nearly always inadequate. He took full names, offences, sentences, dates and places of conviction, trades and personal descriptions. Once these were gathered, they were put on a file which was updated in the event of future misdemeanours. The surgeon-superintendent, who had got to know the convicts best during the voyage, was used by him as by far the most valuable source of information.

Convicts then stayed on board for two or three days until the governor, accompanied by his senior officials, visited the ship, with the surgeon-superintendent in tow, and addressed the men, stressing the need for good conduct. Only then could the convicts set foot on land.

On arriving in Australia, most adult male convicts went straight into the assignment system. This was effectively a system of unpaid convict labour in return for maintenance.

Eden, second from right, in Australia with other convict ships

Convicts were assigned to private masters, who clothed, fed and lodged them in return for their work. In 1838 their weekly rations consisted of 12 lb. wheat, 7 lb. mutton or beef or 4 lb. salt pork, 2 oz. salt and 2 oz. soap. For clothing they were given two jackets, three shirts, two pairs of trousers, three pairs of shoes, and a hat or cap. A generous master might supplement these rations with 'indulgences' of tea, sugar or tobacco as an incentive to good conduct, or as a reward for it. The most sought-after assigned servants were 'mechanics', blacksmiths, carpenters, masons, coopers, wheelwrights and gardeners. In the hierarchy they were considered worth two or three times as much as domestic servants or agricultural labourers, and so were better treated. After all, a master could not compel his 'mechanic' to exercise his skills, so he conciliated him and tried to make life easier for him, often overlooking disorderly conduct, for which mechanics were notorious. Most free settlers welcomed the assignment system, as it provided them with free labour, which they always needed, though the presence of convicts in outhouses or households provided an element of menace.

Assignment went on until the convict reached his release date at the expiry of his sentence, when he would be given a ticket-of-leave. This meant the convict no longer needed to work on assignment to a private master, but could start working for himself for the duration of the rest of his sentence. He had to live in a specified area and his ticket was renewable on an annual basis and could be rescinded at any time. All being well, the ticket-of-leave could lead to an eventual pardon and the right to stay on in Australia as a free citizen, or 'emancipist'. On the other hand, if the convict committed offences while assigned, or proved to be an unsatisfactory worker, this would be delayed and he could be transferred to harsher activities such as the road-building parties or working on a chain gang. Most emancipists started off by keeping a public house and then moving on to owning landed property and farms, sometimes purchasing stolen cattle to get going.

Assignment benefited the government as it cost practically nothing. The government set the hours of work and the rations and provided clothing, but the day-to-day operation of the system was left up to the master. Much depended on his character and temper. Some were good employers, others exploited their assigned servants and relied on coercion and brute force. 'Good conduct' as defined by the master was often a false indicator of merit as it could just mean compliance. If a convict complained of ill-treatment, his complaint was heard before a magistrate, who usually sided with the master, so few did complain. Convicts on assignment could not leave their master's place, earn wages, work for themselves in their spare time, or go anywhere without a pass.

The life of an assigned convict was described by a local newspaper, the *Sydney Gazette and New South Wales Advertiser*, in November 1830. The convict quickly becomes 'a creature of chance'. He may 'fall into the hands of a kind and indulgent master, who will reward his fidelity with suitable acknowledgments, but in ninety-nine cases out of a hundred he will find his employer suspicious, or whimsical, or a blockhead not knowing good conduct from bad, or a despot who treats him like a slave, cursing, and abusing, and getting him flogged for no reasonable cause ... He may be harassed to the very death. He may be worked like a horse, and fed like a chameleon. The master, though not invested by law with uncontrolled power, has yet great authority, which may be abused in a thousand ways precluding redress.' But, as the newspaper went on, the convict was also subject to the caprices of the free population at large. 'Any man can give him in charge without ceremony. If seen drunk, if found tippling in the public house, if met after hours in the street, if unable to pay his trifling debt, if impertinent, the free man has nothing to do but send him to the watch-house and get him punished. The poor prisoner is at the mercy of all men.'

Typical offences committed by a convict on assignment included absconding, pilfering, larceny, insubordination or prevarication, while drunkenness, disobedience of orders, wilful mismanagement of work, or abusive language, profane swearing and insolence were other known misdemeanours. Any of these meant an appearance before a magistrate and was likely to be punished by a flogging or exposure in the stocks. Convicts dreaded flogging most, but the settlers preferred it since it interrupted work less. Flogging in this case was carried out by a convict 'scourger'. Convicts had their own slang for flogging. Twenty-five lashes were a 'tester' or a 'Botany Bay dozen', fifty lashes a 'bob', seventy-five lashes a 'bull', and a hundred lashes a 'canary'. Serious bodily lacerations could result from this, yet such punishments were considered normal and part of the expected routine of convict discipline. A former Van Diemen's Land convict told the reformist writer Henry Mayhew what it was like.

The cats the convicts were then flogged with were each six feet long, made out of the log-line of a ship of 500 tons burden; nine over-end knots were in each tail, and nine tails whipped at each end with a wax-end. With this we had half-minute lashes; a quick lashing would have meant certain death ... When I was first flogged, there was enquiry among my fellow-convicts, as 'How did D (meaning me) stand it – did he sing?' The answer was, 'He was like a pebble', that is, I never once said 'oh' or gave out any expression of the pain I suffered. I took my flogging like a stone. If I had sung, some of the convicts would have given me lush with a locust in it [i.e., a spiked drink] . . . and when I was asleep would have given me a crack on the head that would have laid me straight. That first flogging made me ripe. I said to myself, 'I can take it like a bullock'. I could have taken the flogger's life at the same time, I felt such revenge. Flogging always gives me that feeling.

Road parties were the worst punishment. A convict was worked from sunrise to sunset, was fed with the coarsest food and subject to the most rigid discipline, watched over by a capricious and tyrannical ex-convict as overseer. The parties were herded from one place to another, and either lodged overnight in movable huts on wheels or kept penned into a stockade like animals. Road gangs worked in chains or irons if extra punishment was needed. The weight of these irons varied. A typical case was Joseph Adds, whose irons were found to weigh 13 lb., 12 oz. and were described as 'light' at the inquiry that followed his death in a road gang.

James Backhouse, a Quaker missionary who spent much time in Van Diemen's Land and New South Wales in the 1830s, was struck by the 'strong marks of depravity' on the faces of the road gang members. He felt it came from their ill-use and the way they were punished. 'Misconduct in the gang is flagellation and in some instances they have received from 600 to 800 lashes within the space of eighteen months, at the rate of not more than fifty lashes for one offence.' Backhouse noted that sympathetic free settlers sometimes threw tobacco to road gangs, despite the risk of being fined for it if caught. Backhouse asked to be allowed to give 'religious counsel' to the road gangs. The guards stood by while he did so. 'The soldiers', he complained, 'often use irritating language, mixed with curses, in speaking to the prisoners, which is of bad influence, in hardening them, when they greatly need to be rendered more susceptible of good.'

Road gangs undeniably suffered badly, but life in the penal

A road gang, as seen by James Backhouse

settlements was worse. These were special punitive establishments set apart from centres of population, where convicts who
had committed further offences since arriving in Australia were
sent. Van Diemen's Land had two notorious penal settlements,
at Macquarie Harbour and Port Arthur. Discipline there was so
severe that many considered them 'worse than death'. Macquarie
Harbour, the first to be used between 1821 and 1833, had a horrific reputation. 'The name of Macquarie Harbour', wrote the
contemporary historian Revd John West, 'is associated exclusively with remembrance of inexpressible depravity, degradation
and woe ... There, man lost the aspect and the heart of man.'
Set in a region of tempests, 'its chill and humid climate meant',
West went on, 'that animal life is preserved with difficulty: half
the goats died in one season, and sheep perish: vegetation,
except in its coarsest and most massive forms is stunted and precarious'. These penal settlements were placed in barbaric surroundings so that prisoners dreaded being sent there. So
desperate did men become that many tried to escape. Between
1822 and 1827 over 120 did so, but nearly all perished through
starving in the woods, or even by being eaten by their fellow
escapees or being shot by the military in pursuit of them, or later
being hanged as recaptured bushrangers. Because of Macquarie's
remoteness, in 1830 the governor, Sir George Arthur, decided
to build another penal settlement on Tasman's Peninsula, close

Guard dogs at Port Arthur being inspected by the Franklins

to Hobart. This was Port Arthur, cut off from the rest of the colony by a narrow peninsula guarded by a line of fierce dogs stationed from shore to shore. These dogs were trained to react to the slightest noise and to give the alarm by day or night. So successful were they that only two prisoners ever managed to escape from Port Arthur: one was soon captured, and the other died in the woods.

Escape from Australia itself was virtually impossible. Stringent port restrictions meant that passengers or crews joining merchant vessels were closely watched. However, some convicts did become 'stowaways' and others managed to seize the ships they were working on. The colonial brig *Cyprus* was seized on its way to Macquarie Harbour in 1828 and reached China, with its convict crew pretending to be distressed English seamen. Some managed to get passages back to Britain, only to be found out, tried and returned to Van Diemen's Land. In November 1833, as the Macquarie Harbour settlement was being broken up, a band of eleven convicts seized the brig *Frederick*, on the stocks there, and successfully sailed her to Chile, where four of them were arrested by the captain of Royal Navy ship HMS *Blonde*, and sent back to Hobart to be hanged in 1837. The other six managed to escape and their whereabouts were never discovered. Public executions were used to deter these attempts at escape. Many escapees became bushrangers, living 'wild' in the bush, pillaging and stealing. At a public hanging in Hobart in May 1826 two to three thousand spectators lined the route, including all the local convicts, who were made to watch. The five condemned bushrangers were paraded, hooded and pinioned, through the streets. When they reached their place of execution, the officiating clergyman intoned the burial service and when he got to the final word of the sentence 'in the midst of life we are in death', the traps fell. But these salutary lessons made little impact, so harsh and unremitting was the convict's life.

Women and juvenile convicts fared little better. Once ashore, female convicts were mostly kept in special female quarters. In Van Diemen's Land this was The Factory, a dilapidated structure adjoining the main Hobart gaol. However, outsiders could easily get into this flimsy building. Governor Arthur at first tried moral persuasion, but when that failed he ordered solitary confinement and made the women wear yellow penitential uniforms and have their hair close-cropped. It had little effect, and sexual liaisons with their guards and outsiders continued. The women became noted for their dissolute behaviour. When the Revd Bedford tried to address them in their chapel, the prisoners simply turned their backs on him, lifted up their skirts and smacked their buttocks.

At first juveniles were given no special treatment in Australia and were treated the same as older criminals, but the fear of corruption from these more hardened criminals, which happened on the way out on convict ships, meant that separate establishments were set up for them. In Van Diemen's Land one such was at Point Puer, set up in 1834 on a narrow strip of land opposite Port Arthur. There juveniles were taught to read and write and to learn a trade as tailor, shoemaker, carpenter, boat-builder, mason or gardener for future use in Australia. Again, few ever returned to Britain. Many in any case were orphans or victims of circumstance before they went out, deserted by parents, uneducated, homeless, friendless and unable to earn an honest living.

★

By the time the *Eden* set sail in 1836 approximately 95,000 convicts had already been transported to Australia. During the 1830s, as a result of a series of 'crime waves' in England, urban authorities were getting desperate, and around one in every five convicted criminals was now being sentenced to transportation. Figures for typical years bear this out:

	1826	1831	1840
English prisoners convicted	5,797	13,830	19,292
English prisoners transported	1,054	3,315	4,105

Transportation was no longer just a means of reducing overcrowding in prisons: the policy was also seen as a way to deter crime. More and more the authorities wanted punishment to be exemplary, even for relatively minor offences such as pickpocketing. As the industrial revolution gathered pace and people moved into the cities, crime came to be practised professionally as a way of life. Henry Mayhew and Charles Dickens both attested to this in their accounts of London low life; crime now ran in families, with 'flash houses' harbouring criminals like Snow Hill in *Oliver Twist*, or 'hell houses', the front doors of which opened inwards so that thieves could throw their booty in as they fled. A 'criminal class' had grown up.

By the 1830s notions of class had intruded more and more into British society and the emerging middle class, keen to maintain its dominant position, defined itself by other classes below and above it; hence the emergence of a 'working class', soon to be extended into the looser amalgam of 'working classes'. A criminal class, particularly if allied to the 'dangerous classes', posed a threat to this as well as to property and social order. Even Mayhew could see this. 'I am anxious that the public should no longer confound the honest, independent working men with the vagrant beggars and pilferers of this country; and that they should see that the one class is as respectable and worthy, as the other is degraded and vicious.' Descriptions of the criminal classes were made in language familiar to the industrial revolution. They were seen as 'producing' crime, with their own habitat, milieu and argot. Fagin could be taken as a model for this 'factory' of underage employees – 'and see what a pride they take in their profession, my dear. Ain't it beautiful?' – or the notorious St Giles's area of London, in today's Soho, with its Rookery of squalid thieves' dens and cheap lodging-houses and prostitution.

Attitudes towards criminal behaviour reflected this as well. For much of the early part of the nineteenth century the threat posed by the French Revolution hovered over society, the fear of the mob rising. Repressive measures introduced by Parliament dealt with this threat by criminalizing it. As Robert Hughes wrote in *The Fatal Shore*: 'Thus, it was all too easy to assign criminal propensities to the marginal, the outcast, the rag-and-bones – in short, to those who might be seen as the English equivalent of the *sans-culotte*.' In Britain at this time, in order to have a vote, an individual had to own property. The behaviour of the unpropertied was carefully monitored, to keep them in their place. Yet much of crime, as the records show – and Mayhew is an authority again – was spontaneous theft driven by need. Oscar Wilde was later to remark that 'starvation, and not sin, is the parent of modern crime.'

As the century progressed, people began to fear the moral contagion of crime. But rather than tackle crime at its source, or attempt to understand its causes, transportation aimed to rid society of this moral contagion by shipping the criminal overseas. The policy's psychological appeal was clear. As Hughes goes on to argue, transportation 'answered a deep desire for sublimation and generalisation'. Sublimation meant getting rid of the criminal in a high-minded way, bodily removing him off to the other side of the world in the hope of unspecified better things happening to him there, while 'generalisation' meant that people did not have to face the consequences of crime taking place on their doorstep: it could be wafted away into abstraction. Hughes again: 'Few people want to take direct responsibility for hanging; understandably, they prefer abstractions – "course of justice", "debt to society", "exemplary punishment" – to the concrete fact of a terrified stranger choking and pissing at the end of a rope.' The distant realities of Australia were largely unknown to most British people at the time. Australia therefore provided a suitable setting, as it aimed to make the criminal invisible and harmless, but still a symbol, 'a theatre of horror for a distant audience', as Hughes put it.

Ostensibly, transportation policy was underpinned by the two guiding theories that dominated penal thinking at the time. The first of these was Evangelicalism, which presupposed a divinely ordained, stratified society, where the poor were deferent and the wealthy dispensed solicitous charity. Evangelicals believed Christianity reflected God's deepest purposes and that prisons should reflect this and seek to repair the spiritual and moral deficiencies of each individual prisoner. They feared that industrialization was exacerbating sinfulness and disobedience. Prisoners should be made to take active steps to live in a Christian way and taught skills that would enable them to lead a virtuous, sober and frugal life on release. Suffering in prison was justified, since God on judgement day was going to inflict pain in accordance with previous human conduct. The Evangelical ideal was the dutiful, grateful and obedient reformed prisoner heard to remark at the Evangelical Lord Shaftesbury's funeral, 'Our Earl's gone. God

Almighty knows he loved us and we loved him. We shan't see his likes again.'

The other underlying theory was Associationism, derived from the seventeenth-century views of natural science promulgated by Isaac Newton and others. God was seen as a master engineer who had constructed 'a perfect machine and left it running'. Associationists, such as John Locke, saw the human mind at birth as a blank sheet, a *tabula rasa*, and took the view that human attitudes were formed through the association of sensations and experience, particularly in childhood, and that this process persisted through life. Consequently, to the Associationist, the criminal was one who had learnt, through his earlier experiences, that crime produced pleasure, and that its repetition was likely to produce more pleasure. The first task of prison reformers therefore was to introduce 'a measured quantity of pain over a period of time' so as to reverse these criminal attitudes. The utilitarian reformer Jeremy Bentham used the theory of Associationism as the basis for a new type of penal institution which he called the Panopticon, and subsequently applied the same principle to a variety of plans for reforming institutions. Bentham favoured a carefully regulated regime, whose aim was to ensure that 'things which had been originally objets of desire become objects of aversion and, on the hand, things which been objects of aversion ... become objects of desire'. Associationism and Evangelicalism both agreed about the need for pain, but saw different outcomes for it. Evangelicalism's appeal was to the human spirit soaring upwards towards man's Redeemer, while Associationism's was the more earthbound dictates of an evolving psychology of mankind. Most penal reform in the first half of the nineteenth century reflected one or other of these attitudes. When Maconochie came to formulate his own views, he was of the Associationist cast of mind, believing that prison should prepare the prisoner for release in such a way as to make him unlikely to reoffend, by giving him the strength of mind and inner resources required. At the same time he accepted the right of society to inflict punishment, so long as it was used constructively.

Just when the policy of transportation was at its height, though, its efficacy was beginning to be questioned. Despite the popular belief in the justification, even necessity, of harsh punishments, since the late eighteenth century there had been calls in some quarters for a new approach. England's best-known prison reformer had been John Howard, who, while high sheriff of Bedfordshire in 1773, did what none of his predecessors had done – he actually visited and inspected the prisons of his county. Shocked by what he found, he wrote *The State of the Prisons in England and Wales with some Preliminary Observations, and an Account of some Foreign Prisons*, in which he advocated that prisons should be made sanitary and secure, that the sexes should be separated, and that the prisons should be run by a keeper paid out of the public purse and therefore accountable. Howard's ideas were incorporated into later acts of Parliament, but these were enabling rather than mandatory, and little real change took place. Twenty years after Howard's death, prisons were very much as he had first found them. In 1815, the year of Waterloo, the aldermen of the City of London, in whose prison a debtor had recently died of starvation and two women prisoners had been found with only a rug to hide their nakedness, declared that 'their prisoners had all they ought to have, unless gentlemen thought they should be indulged with Turkey carpets'. This was a refrain that ran alongside much of prison reform, the fear of prisoners being pampered.

Howard's concerns were taken up in the nineteenth century by a remarkable group of Quakers from banking families – the Gurneys, Barclays, Frys and Hoares – with enough wealth and social connections to achieve genuine change. Elizabeth Fry visited Newgate prison, of which John Wesley had previously written that 'of all the seats of woe on this side Hell, few, I suppose, exceed or equal Newgate'. She tended the sick women prisoners, helped mothers there with children, and set up a ladies' committee of Quaker friends to visit. For female prisoners going to the docks about to be transported to Australia, she arranged for closed hackney coaches, with Quaker ladies in attendance, instead of the open wagons previously used, which had been jeered at by the public.

Now the reform movement was gaining a new impetus. An essential part of the theory of transportation was that, once they had completed their sentences, the convicts would avail themselves of the opportunities the new country provided. Yet the system was deliberately so harsh and repressive that they were ill equipped to do so. Few ever returned to Britain, as they had to pay their own passage. And while transportation was meant to deter crime in Britain, reports were starting to come back of increasing crime and lawlessness in New South Wales and Van Diemen's Land. Whatever justification there might be for the cruelty of the system, it was clearly not preparing convicts for freedom after release. The system's inadequacies in this respect were naturally also causing concern among those who had chosen to become free settlers in Australia. Hence such inquiries as the one Maconochie had agreed to carry out on behalf of the Society for the Improvement of Prison Discipline.

Lord John Russell, the Home Secretary, was therefore beginning to think of other, more home-based remedies. His thoughts had turned to building prisons similar to the newer American penitentiaries using the Separate and Silent systems. Prisoners in these were put in cells on their own to reflect on their past misdeeds and to engage in whole-scale repentance, as the word 'penitentiary' implied. Pentonville would soon be the first of these to be built in Britain and the cost would, Russell reckoned, probably be cheaper than transportation, which was estimated to cost the Crown between £400,000 and £500,000 a year.

Russell's interest in reform was long-standing. The third son of the sixth Duke of Bedford, he was delicate as a child and suffered from poor health. His reforming zeal started early. At the age of fourteen, having visited Charles James Fox, then Secretary of State for Foreign Affairs, he wrote in his diary, 'What a pity that he who steals a penny loaf should be hung, while he who steals thousands of public money should be acquitted.' After entering Parliament, Russell became the guiding force behind the 1832 Reform Bill, and gained immense popularity in the country as a result. As Home Secretary in Melbourne's government from 1835 to 1839, he reduced the number of offences liable for capital punishment or transportation. Portraits at the time show him as a bustling, sharp-minded figure, quick and incisive. His presence in the House of Commons was described by Sumner, a contemporary: 'Lord John Russell rose in my mind the more I listened to him. In person diminutive and rickety ... he wriggled round, played with his hat, and seemed unable to dispose of his hands or his feet; his voice was small and thin but notwithstanding this a house of five hundred members was hushed to catch his smallest accents. You listened, and you felt that you heard a man of mind, of thought, and of moral elevation.' Sydney Smith's pen portrait endorsed this: 'There is no better man in England than Lord John Russell, but his worst failure is that there is nothing he would not undertake. I believe he will perform the operation for the stone, build St Peter's, or assume (with or without ten minutes notice) the command of the channel fleet.' He went on: 'Another peculiarity of the Russells is that they never alter their opinion: they are an excellent race, but they must be trepanned before they are convinced.' His grandson was Bertrand Russell, full of the same forceful family traits.

In 1837 Russell set up the Molesworth Committee, whose brief was 'to inquire into the System of Transportation, its Efficacy as a Punishment, its Influence on the Moral State of Society in the Penal Colonies', and then to see how far it was 'susceptible of improvement'. In reality, the committee was set up to justify ending the policy of transportation, which besides failing to reform criminals was felt to be polluting the fledgeling colonial society. Emigrants were being deterred from going to Australia by reports of the dire state of the country. On the other hand, some criminals, especially those with poor prospects in Britain, were reported as committing crimes in the hope of being sent to a country that offered hope of a better life. Sydney Smith put it thus: 'The ancient profession of picking pockets will

Lord John Russell

certainly not become more discreditable from the knowledge that it may eventually lead to the possession of a farm of a thousand acres on the River Hawkesbury.' The committee's chairman was Sir William Molesworth, still only twenty-seven, MP for East Cornwall, an ambitious, flamboyant character who had once been expelled from university for challenging his tutor to a duel. He later edited the works of Hobbes, with whose determinist view of life he no doubt sympathized. The witnesses included Sir Francis Forbes, the Chief Justice of New South Wales, James Macarthur, the Revd Dr Dunmore Lang, James Mudie and Sir George Arthur, Sir John Franklin's predecessor as Governor of Van Diemen's Land. One particularly important testimony was that of the Revd William Ullathorne, then Roman Catholic Vicar-General of Australia, and the author of an anti-transportation pamphlet entitled *The Catholic Mission in Australia*, who left this beguiling description of meeting Molesworth:

> I went to his house, and was amused to find him in a dandy silk dressing-gown, covered with flowers like a garden, and tied with a silk cord with flowing tassels. He had my pamphlet before him, and tried to coach me as to the best way of giving evidence. When we came to one embarrassing point, I told him it was doubtful whether I ought to speak on it. He pulled up his head, gave me a menacing look, and said: 'Do you know how grave would the consequences of your refusing?' I looked into his eyes whilst replying: 'You have read that book, and ought to know that I am not a man to be talked to in that way.' He tried to laugh it off.

The attempt at coaching was an indication of the pre-formed direction the Molesworth Committee was taking. Most of its members had already made up their minds and were opposed to transportation, and the committee had become more an exercise in governmental procedure than a fact-finding mission.

4

Bound for Australia

ON BOARD THE *Fairlie* the Franklin party comprised Sir John, his wife, Jane, his daughter Eleanor, and his two nieces Sophia Cracroft, daughter of his sister Isabella, and Mary Franklin, daughter of his brother James. Jane Franklin was forty-five by the time she set out in the *Fairlie*, and was her husband's staunchest supporter. As she told her sister, 'everybody knows who knows me at all ... that I am devoted soul and spirit to Sir John'. But she had an independent side as well: 'Whenever I think I am imposed upon my spirit rises', she wrote in an early letter to Franklin before continuing, 'if you are a prudent man you will put this letter by and turn it to account on some future occasion when I am in a rebellious mood; and upon this consideration I think you ought to feel infinitely obliged to me for furnishing you with so valuable a document.' Jane Franklin had her two maids with her (one of whom was French and could not speak English) as well as a governess for Eleanor, Miss Williamson, who was soon so seasick she could not teach. 'Eleanor was left to the indulgence of lazy habits & was never so happy as when talking with the young Maconochies, stretched side by side upon cushions on the deck.' However, Lady Franklin soon stepped in and 'promised to take Eleanor in hand again myself'. This 'stepping in' caused friction between them. Lady Franklin's niece Sophia Cracroft noted that 'Eleanor absolutely hates my Aunt'. Jane Franklin was too zealous and interfering as a stepmother,

Jane Franklin

and wanted to bring Eleanor up according to her own high standards. Eleanor resented this, and saw no reason to fall in with her dictates. She adored her father and was jealous of his devotion to her stepmother.

William Henty, who recorded the *Fairlie*'s mid-ocean encounter with the convict ship *Eden*, was emigrating from Sussex, intending to join relatives already out in New South Wales (William's father, Thomas, had brought the first merino sheep out to Australia). Henty recorded the ship's day in his diary. Besides the thirty-six cabin passengers on board, there were many more passengers in steerage, including three pregnant women and fifty-two children. In cabin class the boat seemed overcrowded and there was a feeling that many additional passengers had signed up once they knew that Franklin was on board, hoping for preferment in Van Diemen's Land that way. The ship's day began early:

About 5, the butcher gives his pigs a drive round the deck once or twice; then at ½ past a great clattering begins of knives and forks cleaning, chains clanking, cocks crowing etc. and at 6 the Sailors set to scrubbing the decks overhead with a noise that would out do a ship-load of babies. At 7½ o'clock the Steward's bell rings for the Children's breakfast, and at 9 (called ½ past 8) the Cabin passengers sat down in number about 32 or 33, good Tea and Coffee is handed to us, bread and butter ad lib. Biscuit, hot beef Steaks and cold meat of 2 or 3 sorts.

The main meal was at half past three. On the first day soup and beef 'dressed in three ways' was served. William Henty and his wife, Matilda, found themselves seated at Captain Maconochie's table, 'but rather low at the end' with a set of young men to their right. William looked across and noted Sir John's affability during this first meal, while Lady Franklin's manner seemed 'gentle and kind'. A later collation, or tea, was served at seven o'clock. Then passengers promenaded on deck, followed by evening prayers, read by the Archdeacon the Revd William Hutchins, on his way out to Van Diemen's Land at the request of the Church of England community there. 'His manner very good', wrote Henty. Then grog, a mixture of rum and water, was served. The Hentys had brought their own servants with them, Mr and Mrs Hutson, mainly to look after their sixteen-month-old son and to make their cabin life as comfortable as possible. Extra shelves and hooks were fitted to their cabin and another armchair installed. But cockroaches were everywhere: one even landed with outstretched wings on the gasping Matilda's bare shoulder. The third mate assured them that cockroaches were valuable on board as they kept down bugs: he personally kept cockroaches inside his sea-chest every voyage for that reason.

As the *Fairlie* proceeded down the English Channel, the weather grew worse. A gale blew relentlessly for three days and nights, laying low most of the passengers. As they neared the Scilly Isles, the storms allowed 'no possibility of standing on one's legs', Lady Franklin noted in her journal. Most of the ladies took to lying down out of doors on the poop deck, wrapped in plaids and shawls. A recumbent position and a glass of brandy with Cayenne pepper were recommended for seasickness. As the sea got rougher, the men also braved the tilting decks to join them, and Captain Ager suggested that they should all eat less to aid recovery. William dutifully obliged and cut down on meat, which, he noticed, was already becoming 'too high' after ten days at sea. Once the rough weather abated and the seas died down, a pleasant social life began. Tables at meal times filled up again. William enjoyed the ease and grace of shipboard life. 'Sir John and his lady try to put everyone at his ease and require no State', the archdeacon was 'a *nice* man', still reading his prayers 'most beautifully in a manly rich voice, with a deep fervent manner and so humble and submissive', and Captain Maconochie behaved with 'great attention', while the others were 'as nice people as one could wish to meet with'.

Jane Franklin now came into her own. She was a born organizer and saw the voyage as an opportunity to improve her mind. She took lessons in perspective from a Scottish artist who was emigrating to Sydney. She caught a squid and had it placed under a microscope so that she could draw it. She arranged a Sunday school class for the young children, though she soon found it 'drudgery' trying to 'convey some few ideas into their heads'. She organized evening lectures on deck, and Maconochie, as a former professor of geography at London University, was inveigled to lead these. He chose for his first subject 'The Natural History of Man', delivered 'to a full audience, including the Archdeacon who ... I suspect was a little scandalized to hear that it was possible to find specimens of the human species with tails, & still more to hear Captn M. seriously argue that [there] were strong reasons for believing that we whites owe our colour to our civilization & that if not our first parents yet our antidiluvian [*sic*] ancestors were in all probability black'. His second lecture 'endeavoured to account for the fact of a white skin being the effect of civilization by supposing that the secretion which in the savage blackens his skin, flies off in proportion as he becomes a more intellectual being to his brain & is there converted into the material organ of mind' (the origin, supposedly, of grey matter), while his third touched 'on some rather curious subjects which however essentially belonging to the natural history of man, put the ladies a little to the blush & brought down on his a scolding from his wife'. The archdeacon would not 'give his sanction to any more physical curiosities by his presence', and retired to his cabin. Maconochie afterwards confined himself to metaphysics and phrenology, the recent scientific craze.

The Hentys arranged dancing on board. 'Tonight the party mustered pretty strong, Sir John's piano is brought from below, up on deck, and Miss Kracroft who plays beautifully, is chief musician. They marshal about 7 or 8 couple in country dances, Gaieties & Gravities etc. but Quadrilles are the chief, a Waltz now and then. Sir John and his Lady are great Encouragers, and the Captain, though secretly I imagine no friend to dancing, concurs very readily in the plan ... He declines to dance himself being sure of a gale of Wind if he did such a thing.' Dancing vied with games of leapfrog in popularity. William Henry sat writing his diary in his cabin, wrapped against the cold, recording incidents at sea. In the South Atlantic a ship running before the wind bore down upon them in the middle of the night. Amid noisy uproar from both ships, the *Fairlie's* captain just managed to avoid a collision, while the other ship's captain, in a stream of foul language, refused to give his own ship's name and disappeared into the night. Lady Franklin, too, mentioned this. 'I saw the light alone coming nearer & nearer like the 2 fiery looking & enlarging eyes of a travelling carriage ... The moment was one of intense & even awful excitement & agitation ... Sir John said her behaviour was just like that of a pirate bearing down upon us to throw men on board.'

Other mid-ocean encounters took place. In addition to the *Eden*, the barque *Thomas Parsons, en route* to Britain with a cargo of palm oil from Nigeria, hove to and offered to take letters. The *Fairlie* passengers spent the day busily writing letters home once she was sighted. A week later the *Tigris*, bound for Ceylon, stopped and asked to drop off her letters for quicker dispatch to Britain from the Cape, where the *Fairlie* was bound. Her captain, her surgeon, a merchant and a gentleman travelling for pleasure, who turned out to be an acquaintance of Maconochie, all came across to the *Fairlie* for tea, bringing the *Tigris* mail and a Madeira pumpkin with them.

Theatricals took place on board, none more dramatic than the crossing the line ceremony at the Equator, in which Sir John Franklin refused to take part. The *Fairlie* hove to and a seaman playing Neptune appeared over the bows dressed in his outrageous garb of shells and dried starfish, his oakum beard dripping with sea water, swearing ferociously and guarded by his attendants Queen Amphitrite (dressed as a whore), a judge with a list of those to be baptized, a priest, a doctor, a barber and sundry others, all with painted faces. Anyone crossing the Equator for the first time was duly summoned for trial and judgement. Neptune placed his speaking trumpet close to the initiate's ear and asked him how old he was. The hapless individual opened his mouth only to find a tar brush immediately thrust into it. He was tarred and soaped all over his face, and then scraped dry by the barber with an iron hoop razor. A dozen buckets of water were then hurled over him, washing him completely off his seat, to the accompaniment of sea shanties. The ceremony over, the initiate was made to swear he would impose the same ritual on all future green hands and given his certificate.

In the tropics the thermometer, even in the shade, reached over 100°. The coolest place to sleep was on deck under a wind-sail which gave cover like a tent, yet complaints about the night-time heat were still bandied about at breakfast. The sea was now a dark indigo colour and the effects of the heat on the animals aboard was noticeable. The pigs lost their flesh and their hocks swelled up. Chickens and ducks, crowded so close together, took to eating each other's feathers. Even the cabin cat was affected, and began stretching, mewing and clawing 'in the most melancholy manner'. Sharks were spotted and passengers hurried up on deck to watch as sailors prepared hooks with pieces of pork. No sooner was the bait over the side than the pilot fish accompanying the sharks approached it and, after examining it, swam back towards the sharks to report their discovery. The leading shark took the bait and the sailors on deck, whooping and hallooing, hauled the 'sea lawyer' up on the deck. Lady Franklin gleefully reported seeing a shark 'drawn up with much composure' as she watched out of her cabin window, which she feared the victim's tail might smash. The shark was quickly dispatched with a pole-axe and his stomach, or 'glory hole', opened, but little was found except a piece of old rope and the half-digested skin of a ham, which had been thrown overboard the day before. The shark's flesh was cooked, and even Lady Franklin was not too squeamish to eat it at the next morning's breakfast. It was 'rather flabby and coarse-grained'.

Altogether Lady Franklin was enjoying the voyage. 'I was perhaps the only person in the ship who if the power of arriving in a week instead of a fortnight had been mine, would not have cared to secure the shorter period.' Her thoughts were beginning to turn to how she would fare as a colonial governor's lady. She used the Maconochies, especially Mary, as a sounding board. 'I had long begun to find much pleasure in her & Captain Maconochie's society, & to see in them new virtues & endowments, & my only unpleasant sensation in my intercourse with them was this, that I did not feel sufficiently careless of their opinion of me, & had some solicitude that they should not by observation discover me to be less favourably organised than my cerebral development indicated.'

As they neared the Cape of Good Hope, Lady Franklin noted: 'The last days of fresh meat aboard. We were reduced to the two remaining fowls on the Sunday. Next day dinner was reduced to soup, salted tripe and ham with the usual accompaniments of plum pudding and champagne.' They had caught another squid, which had afforded them 'much amusement'; its tentacles were 'all cut off and everybody obtained a few'. Table Bay came into view, its shoreline thickly studded with white Dutch-style villas, while beyond lay the imposing Table Mountain, capped by cloud. On anchoring, they were surprised to find the *Eden* and *Tigris* there, neither of which had planned to stop. Scurvy had broken out on board the *Eden* and had already carried off one convict, his constitution weakened by a refusal to eat on board his hulk in Portsmouth, 'brooding over some secret grief', as the surgeon-superintendent put it. Another prisoner had died of fever off Madeira, and a third had suddenly decided to put an end to his existence by strangling himself from a beam in the prison one night with his own handkerchief 'in a fit of despondency'. The *Eden* had come into port to load fresh provisions, desperate now to prevent future outbreaks of scurvy.

The *Fairlie* had a three-week stopover at the Cape. The Franklins and Maconochies stayed in lodgings in town, and after dispatching their laundry 'as a matter of urgency' set off exploring. Their main objective was Table Mountain, which Lady Franklin was determined to climb. A challenge was issued by her at a dinner party and she audaciously climbed it at three o'clock the next morning, despite protests from Franklin and Maconochie. She went ahead with her small party, taking five hours for her ascent and three for the descent since she stopped on the way down to pick flowers to illustrate her botanical notes in her journal. The archdeacon was in her party, 'spudding lightly down the steep, with an umbrella in one hand & a bundle of white chrysanthemums in the other'.

For the Hentys the Cape stay was not a happy one. Much of William's time, as well as Matilda's, had been devoted on the trip out to the care of their ailing son Willy, already ill when the voyage started. The ship's doctor had given him laudanum and spirits of lavender, but his health never improved. His hands contracted and his feet and ankles became so swollen that they could not bear to be touched. The doctor thought it was rheumatism, caused by a damp cot just off the wet floor of the cabin. His parents hoped the stay at the Cape would give him some respite. As they neared the Cape, William in his diary described his son as 'still a great invalid', weak and in pain, with a heat rash and festering gums and a cough that would not go away. After leaving the Cape, William and Matilda found their baby still distressed and summoned the ship's doctor, who gave him some medicine to relieve him. After washing their baby, they put him back down into his cot and his low fretting sounds ceased. Thinking he was asleep, Matilda was about to leave when, taking a last look at him, she called out to William. Together they looked again and saw that their beloved son had just died. At his funeral next day a small coffin made from wood provided by Captain Ager was used. William's diary entry for the day simply records the time and the place, the latitude and longitude and the place in mid-ocean where his son's coffin was consigned to the deep.

After Cape Town the *Fairlie* experienced some 'real Cape weather', and the ship was battened down for a week, shipping water all the time, with the floors of the cabins awash. The emigrants in steerage suffered worst from the lack of air and light. Yet once through these high southern latitudes, the Australian coast soon came into view. Unusual bustle took place and freshly laundered petticoats and gowns fluttered on deck in the breeze. Down below in the emigrants' quarters wives were up to their elbows in suds, as they got their shore clothes ready.

*

The *Fairlie* arrived at Hobart, Van Diemen's Land, on 6th January 1837, four months after leaving Portsmouth. Lady Franklin wrote 'we are happily arrived at our destination after a brisk but rather stormy passage from the Cape of five weeks & two days. It is now eight in the morning, & at eleven the members of the Executive Council with the Commandant of the Troops ... come on board, & then Sir John makes his public landing, while we ladies walk quietly through the garden to the Government House.' Hobart had been spruced up for his benefit. 'The place looks beautiful ... & every body seems in high spirits.'

Franklin's first days were ceremonial, with Maconochie at his side. They went inland to Launceston, the second largest town on the island, which they entered triumphantly with an escort of three hundred horsemen and seventy carriages. Mary Maconochie noted her husband's contribution to Franklin's reception: 'Sir John was received with perfect rapture; Alexander's addresses, written in his name, were hailed as a new order of things, and his tour through the Island was a perfect triumph.' Lady Franklin too noted that the island 'seems to be in a most flourishing condition – every body growing rich'. It was true. Settlers had done well out of the colony and had been able to line their pockets handsomely through the sale of land for the burgeoning infrastructure of roads, buildings, mills, churches and schools. Van Diemen's Land was still 'an infant society' as Franklin's friend Thomas Arnold, headmaster of Rugby, called it in a letter to him: it had been founded only thirty-five years earlier, in 1803. In 1837 the population of the island was 50,000, half of them free settlers (a quarter of whom were women), and half convicts (of whom only a tenth were female).

As Governor, Franklin would have overall control of all the island's affairs, civil, penal and military, a job that called for a delicate balance since the civil and penal systems, in particular, often presented conflicting demands. The governor was directly answerable in London to the Secretary of State for the Colonies, to whom he sent regular dispatches, but it was understood that he had at times to use his own discretion, and different secretaries of state allowed varying amounts of autonomy to their colonial governors. The whole national penal system, however, came under the jurisdiction of the Home Office, and decisions taken by the Home Secretary in the area of colonial penal administration were invariably accepted by the Colonial Office and relayed on to the local governor, adding to the number of potentially conflicting demands needing to be reconciled.

Five days after his arrival Franklin gave a reception at Government House. Over 600 people were invited, but leading colonists were not pleased by this. One of them, Alfred Stephen,

a newspaper owner, mentioned in a letter home that the tradesmen 'who graced the drawing-room and were duly presented to
Sir John and Lady Franklin' included an ironmonger, several
linen drapers, a greengrocer and a boot-maker. 'Such a levee was
never before witnessed in the colony.' However much an 'infant
society', Van Diemen's Land was already riven with its social
stratification, but Franklin had never had charge of a British
colony before and he was probably following naval tradition by
inviting the whole crew. It was a miscalculation, since Van
Diemen's Land, like many an emerging colony, was particularly
self-conscious over the minutiae of social etiquette, a touchiness
that stemmed both from the colonial wish to aspire to a higher
social status abroad than in Britain and, in this case, from the
hierarchical structure already put in place by Franklin's predecessor, Sir George Arthur.

Arthur had first come out to Van Diemen's Land as Governor
in 1824, and twelve years later the imprint of his determined and
ruthless rule was still visible. Contemporary portraits show him
when he first arrived as a forty-year-old, lean-featured man,
with dark hair retreating from a high forehead, dark, frowning
eyebrows and the fashionable mutton-chop whiskers of his day.
An aquiline nose, firm lips and a resolute chin completed the
picture. Indeed his looks matched the image he wanted to create
– masterful, exacting and faintly disturbing. Arthur made his
presence felt in the settlement by riding around everywhere on
horseback, his black frock-coat buttoned up to the neck, glisten-
ing sword down the side of his red-seamed trousers. He preferred surprise visits and would arrive unannounced at, say, the
gates of the female penitentiary, accompanied by an aide, and
then hurry through the entrance gate, nod condescendingly to
the superintendent and examine and pry into everything; the
cells, yards, wards, drains, spinning lofts, washing and cooking
departments, hospital and nursery – each was given the minut-
est inspection. A few quick remarks and he was off again to write
down all he saw. His lengthy dispatches to Britain were full of
details from magistrates' reports and from superintendents of

Governor Arthur

gaols, and minutiae such as the full composition of road and chain gangs. Nothing missed his glance. An ultra-efficient administrator, he personally initialled all documents and oversaw tickets-of-leave, pardons, sentences to hard labour and, especially, executions. In fact, he meddled in everything and his large sloping handwriting was frequently scrawled across other people's reports, demanding explanations.

Arthur was an army man at heart, a martinet. His first experiences of colonial Government had been in Jamaica, followed by eight years as Governor of British Honduras. Aware of the ins and outs of colonial government, his appointment to Van Diemen's Land came, it was said, after he had 'haunted' the

Colonial Office in London. 'Promotion was my idol', he once admitted. Arthur's abrasive manner and brusque temper upset the settlers, by whom, as the historian of Tasmania L.L. Robson writes, 'he was hated with an intensity of which only the neurotic and grasping settlers of Van Diemen's Land were capable'. His priority was always the smooth running of penal establishments: he was there, as he saw it, 'not to build up a free community, but to hold in check the criminality of an empire'. Convicts 'should be kept rigidly at the spade and pick-axe and wheel-barrow . . . from morning till night'. The welfare of colonists came second. Settlers resented this, comparing it unfavourably with their treatment under his affable predecessor, William Sorell.

To make his system work, Arthur placed friends and family in preferred positions. His nephew-in-law John Montagu became Colonial Secretary and another nephew-in-law, Matthew Forster, chief of police. Appointments such as these became known as the 'Arthur faction', an inner clique obedient to their master and ruled by sycophancy and favouritism. Anyone left out felt excluded and Arthur was ruthless with those who displeased him. One settler had his assigned servants removed simply for being associated with a hostile newspaper, the *Hobart Town Gazette*. Arthur was an Evangelical and had little sympathy with laxity or weakness, yet a new colony such as Van Diemen's Land was bound to be full of irregular behaviour. Contemporary newspapers abound with accounts of drunkenness, pilfering and general unrest. Arthur would have none of this. Although men greatly outnumbered women and marriage tended to be the exception and concubinage the rule, Arthur could not abide this situation. Since he himself was comfortably married and the father of twelve children, why could others not do likewise? Entertainment at Government House tended to be on the staid side.

Convicts had to be kept in their place, or, as Arthur put it, 'on their proper level'. It was 'insulting to his feelings' that a document sent to him had actually been copied out by a convict clerk. The fact that government officials had also held a conversation about their differences of opinion with him in the presence of a convict was conduct which 'strikes at the root of all decency'. He informed the government in London that 'no emancipist or time-expired convict has ever been received at my table, none have been promoted to a higher municipal office than that of constable, nor have they, nor any prisoners, ever been suffered to be the channel through which either the favours or orders of the colonial government have been conveyed.' The idea of reforming, or even rehabilitating, convicts was not for him. He adhered to the view that transportation was to be used at all times as a deterrent to further crime.

Insubordination, however, did at times raise its head. At a race meeting in Hobart in 1830, a toast was drunk to 'The Turf, and may its opposers be under it!', a clear reference to Arthur, whose objection to racing and such other loose activities was based on his fear of a weakening of discipline. But his methods of enforcement were not always as Christian as they ought to have been. Some were decidedly underhand, such as informing on others, a device he actively encouraged. Convicts, on his orders, were expected to watch and report back on the misdemeanours of their fellows in the belief this would lessen their own punishments. Religious instruction, which he made compulsory, was slanted to remind convicts of their degraded state, so that the severity of their punishment was fully brought home to them. Convicts were there to suffer. Such an autocratic system meant that Arthur's own intolerance and harshness got passed down the line, and at the very lowest level where convict met enforcer, much cruelty ensued. The ruins of Arthur's penal establishment at Port Arthur on the isolated Tasman Peninsula, where discipline was made as ruthless and severe as possible, remain there today, a chilling reminder of his excesses.

By the time Franklin arrived, Arthur had ruled Van Diemen's Land for twelve years, a double term of office. He left a rich man, mainly through land sales, and in his typical meddlesome way, he also left a letter of instruction behind for Franklin at Government House. 'It would certainly be unwise in you, as it

Port Arthur penal settlement

would be unwarrantable in me, to expect that you should involve yourself in any individual controversies on my behalf, so that if my supporters become your supporters I shall very sincerely rejoice, provided you can secure them without weakening your influence in other quarters.' He was trying to 'fix' Franklin before he started. Arthur's loyal followers, his faction, were still in the main positions of power, John Montagu as Colonial Secretary and Matthew Forster as chief of police. Arthur's opponents, on the other hand, had welcomed Franklin's appointment, hoping that this change would be in their favour, flattered that a man of his fame had been sent out to them.

In reply to Arthur, Franklin wrote: 'I feel that I have an arduous task before me and that I shall require the constant assistance of all around me and I am truly happy to find Mr. Montagu quite ready to afford me his best assistance.' He was playing for time, prepared at this stage to keep an open mind, like a sea captain getting used to the feel of his new ship. Looking back, he later wrote: 'On arriving in the colony, fully aware of the strong feeling which existed and to which repeated allusions were made in the addresses with which I was presented; aware, too, of that which was expected from me in counteraction of the policy of the late administration and that it was my duty to be on my guard against the errors into which any hasty judgement on this head might easily lead a man of my inexperience in colonial government, I determined not to disturb the policy of my predecessor without necessity, yet to lose no time in learning and judging for myself.'

The initial plan then was to keep the ship running while learning all about its particular idiosyncrasies. In his first speech to the legislature, Franklin spoke about developing the as yet unexplored areas of the island, and of establishing an adequate educational system. This long-term view of the job as a form of stewardship, keeping the colony in trim for the next man, meant little to the Arthur faction. They had no intention of staying long in Van Diemen's Land, and immediate profit was much more their concern. In his first speech Franklin made no mention of convict establishments, which had always been Arthur's primary concern, so the Arthur faction could see things were going to be different. But although anxious to secure their positions, Montagu and Forster soon summed up Sir John Franklin as an easy-going individual, someone they could manipulate.

A greater threat to the *status quo* was Maconochie. Montagu himself wrote to Arthur soon after Franklin's arrival: 'I like Sir John very much. He is open, generous, firm and perfectly honest – but he is in very bad hands, and his Private Secretary, who is a very different person, will ruin him in twelve months and make his Government a bed of thorns.' This was a clear reference to Maconochie, whom they both quickly recognized as their main enemy. Another member of the Arthur faction, Chief Justice Pedder, described Maconochie in a letter to Arthur as 'a cool-headed, shrewd, ambitious, meddling Scotchman'. To this cabal Maconochie was a dangerous rival, close to the throne. They saw him as a man of intellect, with ideas of his own, inimical to theirs – a liberal, a Philosophical Radical, with his own notions about the rights of convicts.

Maconochie had not been idle in his first days at Van Diemen's Land. He and his family were living in Government

House with the Franklins and he therefore knew all about the Arthur faction and its machinations as he set about his research for the Society for the Improvement of Prison Discipline. The society's commission was ideally suited to one of Maconochie's temperament, as he could use the same questioning, investigative ability he had used at London University and, indeed, for the Royal Geographical Society. He set about his task with an open mind: he had 'few or no strongly conceived opinions' on the subject of transportation, and no particular prior interest in penal science. An essay he had written in April 1836, *Thoughts on the Introduction of Representative Government into the Penal Colonies in Australia*, had expressed the view that colonies should 'shake off the taint of discretionary administration in whatever shape', but this was more about methods of colonization than convict management.

Maconochie started visiting convict barracks, speaking to superintendents, checking up on how the assignment system was put into practice, seeing how convicts were selected, interviewing both assigned convicts and their masters, and visiting chain gangs, road parties and anyone else involved with the convict system. But he quickly sensed that the Arthur faction were trying to block his efforts. They looked down on him and started treating him dismissively. What was a private secretary on £300 per annum doing trying to probe into their affairs?

The situation was putting Franklin in an awkward position. A naturally affable man, Sir John had none of Arthur's severity: Lady Franklin's nephew Frank Simpkinson, who served under Sir John in HMS *Rainbow*, remembered his nervousness of flogging. 'Whenever he had to carry out this revolting punishment, poor Sir John was trembling from head to foot.' He sought always to get on with others, irrespective of their differences – Simpkinson also noted that Franklin disliked confrontation and that 'chicanery ... made him ill, and so paralysed him that when he had to deal with it he was scarcely himself'– but Maconochie's involvement in local affairs was in danger of stirring up resentment and factionalism. Franklin valued

Maconochie's friendship and had asked him personally to come out to Van Diemen's Land and he sensed Maconochie's heart was in the right place, but he still had to rely on the Arthur faction to help him run the colonial government. Maconochie, he wrote, 'took on almost all subjects of local policy a different view from my own and maintained such very opposite sentiments on the important questions of the management, treatment and discipline of the convicts to mine and those gentlemen in the Colony best informed on these points.'

Maconochie, from his side, was distressed that Franklin wasn't supporting him more and seemed unable to see through the Arthur faction. He felt Sir John was too easily susceptible to their flattery. Maconochie wrote to their mutual friend George Back, the Arctic explorer, about this.

For he was completely puzzled, and I saw through the whole almost at a glance – I do not impute blame to him, or assume merit to myself on this account; the respective results were the mere effect of our different stages of preparation to look on what was new – he had none at all, and I had a great deal. He was completely bewildered while I had all my wits about me. He was received with a degree of enthusiasm consequent partly on the unpopularity of his predecessor, partly on the favourable prestige attached to his own name – and he became really half-wild upon it, and upon the gross adulation, the 'bowings', the presentations, the 'Excellencies' lavished on him by the Government officers, who read him in a moment and were delighted to find the measure of his foot so easily. I was a looker-on all the while, neither sharing in the applause nor constitutionally very likely to be imposed on by it – I read it thus at its just value, and tried to expose it equally to him, but that was hopeless. It was like trying to force a piece of barley-sugar out of a child's mouth.

The Arthur faction now tried to split them, and Maconochie soon found himself in an invidious position. As his inquiries proceeded, and he saw more and more of the need for reforms, he knew that advocating these was likely to be incompatible with his role as private secretary. An added complication was that his position had never been properly clarified, since it was a private arrangement between Franklin and himself rather than an official one. Furthermore, he and Franklin had a prior understanding that, once in Van Diemen's Land, he would be helped to find a post commensurate with his abilities, as the post of private secretary was seen as a stepping-stone to more remunerative things. Franklin had even discussed this with Lord Glenelg before leaving Britain, and Glenelg had agreed that the post of secretary alone was not sufficient for a person of Maconochie's 'acknowledged talent and character to accept'. Maconochie had told Back he had been promised a 'prominent and important office in the colony as soon as possible – it was never dreamed that I was to remain permanently as a Household drudge'. Franklin had taken steps to do this soon after arrival and had written to Sir Richard Bourke, then Governor of New South Wales, suggesting Maconochie for a post in the newly colonized Port Phillip, later to become Melbourne. In fact, Maconochie went across to Port Phillip as early as March 1837 as a stand-in for Franklin, who was too busy to leave Van Diemen's Land. Bourke had told Maconochie: 'I can assure you it would give me infinite satisfaction to be the means of introducing into those incipient communities of Port Phillip and the southern districts of New South Wales, or to any share in the management of our colonial affairs, a person so qualified as yourself', but he then added, 'I fear I have nothing to offer that would be deserving of your acceptance.' So Maconochie had to make do with his present position.

While Maconochie was away, the Arthur faction had made full use of his absence to stir up trouble, as Mary Maconochie related to Back:

> Captain Maconochie was absent about three weeks. On his return he found things totally changed, Sir John listening or giving credit to the most absurd tales against him, the duties of his office all curtailed, business usually transacted through him was now ordered to

the Colonial Secretary's Office. Everything was to be kept a dead secret; whatever Alexander said or did was an improper interference. He was an injudicious person whose judgement could not be relied upon. That he was a perfect radical, was prejudiced against Colonel Arthur, encouraged all the disaffected, and promised what he could not perform. To enumerate the one half of the falsehoods got up against him would indeed be a miserable occupation.

The situation was becoming polarized, putting more pressure on Franklin. He and Maconochie were still living under the same roof and frequenting each other's company, as this vignette of a visit to Government House by the Quaker missionaries Backhouse and Walker in April 1837 shows:

> At half past six we repaired to Government House, to dine with Sir John and Lady Franklin. Captain Maconochie with his wife and large family, principally of daughters, and a few others, were present. The Governor, as well as Lady Franklin, is particularly affable, apparently seeking to please and accommodate himself to all, so far as he can do so without compromising his character and proper dignity; and this disposition, in conjunction with an honest straightforward manner in matters of business, has had the effect of conciliating the favourable opinion of the public almost universally. After dinner we were ushered into the drawing-room, where the junior members of the two families, of Sir J. Franklin and Captain Maconochie, were seated round a large table, employed in several ways with the needle, books, &c. The absence of all ostentation or display, and the exhibition of social and domestic comfort in the family which ranks highest in the land, struck me as particularly pleasing. At nine o'clock the domestics were assembled in the drawing-room, while Sir John Franklin read a portion from the New Testament and a form of prayer. The whole was conducted with great decorum, especially on the part of the Governor, who appeared to feel what he read. I had much discourse with Captain Maconochie on the penal discipline of these colonies; and it was not a little gratifying to remark his deep interest in this subject, and the pains he must have taken to possess himself of the information he had acquired, and by which he has arrived at conclusions equally just and comprehensive.

Franklin had no objection to Maconochie consorting with more open-minded colonists such as Alfred Stephen and Thomas Gregson, men whom he liked and respected and invited to his own home, but it distressed him to see Maconochie spend more time in the company of opponents of the government. Maconochie, however, saw this simply as doing his job properly, acquiring information from all sides and finding out as much as he could about convict management. By the end of May he had summarized these findings in his first report, ready for Franklin to see. Maconochie's survey had taken in Van Diemen's Land as a whole, since the convict system could not 'be well appreciated without connecting it with the whole social edifice of which it forms a part'. His conclusions were 'extremely unfavourable ... to the present convict system' as he described in a key passage:

> The fretfulness of temper, then, which so peculiarly characterizes the intercourse of society in our penal colonies, may be attributed, I think, almost exclusively to their convict system. Degraded servants make suspicious masters and the habit of suspicion being once given, masters soon learn to suspect their equals and superiors as well as their inferiors ... the total disuse, moreover, of moral motives in the domestic relations of life, and the habit of enforcing obedience by mere compulsion, give a harsh and peremptory bearing in all transactions, which being met by a corresponding tone in others (the upper classes acting and reacting on each other exactly as the lower), every difference of opinion constitutes a ground of quarrel, and disunion becomes extensively prevalent.

He saw the convict system as 'cruel, uncertain, prodigal' and as bringing about neither reform nor example. It was maintained 'by extreme severity' and by a 'severe coercive discipline, which defeats, in consequence, its own most important objects; instead of reforming it degrades humanity, vitiates all under its influence, multiplies petty business, postpones that which is of higher interest, retards improvement, and is, in many instances, even the direct occasion of vice and crime.' This was strong stuff, and bound to hit its local Van Diemen's Land readers hard.

Maconochie felt he was being as accurate as he could. He was, he claimed, 'no sentimentalist' and fully subscribed to the right 'claimed by society to make examples of those who break its laws', so that others 'may feel constrained to respect and obey them'. Next came his crucial sentence:

> But individuals thus sacrificed to what is, at best but a high political expediency (for vengeance belongs to another) have their claims on us also, claims only the more sacred because they are helpless in our hands, and thus helpless we condemn them for our own advantage. We have no right to cast them away altogether. Even their physical suffering should be in moderation, and the moral pain we must and ought to inflict with it should be carefully framed so as if possible to reform, and not necessarily to pervert, them. The iron should enter both soul and body but not so as utterly to sear and harden them. Another world should be thought of.

He was already moving in the direction of reform, while not losing sight of the need for punishment. 'Punishment may avenge, and restraint may, to a certain limited extent, prevent crime; but neither separately, nor together, will they teach virtue. This is the province of moral training alone.' This was to be his real emphasis, and the great gap he could see in the present arrangements. He was shocked, as any perceptive visitor from Britain might be, at the difference between what he had thought was going on in Australia and the reality. He felt he had to do something about it. Most previous visitors had acquiesced, or shrugged their shoulders.

Maconochie's views were corroborated by another outside observer, an English Treasury official, George Boyes, who spent nearly thirty years in the colony:

> The people of this colony very much resemble the Americans in their presumption, arrogance, impudence, and conceit. They believe they are the most remarkable men on the Globe, and that their little Island 'whips all Creation'. They are radicals of the worst kind and their children are brought up in the belief that all

Governments are bad – that they are deprived of their rights, and that they are ground and oppressed by the Mother Country, and mocked by the Officers sent out from England to rule them. Their views are of the narrowest and most selfish kind. They are incapable of any generous sentiment, and ever ready to impute the basest motives to their fellow colonists. Lying, slandering, envy, hatred and malice are their daily aliment, and the consumption is incredible.

Franklin, cautions as ever and sensing the possible ramifications of Maconochie's report, circulated it first among the principal officials of the colony, asking for their comments. Most, especially Montagu, were hostile. The chief of police, Forster, ignored Maconochie's findings and suggested other amendments of his own, observing slyly that the latter were not theoretical but founded upon actual experience. The Principal Superintendent of Convicts, Josiah Spode, sided with Forster. Captain Cheyne, however, who was Director-General of Roads and Bridges, agreed mostly with Maconochie. A fellow Scotsman, he too deplored the waste inherent in the convict system.

Franklin passed these comments back to Maconochie, who now produced a supplementary, or second, report. In this he included proposals to remedy the situation, including the first outlines of a key feature of his approach, the mark system. Each prisoner would have to earn a fixed number of marks according to his sentence – Maconochie reckoned 6,000 marks for a seven-year sentence, 8,000 for fourteen years, and 10,000 for life. The prisoner would be paid an agreed daily wage of, say, eight or ten marks for approved work, with additional marks being awarded or deducted according to his conduct, and once he had earned the required number of marks, he would qualify for his ticket-of-leave. Additional marks could also be earned by extra work done out of hours. Food rations and other commodities such as tobacco, but also including education, would have to be paid for out of the marks earned. This would give prisoners a choice, and an experience of self-denial if they chose it, in anticipation of the time after release. The point Maconochie was making, and this is where his 'moral reform' came in, was that each prisoner should be able to influence and reduce the length of his sentence.

The second report was even more polemical in tone than Maconochie's first and brought a sharper response, from Forster in particular. Maconochie compared Forster's reaction to that of a lamplighter in London before the era of gas, old-fashioned and out of touch, and described him as someone to whom the pages of the 'much abused, often soiled, but always beautiful book of human nature were sealed'. Montagu, the Colonial Secretary, joined in, as did the Military Commandant, Major Ryan, with Montagu expressing grave alarm for the safety of the lives and property of settlers if any of Maconochie's recommendations were adopted. Franklin added his own contribution and observed in his minute: 'Much of whatever is practicable and expedient in the scheme proposed by Captain Maconochie already exists in the arrangements now in operation.' It was an evasive, sitting-on-the-fence reply: Franklin was still trying to juggle the interests of all concerned.

Maconochie knew that change would be resisted. 'No one can be more sensible than myself, that the process of transition from the present to an improved convict system would be delicate ... But the object is, first, to establish principles, and only subsequently to devise the means by which to bring them into operation.' The establishment of new principles was the core of his first reports. Maconochie gathered these papers together and gave them to Franklin for onward transmission to Britain. But Maconochie had thrown in one or two extra items without properly telling Franklin about them, a sign of his growing impatience, and of his wish to notify those in London of what was really going on.

The package of papers Maconochie sent home were his 'Report on Convict Discipline' (the replies to the Society for the Improvement of Prison Discipline questions), his supplement to this, and a reply to 'Observations on the Report by Mr. Forster'. He also included a summary of his main report as well, which he sent to Sir George Grey, partly out of fear that his package would otherwise 'perish in the Colonial Office from its own intrinsic gravity' and partly in response to Grey's request to be notified of the contents of such reports. This summary was to be the controversial document, partly because its contents were not actually read by Franklin before being sent back to Britain.

Franklin was disinclined to send Maconochie's reports back home in any case because, as Mary Maconochie wrote in a later letter, 'his, Alexander's, opinions were unfavourable to the present mode of management', and 'offended the authorities here'. Franklin's indecision may have influenced Maconochie's determination to press on. Maconochie knew that if he did not push it through, Franklin might stall for ever. Maconochie explained his inclusion of the summary in his letter to George Back. 'I took it accordingly to Sir John, told him it was to Sir George [Grey], and that it was an abstract of my other papers; begged him to forward it, and had a warm discussion with him on the subject. At length he consented, but at the moment wrote a private note to Sir George telling him that he had not seen it, knew nothing of its contents, and begging him to give it no priority of examination.' Franklin's own covering letter had urged that the materials should not be sent to the Society for the Improvement of Prison Discipline 'before they have been examined carefully by some confidential person of your department. The printing and promulgation of such opinions would undoubtedly give pain to many respectable inhabitants here.' Concerning the summary, he wrote: 'Captain Maconochie having offered his original opinions in three separate papers has drawn up a precis of them – which at his request I forward by this conveyance. I have not read it.' Franklin then sent them off by the next outgoing ship. This was on 7th October 1837.

In Maconochie's summary assignment was described as a system akin to 'slave labour', where 'no wages are allowed to be given, nor is any other moral impulse employed, excepting the remote hope of indulgence after four, six, or eight years, according to the original sentence'. Men lived 'in the roughest manner', sleeping in outhouses, six, eight or more at a time, on earthen floors. Their morale was low and 'all fly to liquor, whenever they can obtain it, to down humiliation and care.' The high incidence of drunkenness in Van Diemen's Land was already one of the strongest arguments against transportation. Moreover, even when a ticket-of-leave was obtained, the convict could not acquire property and could easily lose his ticket through 'trifling irregularities'. For the convict 'a feeling of self-respect is speedily lost amid the humiliations and inconveniences inflicted, and irritation, recklessness, insubordination, disgraceful punishment, furious resentment, drunkenness, theft, and prostitution, compute the sacrifice.' Evil was passed down the line: the convict masters acquired the reputation of being 'slave-owners', and overall there was a 'harsh, peremptory, and overbearing character to the whole intercourse of society'. The whole system was wrong, as Maconochie saw it. The punishment meted out to prisoners for their past offences was also supposed to be a means of improving their future conduct. The paradox was not sustainable and for Maconochie punishment needed to go hand in hand with reform.

Maconochie's remedy was to separate the two and make sure each was 'distinctly pursued'. Prisoners should be 'punished for the past, and trained for the future' via a staged treatment process. This was where his mark system came in. In Van Diemen's Land prisoners had often said to Maconochie 'What's the point? However hard, or well, I work, my sentence will never be reduced.' They had always felt it was not worth making any effort at self-improvement.

But Maconochie's reformist ideas needed the right sort of institution. Maconochie felt punishment for the past should initially be 'inflicted in seclusion from the free population, at stations appointed for the purpose in each penal colony'. The first punishment stage should consist of hard labour, enforced, if necessary, by physical means, so that convicts' minds might be 'humbled'. After that, the 'most stringent system of moral influence that can be devised should be here brought to bear on the prisoners to induce them to behave well, and work out their further liberation, on tickets of leave, by inspiring a just confidence in their future good intentions'.

Prisoners would thus be involved in their own future welfare. After the initial punishment period, prisoners would be grouped in parties of six 'who should choose each other, and agree to run the chances of their future probation together'. This connecting of one person's fate with the others was a repeat of his Quebec experiment.

> These parties, then, of six should be reckoned with every evening by the superintendent under whom they may be employed in the Government works, and should receive marks in his book to their credit or discredit, according to their conduct. If they have been orderly, obedient, zealous, attentive, active, industrious, cleanly in their persons and rooms civil, temperate under provocation, punctual in their attendance at prayers, school, work, &c., or have in any other way deserved commendation, they should be gainers accordingly; and if, on the other hand, any *one* has deserved censure, his party should suffer in proportion.

Group pressure was being put to good purpose 'for only thus can the utmost exertions of a whole party be ensured to reclaim a bad man'. At a later stage, when prisoners were approaching their freedom, they should be given training for this, should be 'habituated to feel tolerably free', so that 'its entire acquisition may not intoxicate them'. Again it was a staging process, rather than a sudden transition from prison to freedom.

Maconochie knew the cost would be high, and that the British government would be worried about this. However, the present system was so unproductive and caused so much crime – with its attendant police costs – that money was now being badly spent. Maconochie felt sure that his system, founded in large measure on moral influence, would be less expensive than one of pure physical restraint. Furthermore it would produce 'a smiling prospect for the future out of the moral gloom which now hangs over ... England's colonial children'. This was his hope, his widening vision. Convicts should set out to win their

own regeneration not in a selfish way but by earning their way
back to society through cultivating new 'social virtues'. This was
transforming one of the central paradoxes of the transportation
system, what convicts were meant to do at the end of their sentences. Maconochie wanted them to be properly equipped to
join in the emerging 'infant society' of Australia.

With his summary, Maconochie attached a letter to Lord John
Russell, responsible for penal affairs as Secretary of State for
Home Affairs. He asked Grey to read it with the other papers,
adding that 'if there was impropriety' to give them another direction 'or suppress them altogether' and if not, then to forward
them all to Russell. In his letter he reminded Russell of the
circumstances surrounding his report, how he had been asked by
the Society for the Improvement of Prison Discipline to
comment on the working of the existing convict system in Van
Diemen's Land and how, on referring this request to Sir George
Grey, 'I was directed to consider the subject as one on which
information was much wished, but to correspond directly concerning it only with His Majesty's Government.' Maconochie
was here deliberately addressing Russell as the most senior
person available, keen once again to go to the top. His letter
mentioned the 'variety of documents, some from myself, others
from the local authorities here' – a reference to the minutes from
Forster and other such contributions – 'partly because the interest you take in it is known to be personal as well as official'.
Maconochie sensed that Russell might be the right person to
share his views. He was right, for Russell was now coming to a
conclusion of his own on the subject of transportation.

5

Change of Direction

AFTER BEING MINUTED by James Stephen, Under-Secretary for the Colonies, Maconochie's summary and proposals were sent on to Sir George Grey on 16th February 1838 and to Russell at the Home Office on 5th March 1838. Stephen's note to Russell added that the letter 'by Captain Maconochie, R.N., Private Secretary to the Lieutenant Governor of Van Diemen's Land', contained 'some valuable remarks on the system of secondary punishment in operation in that colony'. Russell saw the documents four days later and leapt upon them. He immediately sent them off to the government printer with the firm instruction: 'This is to be printed immediately Stat. [ionery] office and proof sent to me.' This was a momentous move, as Maconochie's seemingly private communications were now suddenly being made into public documents. As Robert Hughes says in *The Fatal Shore*, 'If any moment can be said to mark the peak and incipient decline of transportation to Australia, this innocuous act marked it.' Russell, always something of an opportunist so far as Parliament was concerned, had quickly realized how he could best use Maconochie's documents. He could put them before the Molesworth Committee as firsthand evidence from a seemingly reliable authority on the spot.

The Molesworth Committee witnesses had all aired the general disenchantment with colonial life. In its final report towards the end of 1838 this was put as follows: 'It is difficult to conceive how any man ... merely having the common feelings of morality, with the ordinary dislike of crime, could be tempted, by any prospect of pecuniary gain, to emigrate, with his wife and family, to one of these colonies, after a picture has been presented to his mind of what would be his probable lot.' The committee heard that

> To dwell in Sydney ... would be much the same as inhabiting the lowest purlieus of St. Giles's, where drunkenness and shameless profligacy are not more apparent than in the capital of Australia ... every kind and gentle feeling of human nature is constantly outraged by the perpetual spectacle of punishment and misery – by the frequent infliction of the lash – by the gangs of slaves in irons – by the horrid details of the penal settlements; till the heart of the immigrant is gradually deadened to the sufferings of others, and he becomes at last as cruel as the other gaolers of these vast prisons ... The whole system of transportation violates the feelings of the adult, barbarizes the habits and demoralizes the principles of the rising generation; and the result is to use the expression of a public newspaper, 'Sodom and Gomorrah'.

Maconochie's own findings had echoed this. The Molesworth Committee's conclusions were that transportation should be stopped for its 'inefficiency in deterring from crime, and remarkable efficiency ... in still further corrupting those who undergo the punishment'.

One of Maconochie's proposals to Russell was that an outsider of high rank could be sent out to Australia to sort the situation. 'Could not some nobleman or gentleman of high rank, talent, and estimation be induced to come out for a few years on a mission of so great interest and real importance? Could not Mr. Craufurd [William Crawford, secretary of the Society for the Improvement of Prison Discipline and author of an important report on the American prison system] or some equally well informed individual in penal science and practice, be induced to accompany him?' This would get round the ten-month delay between decision and action, with colonists hanging about waiting for authorization from London, the bane of colonial life. 'References home for every trifling step requisite would be interminable, and would, moreover, almost certainly lead to error.' With a competent presiding authority on the spot, Maconochie urged that changes might quickly be implemented. This may have planted a seed in Russell's mind that Maconochie could indeed be that man.

On 6th March 1838 Maconochie sent a further paper to Grey, this time on the subject of Sir George Arthur, roundly condemning his character and regime. Why did he send it? Nobody had requested it. Perhaps Maconochie thought it would add conviction to the papers he had already sent to the Colonial Office in October 1837, and support his position as a valuable commentator from overseas. It was marked 'private', but Maconochie must have felt slightly uneasy about this as his covering letters states: 'I am somewhat embarrassed about sending this to you, yet I think you ought to have it.' He then goes on:

> I have it marked 'private' – not because I have the slightest objection to its being shewn wherever it may be desirable to shew it – or that I am unwilling, or afraid, to be answerable for its statements – or that there is a word in it that I do not most conscientiously believe to be both true and important – but simply, that I may put it entirely in your power to communicate it elsewhere, or not, as you may think best for the public service. I most unqualifiedly entertain the sentiments contained in it; and in my private correspondence I have not scrupled to say so where occasion has offered. But publicly I have no wish, and can have none, to press them.

It was an early example of his incipient verbosity, which was to dishearten government officials in Whitehall. Of course he was not to know at this stage that his earlier papers had already been published and been made public property by the Molesworth Committee.

Maconochie's paper on Arthur, after reaching London, went as usual first to James Stephen, under-secretary at the Colonial Office, who sent it on to Grey on 18th July 1838 with the following comments:

I presume that the first part of the enclosure [these were further comments from Maconochie on convict management] should be communicated to Ld. John Russell, and the Transportation Committee. I think however that the appendix, which is marked 'private', could not properly be disposed of in that manner. I think it should not even be left among the records of this office. Capt. M addresses you not in your private but in your official capacity and it is in my judgement a serious abuse of the freedom of official communication to employ it as the channel through which a philosophical analysis of the character of a gentleman formerly an officer in the colony, is to be conveyed to the Govt. The philosophy such as it is, seems to me sadly out of place, nor can I very much respect the good sense of any man who can indulge himself in such a recreation on such an occasion. To communicate his charges to General [*sic*] Arthur could do no good for they are too vague to be answered and at the same time are so exceedingly strong that probably no human being could maintain his patience and self command on reading such a censure on himself drawn up for no one purpose, but to exhibit the cleverness of the accuser. Ought not Capt. M to be admonished against the multiplication of such documents?

This note from Stephen is important as it marks the beginning of his growing animosity towards Maconochie, a feeling that was to play an increasingly important part as Maconochie's stay in Australia unfolded.

James Stephen was the third son of an MP with the same name and grew up in a reforming milieu: his father was a close friend, and became the brother-in-law, of William Wilberforce. The Stephens belonged to the Clapham Sect, a group of Evangelical Christian Philanthropists. James, the son, was a convinced Evangelical all his life. He joined the Colonial Office at the age of twenty-four, in 1813, and soon became permanent undersecretary there. Many saw him as one of the greatest civil servants of the nineteenth century. Successive ministers came to depend more and more on Stephen, and his character and talents fitted him well for this role. He knew his place, he was greatly experienced, and he enjoyed wielding power. During his time

James Stephen

the Colonial Office was faced with rapidly expanding respon-
sibilities in Africa, Canada, the West Indies and Australia. Not
surprisingly he soon earned the nicknames of 'King Stephen',
'Mr Over-Secretary Stephen' and 'Mr Mother Country', so
great was his influence. Henry Taylor, his admiring colleague,

remarked that for more than a quarter of a century Stephen 'more than any one man virtually governed the British Empire'. Within the Colonial Office, Stephen was indefatigably hard-working, insistent on formality but not good at delegation. Painfully shy, he found relationships with all but a few intimates difficult. He would not have liked Maconochie or Maconochie's type, for they were too loose, too ambitious, too free-thinking.

Stephen was deeply religious, and regularly contributed articles to the *Edinburgh Review*. He was ascetic by temperament and it was said of him that he 'once smoked a cigar and found it so delicious that he never smoked again'. After the Colonial Office he became regius professor of modern history at Cambridge, and of his five children the most notable was Leslie Stephen, first editor of the *Dictionary of National Biography* and father of Virginia Woolf.

By the time the Molesworth Committee's final report was published in August 1838, word of its likely contents had already leaked back to Australia. The colonists in Van Diemen's Land were alarmed and furious at the way their methods and morals were being discussed. The report eventually mentioned the 'progressive demoralization both of the bond and of the free inhabitants'. When they read this, it was too much for them. The relationship between colony and mother country had always been crucial to them as free settlers. Like colonists everywhere, they had gone to Australia to live out social aspirations not always available to them in Britain. Having moved up a notch in the social strata, for their world now to be so disparaged by their 'mother' country was unbearable. They were alarmed, moreover, at the prospect of an end to the assignment system, on which they relied more heavily than did the relatively developed New South Wales. Their vituperation was levelled against the Molesworth Committee and, when the full contents came out, particularly against Maconochie, whom they saw as having been the instigator of this misrepresentation. Franklin first learnt of the committee's findings through the English newspapers, and particularly *The Times*, when they reached Hobart. Lengthy descriptions of the committee's proceedings and accounts by its witnesses filled their pages. Maconochie's reports were mentioned, with the condemnatory description of Van Diemen's Land. Now uproar broke out and Maconochie was accused of going behind Franklin's back, of smuggling his report back to Britain under the guise of official papers. He became everyone's favourite target, as they heaped onto him all their guilt and anxiety at their involvement in the treatment of convicts.

Franklin now found himself in an untenable position, feeling he would have to dispense with Maconochie as private secretary if he was to continue as Governor. This he did on 21st September 1838. He wrote to their mutual friend Sir Francis Beaufort thus: 'As soon as I discovered that I had been the unconscious means of sending through Sir George Grey to Lord John Russell a summary of his Papers on Prison Discipline which had never been shewn me, I could no longer submit to such a want of confidence and propriety in my Private Secretary.' He sent Maconochie his dismissal by internal letter at Government House, and within five minutes an answer came back from Maconochie 'intimating that he would soon think better of it and asking Sir John not to drive him out that night'. Lady Franklin felt this was being altogether 'too theatrical', as she told her sister, but agreed that this was 'an unkind and unhandsome cut'. She sent for Maconochie and together they went to see Mary Maconochie. Maconochie had 'a few words in private' with his wife, first explaining his dismissal. Mary Maconochie was clearly shocked by the news: Lady Franklin described her 'as cold and immoveable as a stone', feeling 'wronged and full of disdain' and 'scarcely moved even by my emotion'. Mary Maconochie's response was all the keener as all along she had doubted the wisdom of Maconochie's coming out to Australia to be with Franklin.

Lady Franklin was plunged into a crisis. As she told her sister Mary, 'the subject so absorbs my mind that I can scarcely think of anything else', and she wanted to be 'the mediator and friend towards them'. As often happened with her in moments of stress, she now felt 'unwell' and retired to her room. Mary Maconochie visited her there and Lady Franklin suggested that the Maconochies should go to their mutual friends the Gregsons the next day and stay with them while looking for a new house. Maconochie still hoped he would be 'restored' to Franklin's favour, and Lady Franklin, when she came down to say goodnight, felt it necessary and her duty 'to assure him that there was no chance whatever of it happening'. Mary Maconochie agreed with her. 'Better not,' she said, 'much better not.'

The Maconochies left the next day, with Mary Maconochie 'entreating' Lady Franklin not to attend their departure, but Maconochie went to see her and 'embracing me most affectionately, too much so I thought to be sincere, begged me to deliver a huge letter he gave to my hand to Sir John'. The Franklins read Maconochie's letter that evening but it only made matters 'decidedly worse', according to Lady Franklin. The tone of the letter was 'not merely of the most earthly quality but of absolute disrespect'. Maconochie's self-conceit stood out, he was 'magnifying his own consequences'. Maconochie was probably being defensive as he undeniably felt hurt. However, Franklin, as Lady Franklin reported, still 'dwelt on his friendship with him' and was inclined to be lenient. The Franklins set about composing their answer to his letter together but 'Sir John cut short his task at rather a later bed hour than usual' while his wife sat up 'until Monday morning sun's traces came through my window blind' composing it, indomitable as ever. The reply to Maconochie was dispatched by constable to the Gregsons' house the next morning. In the evening, when the executive committee met, Franklin read to them both his letter and Maconochie's. There was more indignation at Maconochie and his presumption of Lady Franklin's support.

Maconochie now sent home a long exculpatory letter to Lord Glenelg and another to Sir George Grey, vindicating, as he saw it, his conduct. Maconochie was still bemused by the strength of the reaction against him. His view was that he had kept to his side of the bargain so far as the Society for the Improvement of

Prison Discipline and the Colonial Office were concerned, as he wrote to Lord Glenelg: 'His Excellency Sir John Franklin views my conduct in this particular with extreme displeasure. He considers it to have been disrespectful both to Your Lordship and himself – that it has given my views an advantage over others better, or at least equally entitled, in his opinion, to early consideration – and he has, in consequence dissolved my official connection with him.' He was particularly vexed by insinuations being made against him. 'It has been imputed to me, that I have been unguarded in expressing my opinions here – but on the contrary, scarcely any one knows them, which I much regret.' It was a fair point, since no one in Van Diemen's Land had properly read what he had sent home and all were basing their reactions on newspaper reports. Everyone there was still waiting to see the official publication of the Molesworth Committee. Moreover, Maconochie could hardly be blamed for the use of his report and summary by the Molesworth Committee, as the decision to print it had been taken on the spur of the moment by Lord John Russell. Maconochie reminded Glenelg in his letter that the Society for the Improvement of Prison Discipline had asked him to report on the operation of the penal system in Van Diemen's Land as 'a *private*, an *individual* task'.

A week later Maconochie returned to Government House requesting to see Lady Franklin, and an interview took place in the library. Maconochie regretted what he had done concerning the use of her name; he said that his recent letter had simply been an outpouring of his feelings, and he acknowledged his error in writing directly to Russell without forewarning Franklin. But there was no hint of regret. 'He took this without a word of remorse but seemed to excite his spirits as he talked with great enthusiasm about his system, the glory of which would come to be recognised.' Maconochie was still convinced of the rightness of his position and saw no reason to back down.

The Maconochies now moved to a new 'pleasant house' in New Town, two miles away, although Maconochie still expressed himself 'constantly anxious to remain on amicable terms', as

Lady Franklin noted. She was drawn to Maconochie, whom she perhaps saw as a more dynamic, controversial figure than her husband. Most of the island's inhabitants, however, remained hostile to him. John Montagu, the Colonial Secretary, never allowed his animosity towards Maconochie to wane. Writing to Franklin about Maconochie, Montagu said: 'I consider the day of your separation from him the most fortunate of your life'. Local newspapers varied in their responses. The *True Colonist* took Maconochie's side and praised the 'open candour of his character – his unassuming demeanour to all classes – and readiness to oblige and advise the humblest supplicant to the Government for justice, or on other business,' and contrasted his character with the 'mystification and concealment – the overbearing presumption – the low and detested system of political deception, intrigue and artifice, which were the specific characteristics of Colonel Arthur and all his official clique'.

However, Maconochie recognized in private that his actions had not been blameless, and admitted as much in letters to Britain. To George Back he put it thus: 'I do not consider myself faultless in them – on the contrary I would give a right arm to recall some of them – yet were they all *virtuously* purposed, and at the moment wore a much more favourable aspect . . . I did not tell Sir John that the MS contained a hypothetical Letter to Lord John Russell. I am more sorry now for both circumstances that I can express . . . I was a solitary Abolitionist amid a host of slave-owners and drivers . . . the more lofty and laudable my purpose, the more ready, I fear, was I to look with indulgence on the means which appeared to be required to attain it.' Maconochie also recognized in these letters that his dismissal had been inevitable. Writing to his successor at the Royal Geographical Society, Captain Washington, he said: '[Franklin] might have been more friendly in the manner in which he went against me; but in the matter itself, he could no more act other than he has done than he could fly.' The quarrel with Franklin 'has been unavoidable, neither all his fault, neither all mine, nor all between us. And Time will yet make all apparent.' Yet

Maconochie was clearly exasperated that Franklin had not been robust enough, or used some of his old naval determination in handling Van Diemen's Land affairs.

Mary Maconochie backed her husband up. As an army officer's daughter, she was always a shrewd and realistic observer of her surroundings. She saw things steadily and saw them whole. She had all along doubted the wisdom of going out to Van Diemen's Land, as is clear from a letter she wrote to George Back, in which she mentioned her affection for Jane Franklin – 'for Lady Franklin I shall ever feel warmly attracted' – but revealed that she had never held Franklin in high regard: 'For Sir John, I never thought much and since our sojourn here less and less'. Gradually the Maconochies were being ostracized. Not wishing to stir up further controversy, Maconochie turned down invitations from friends, kept to himself and wrote copiously. He put together a collection of his various papers, including the summary of his 'Report on Convict Discipline' and other items stressing the superiority of moral influence to physical coercion in convict management, and had them published on 30th November 1838 in Hobart, as *Thoughts on Convict Management and other subjects connected with the Australian Penal Colonies*.

Mary Maconochie described their situation in her letter to Back: 'We see few people and go nowhere, your friend Alexander is like a Lion at bay, deafened by the barking and yelping of the curs about him, but in no other way stirred from his steady honesty of purpose – he must bide his time and pay the penalty.' She referred to him as 'so noble an animal' having to contend with 'the continued tissue of falsehood, suspicion and unworthy accusation continually poured forth'. It was important to show that she still had faith in her husband: 'In my hours of feeble hope, frightful visions pass before me, but for the most part I am hopeful; he has powers to force attention with common fair play; this he has not yet had, but the cause of truth and humanity can never altogether fail, and though it may be long deferred and most painfully so for us in every way, yet a time must come when his merits are known as they ought to be. In the meantime it is a most cruel position to place us in, in an expensive colony, and our young family to educate and there are no advantages for them here in any way.' Financially, matters were indeed becoming pressing. They had made some money out of land speculation but had only recently learnt that the person they had entrusted their financial affairs to in London, a Mr Bradbury, formerly Maconochie's clerk at the Royal Geographical Society, had failed to use the money to settle their outstanding debts and had instead pocketed the money himself. Now with six children to look after – they had all just been ill with a fever that had also struck down fourteen residents in Government House – Mary Maconochie's hands were full.

Maconochie, sustained by his wife, was determined to combat adversity and profit from it. In an important letter of 29th May 1839 to Captain Washington he wrote of his continuing commitment to the reform of the convict system. 'That cause has now got me complete. I will "go the whole hog" on it. I will neither acquiesce in the moral destruction of so many of my fellow beings nor in misrepresentation made of myself, without doing *everything* that may be necessary or possible to assist both. "Thrice armed is he who in his cause is right" – and I am more than right in mine.' He was now bracing himself to stand out against the crowd and pursue his own beliefs. He was pleased by some recent newspaper reports, which seemed to vindicate him and by news of the Molesworth Committee's findings: 'Lord John Russell's Minute to the Transportation Committee recommending my views and plans has given me great hopes.' He would wait and see what happened. 'I give myself twelve months to see this through. Within that time I shall hang loose, involve myself in no permanent office but be perfectly quiet, giving no offence.' He had 'no disposition' to become a settler; after February next he would return to 'take my chances in England'.

Lady Franklin remained an ally. Writing to her sister, she explained: 'There was something so much more liberal and conciliatory in his policy, such a freedom from colonial suspicion and narrowness of views and personal spite and hostility, so much more philosophy, and so much less apparent self-interest that I could not but value his union with us and deplore his separation.' Lady Franklin regretted that the two families now saw less and less of each other.

> The Maconochies and I have not seen each other for the last seven months . . . and I assure you I suffer from it – I have a growing desire to stumble in their way – to be able to look at and speak to them. I am a poor, soft-hearted creature that can never cease altogether to love those I have once loved . . . You will be tired of my eternal talk about the Maconochies – yet consider that they lived nearly two years with us as one family, and that now, in the same country, in the same town, I never by any chance obtain a glimpse of any one of them.

Early in 1839 Montagu sailed for Britain on eighteen months' leave, ostensibly to arrange for his sons' education. Mary Maconochie never had any illusions about Montagu, as she mentioned in a letter to Back about his visit to Britain: 'You will probably meet our deadly enemy Capt. Montagu – that snake in the grass, sleek, smooth, & slippery, a specimen of our Genus homo well worthy of the attention of the naturalist . . . like many noxious animals he has the power of soothing & fanning his victims to sleep, never attacking openly or boldly . . . But from close & repeated examination, it is found he possesses *invisible* tentacula, which come from many quarters, puncturing, & injuring the victim, gradually destroying & undermining its character.'

However, as 1839 drew to a close prospects brightened for Maconochie. Action on the Molesworth Committee's report had started. Transportation to the New South Wales mainland was to cease on 1st August 1840, and convicts sent out from Britain would be sent instead only to Van Diemen's Land and Norfolk Island. Lord Normanby had now replaced Lord Glenelg as Secretary of State for the Colonies (Glenelg had been sacked for incompetence by Russell) and he issued guidelines on how the new policy was to be carried out. He had written to the new Governor of New South Wales, Sir George Gipps, on 11th May 1839: 'With respect to Norfolk Island, it is the intention of Her Majesty's Government that an essential alteration should be made in the system of punishment pursued there. The healthiness of the climate, the fertility of the soil, and its entire separation from intercourse with ordinary emigrants, render it peculiarly fit for the reception of a large number of convicts, subject to careful superintendence and discipline, and for whom regular means of employment must be provided.' The 'careful superintendence' was an opening for Maconochie, as Normanby further suggested that the superintendence should be entrusted to an officer, 'who should feel a deep interest in the moral improvement of the convicts, and be disposed to devote his whole energies to this important object'.

Normanby, in a confidential memorandum, actually recommended Maconochie for the position but left it up to Gipps to finalize the decision. Gipps sent his dispatch across to Franklin, letting him decide whether to offer Maconochie the post. When he did so, Maconochie accepted with alacrity. Franklin wrote to his old naval friend Francis Beaufort in November 1839 with some relief. 'You will rejoice to hear that Maconochie has rec'd from Sir Geo Gipps the offer of the appt to Norfolk Island with a salary of £800 per year ... you can imagine the gratification I felt ... I sent for him at once and placed before him the whole of the official correspondence as well as the letter of Sir George Gipps ... I trust he may soon be established on the island and I most heartily wish him all the success he anticipates in the working of his system.' Once Franklin had offered it and Maconochie had accepted it, the 'estrangement which had for above a year existed' between them ceased.

Maconochie hurried across to Sydney to see Gipps, feeling he could best discuss the appointment in person. Maconochie held a high opinion of Gipps, to whom he would be accountable, and whom he thought 'a most excellent man, just, equitable, and high minded'. Gipps received him in 'a very kindly fashion'. As they discussed the operation of Norfolk Island, Maconochie's main objection was to the continued presence alongside the new batch of convicts of the 'old hands', hardened prisoners who had been sent there for reoffending since arriving in Australia. If he was to try out his mark system properly, he would be much better off with just 'new' prisoners. His line was that 'to coop up 1,500 men on a small island under two systems, one thought more advantageous than the other, would certainly breed jealousy and quarrelling between them and infallibly injure both'. Gipps, however, could not permit this, as he had no authority to withdraw the 'doubly convicted' reoffenders. Maconochie offered to give up Norfolk Island instead, 'and try my experiment on a much smaller scale in some retired nook in New South Wales, rather than be under the necessity of keeping up two systems at once'. But this proposal was not granted either, and 'though already foreseeing the rock on which I should ultimately split with Sir George, I was forced to acquiesce'. Maconochie acquiesced because in any event he now very much wanted to try out his new system, aware that he might not get another chance to do so.

Gipps said he had given Maconochie's suggestions his 'very mature and anxious consideration'. With regard to the doubly convicted felons on the island, however, he said his hands were tied since their presence there had been 'undoubtedly known to Her Majesty's Government when Norfolk Island was selected'. For Gipps, only recently appointed, to countermand directives from London would have been too risky but also out of character. He was four years younger than Maconochie, the son of a vicar. As a soldier, he had fought with Wellington's army in the Peninsular campaigns but missed Waterloo as he was preparing fortifications at Ostend at the time. He was then sent to the West Indies, where he showed much administrative ability. Indeed his reports to the Colonial Office so impressed senior ministers that he was recalled to become private secretary to Lord Auckland, First Lord of the Admiralty, and afterwards spent two years with the Gosford Commission in Canada; once

Sir George Gipps

again his able memoranda in the Gosford report were praised. He was knighted, promoted major, and then appointed Governor of New South Wales on 5th October 1837. He had arrived in Sydney with his wife and son on 24th February 1838, to find a city of 22,000 people and of strong contrasts. Alongside the impressive Government House, where they lived, were grog shops and disorderly houses. Animals roamed the streets and there was no sewerage. It was a society at war with itself – officials clashed with other officials, merchants fought merchants, squatters despised townsmen, freemen hated emancipists, emancipists hated convicts, and the convicts hated everyone. Gipps had several immediate problems to deal with, not least those of the 'squatters', sheep farmers seeking security of tenure. He set to work, but like many intelligent people was impatient and short-tempered. He hated delays. Lady Franklin met him in Sydney and found him 'somewhat peppery ... straightforward and frank when answering questions, but asking none himself'. She also thought him good-hearted and utterly devoted to his wife, and that they were both devoted to their son. In his private letters a whimsical sense of humour is apparent. Having in his role as governor to serve two masters, Crown and colony, was proving a difficult task. With communication between Sydney and London slow and uncertain, he often had to act independently, and defy both Whitehall and the colonists. His task was made no easier by the frequent changes of secretaries of state over him – first Lord Glenelg (1835–9), then Lord Normanby (February–September 1839), Lord Russell (1839–41), Lord Stanley (1841–5), and finally Gladstone (from 1845) – but the permanence of James Stephen as under-secretary helped maintain consistency. Gipps treated the Colonial Office with marked respect. His dispatches were models of their kind, and he knew the office's real priorities: 'My whole official experience teaches me that in Downing Street at least the Governor who keeps his government out of debt is the best.'

Gipps was determined to support Maconochie, as his dispatch at the time to Russell shows. 'I cannot conclude this despatch without expressing my hope that nothing contained in it may lead your Lordship to consider me as in any way indisposed to see Captain Maconochie make trial of his system under the most favourable circumstances, and such as he may himself entirely approve.' Gipps backed this up by saying that though he may have had doubts of 'any great results being produced by it, or rather results upon a great scale, I have great faith in the principles on which his experiments are to be founded', an early example of Gipps's equivocation. For while he may have admired Maconochie's strength as an innovator, Gipps wanted to make sure he was not caught out and that the government in London knew he could foresee the risks.

Looking back on their first meeting, Maconochie summed up the differences between himself and Gipps. 'His idols were order and discipline, to attain which his tendency was to severity, and . . . he over-valued mere authority and under-valued what I called means of persuasion, on which, moreover, I rested almost my whole system.' Maconochie was a pragmatist and wanted to work things out as he went along, by 'means of persuasion'. He confirmed his acceptance of the post, writing to Gipps saying how pleased he was at appointment and in 'the confidence so reposed in me; it gives me both pride and pleasure, and I pledge myself to devote my whole energies to the interesting and important object thus set before me'. He still worried about maintaining any 'effective separation' between the two groups of prisoners there – the reoffenders and the new arrivals – since there would be 'wicked purpose' in one group and 'active curiosity' in the other.

Russell, approved of Maconochie's appointment. 'It is the intention of Her Majesty's Government that Captain Maconochie's plan should be left to be tried by himself, and that the experience of that trial should guide the further proceedings.' But Russell did not answer Maconochie's principal objection. With Gipps claiming no authority to resolve it, the issue had been fudged, as so often happens with innovative schemes set up to remedy a failing situation.

At the end of 1839 Maconochie returned from Sydney to Hobart to fetch his family. They had been in Australia for three eventful years, but now a new adventure was beckoning. While waiting for their ship to Norfolk Island they stayed for a month in Sydney. It was a raw, bustling, cosmopolitan place and

Maconochie's children relished this after the quieter atmosphere of Hobart: the two eldest, Mary Ann (or Minnie) and her sister Catherine, were now seventeen and fifteen respectively. They were a close-knit family, their education largely home-based and with a strong parental input.

One of the people Maconochie came across in Sydney was William Ullathorne, one of the key witnesses to the Molesworth Committee, who was shortly to return to Britain. They talked inevitably of Norfolk Island, and Ullathorne told Maconochie of his visit there in 1834. Ullathorne was a Yorkshireman, who, like Maconochie, had gone to sea as a young man. By a curious coincidence his mother was a cousin of Sir John Franklin, brought up next door to him in Spilsby, Lincolnshire. At the age of seventeen Ullathorne had a sudden religious conversion to Catholicism and entered the Benedictine monastery at Downside. At the age of twenty-five, having been ordained, he was sent out to Australia to join the new Catholic mission there. Ullathorne, who had already criticized the transportation system in his *The Catholic Mission in Australia*, had recently written a further pamphlet on *The Horrors of Transportation*, published in 1838. All this was fresh in his mind when he met Maconochie in 1840.

> Prior to the commencement of his experiment, he [Maconochie] had done me the honour by letter, as well as by interview, to ask my frank opinion of his plans ... struck by his mild and open bearing, I gave him my opinion as frankly as he asked it, and much in these words. Your system, I said, embodies elements of the utmost value, but it appears to require provisions of a more astringent virtue. Besides, in Norfolk Island, you will have the worst and most inveterate criminals, the scum of the Penal Settlements, to deal with, and you will have hard and unfit instruments in your co-operators. They, and not you, will be in hourly contact with the men, and yet what you want is to carry your own spirit everywhere. Could you be your own wardens and overseers, you might succeed; provided at all events, that these double-dyed felons were made to feel that behind all your kindness there exists a desperate resolution, as prompt, if the necessity comes, to cut them down, as to encourage and reward them.

The Revd William Ullathorne

Mindful of Ullathorne's advice, Maconochie asked Gipps for 'intelligent superintendence' to carry out his plan – in other words, proper assistants, men 'of liberal minds, not wedded to any particular system, yet reasonably hopeful and zealous in the prospects of this one'. It was a sensible precaution, but Ullathorne's warning proved prescient as Maconochie was to have much trouble with his 'wardens' and the existing 'old' staff on the island, whose views rarely matched his. The chief of them was the Superintendent of Convicts, often a retired military man in need of the money, whose assistants would also be retired NCOs. It was not a pleasant job nor an easy one, and the staff usually felt happiest when running things along military lines. In Maconochie's time the Superintendent was William Foster, described as 'an elderly man who has seen much military service, is addicted to intemperance, indulged in prolonged fits of insobriety, the effect of which had been to impair his health and render him unfit to discharge his duties; he is frequently confined to his bed by serious attacks of illness of some duration'. Many of the warders and lesser overseers were ex-convicts who had completed their sentences and elected to stay on in the island, since the mainland was unlikely to offer a more attractive alternative. As Maconochie found for his regime, these ex-convicts were often the best staff, as they understood the convict mentality.

In Sydney, Maconochie arranged for other senior staff appointments: notably James Reid as Assistant Surgeon and John Simm as Overseer of Works, or rather, as Maconochie foresaw, Overseer of Marks. Reid was to get just over £100 per year and Maconochie's own salary was a respectable £800 per year. Gipps, however, was behind another appointment, Charles Ormsby, with an Irish police background, as Maconochie's deputy. Gipps planned for Ormsby to look after the 'old' prisoners while Maconochie tried out his innovative system with the 'new'.

Before leaving Sydney, Maconochie regularly consulted Gipps and, as a foretaste of what was to come, bombarded him with memoranda. One was on the 'social management of a large insular establishment', another on the method of exchanging marks for indulgences such as tea, sugar or tobacco, another on the remission of punishments, another on sending female and juvenile convicts to the same island establishment as males and yet another commenting on Russell's views on the abolition of transportation. Maconochie was an inveterate memo writer, and his sprawling handwriting gives an indication of the speed at which he wrote. In the memo on 'social management' he argued that his new system would be cheaper than a coerced one, as his labour would be free and more productive since it would be stimulated by the same motives as 'animate industrious life in free society'.

Maconochie's idea of introducing female and juvenile convicts to Norfolk Island was turned down by Gipps. Maconochie argued that 'it is vain expecting improvement in the morals of this Colony except on the basis of families.' The family was the 'cradle of order and morality', whereas a place full of unmarried men was the 'cradle of disorder and immorality'. Gipps felt that it would be dangerous to have women convicts there, as much because of the presence of the military as because of the male convicts. Gipps, however, granted Maconochie's request to set up a proper library and to encourage music on the island. Maconochie told Gipps that he had already pre-empted this by buying 'the entire stock of Mr Ellard, music-seller, now leaving the colony for England', including blank music sheets which the 'old, lame, sick or infirm prisoners' could use for copying out.

For the library Maconochie asked for a wide selection of reading matter: the *Farmers' and Mechanics' Magazine* as this would benefit 'the minds of men in very humble life, and otherwise remaining illiterate', as well as Loudon's works on agriculture, gardening and cottage architecture, Davy's lectures, Cobbett's *Cottage Economy* and assorted guides to subjects such as brewing, baking and farriery. 'An uneducated man is newly born when his mind is thus awakened.' Moral and religious works should be 'narrative as well as didactic', and he wanted some works of 'controversial divinity' as this encouraged polemical discussions and would open the mind to a 'perception of the value of minute distinctions, and fix it on its highest interests, even through the medium of error'. Books of narrative and moral tendency were to include *Robinson Crusoe*, which would teach 'energy, hopefulness in difficulty, regard and affection for our brethren in savage life, &c'. Accounts of Pacific Ocean voyages such as Cook's were recommended as 'the mind of the whole white race in this hemisphere wants softening towards its aboriginal brethren.' National poetry – 'Dibdin's and Moore's Songs, Burns's, Scott's, and Crabbe's Poems, the Waverley Novels, Miss Edgeworth's Works, Miss Austen's, Miss Mitford's, Horace Smith's, &c' – would be useful in providing images of home life, which were 'too much wanting in the individual experience of our lower and criminal classes'. But Maconochie was not so sure about plays. 'Shakespeare's Plays ought to be included . . . though I fear, rather than hesitate, to recommend many more. The English drama is often licentious; but substantially its tendency is moral.'

Maconochie's educational programme aimed to bring out powers that he believed were 'unawakened' in individuals. This was education in its literal sense of bringing out, releasing people's potential. 'Minds thus once touched will expand almost as the tree shoots.' Music was needed for its uplifting and humanizing powers, its ability to 'wean the minds' of those with 'social weakness' from 'former low amusements' to others 'higher and less dangerous'. It was also a social occupation and its acquisition difficult, so this would be good training in 'pace and perseverance'. Seraphines, a type of reed instrument, were asked for, if organs were not available, plus an assortment of 'the usual band instruments'.

Gipps read his proposals and granted these specific requests, making sure his own written replies to Maconochie were also sent back to London for Russell to read. Gipps assured Russell that he had considered it right to give Maconochie all the support in his power 'and every reasonable facility for doing it in his own way', but said he could not accede to the proposal that marks could be exchanged for indulgences. He would consider it only if 'it was absolutely necessary in order to give his system a fair trial'. This was more of a concession than it seemed, for Gipps knew it was fundamentally opposed to the government view that every transported felon should, for two years at least, be punished and receive no indulgences whatsoever. Under Maconochie's scheme marks could be used to purchase benefits sooner than that.

Maconochie's final memorandum proposed an idea more familiar to modern approaches. 'I have little doubt that after a time another arrangement might be made. Private capital might be admitted into our penal establishments under adequate regulation, the Government funding only buildings and labour at a fixed rent.' This would give 'greater simplicity to the public accounts' and the 'work so conducted would be more varied, more judicious, more enterprising at the same time, and more economically, therefore more instructively, prosecuted by private hands than under any public management.' Another innovative idea was his suggestion that second offenders, the 'doubly convicted', should be branded or tagged, another idea ahead of its time. They should be marked with 'a small private brand (as between the toes or elsewhere), which shall be invisible unless specifically sought for, but yet shall identify cases of second conviction in any part of the world.'

Maconochie was nothing if not persistent, as Gipps soon became aware. He was also impatient to get started and wanted to put his plan into full operation. He took the view that the Molesworth Committee had endorsed his ideas and that his appointment, actively supported, as he thought, by Russell, meant that his views were being used to herald a new era in convict treatment. His reading of this led him to proceed full ahead. Gipps never really clarified this with him, nor established the amount of discretion he was permitted in putting his system into practice. Gipps sent Russell a dispatch on 25th February 1840 emphasizing the trial nature of this experiment and adding: 'Captain Maconochie avows his opinion that the first object of all convict discipline should be the reformation of the criminal. This opinion, however agreeable it may be to the dictates of humanity, is not, I believe, the received one of legislators, who rather require as the first object of convict discipline that it should be a terror to evil doers.' This was the unresolved crux of the matter. Gipps seemed to be pulled in two directions at once, siding partly with the view that Norfolk Island should be kept as a place of ultimate deterrence and partly with the hope that Maconochie would somehow produce another alternative.

Gipps also explained to Russell why he had decided to stick to Norfolk Island:

> I feel persuaded that Captain Maconochie will have far better chances of success at Norfolk Island, than he could possibly have had, if his experiment had been tried, as he once expressed a wish it should be, on the roads in New South Wales. In such a position he would have been constantly overwatched by a jealous, and even a hostile public: every failure, however trifling, would have been exposed, exaggerated, and turned into ridicule; and his own attention would have been constantly withdrawn from the object to which it ought solely to be directed in order to defend himself against the attacks, whether well or ill founded, with which he would have been assailed.

Gipps was right; the New South Wales settlers certainly would not have taken to such an experiment.

Maconochie had also sent Gipps a plan for a new gaol to be build on Norfolk Island at Longridge, the agricultural station where the new prisoners would be based. He knew that reform was not just about individuals but depended on the nature of the institution itself. He wanted to cultivate an *esprit de corps* and to bring this about the buildings needed to allow 'moral, religious, and other intellectual stimulus and instruction'.

> My plans then for a penitentiary would be of a long narrow hall, perhaps 30 or 40 feet wide, by any length, and divided across this length into chapels, say 50 or 60 feet long each. Between buttress walls outside of these, I would erect my separate cells, probably in three rows, varying in security and comfort as may be deemed expedient (thus the upper row may be the most secure, and lighted only from the roof; the second have a cheerful look out, and the lower have small gardens, and be secured by a simple latch on the door, &c.), and all provided with a door from the chapel (and light open iron rail galleries in it), to enable the clergyman and his assistants to visit them, and with a window of ground

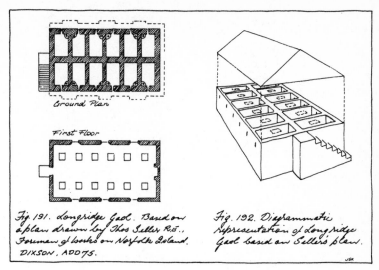

Ground Plan
First Floor
Fig. 191. Longridge Gaol. Based on a plan drawn by Thos Seller R.E., Foreman of Works on Norfolk Island.
DIXSON, ADD 75.
Fig. 192. Diagrammatic representation of Longridge Gaol based on Seller's plan.
JSK

Longridge cells as designed by Maconochie

> glass, or a wooden panel, by sloping which a voice from the pulpit or reading-desk may be easily heard by the prisoners within them.

The idea of reading to prisoners was a way of using their time in a more beneficial way. Clergymen would have a useful role in this, providing readings of an uplifting and moralizing nature, but the real innovation was the prisoners' freedom to choose whether or not to listen to them.

6

Norfolk Island

CAPTAIN COOK FIRST saw Norfolk Island at daybreak on 10th October 1774. He and his party, *en route* from New Caledonia to New Zealand, were probably the first white men to set foot on the island, which had hitherto been used only as a stopover by seafaring Polynesians. Cook named the island after his patron, the Duchess of Norfolk, and he noticed the fertility of its volcanic soil, its flax plants and its giant spruce, now known as Norfolk Island pine. Accompanying him ashore was his astronomer William Wales, a fellow Yorkshireman, who wrote: 'I saw many trees which were, breast high, as thick as two men could fathom and at the same time exceeding straight and high.' Cook felled one to replace a topmast on his ship, and the ship's carpenter was impressed by its quality.

The island was five miles long and three miles wide. At its centre rose two elevations of over 1000 feet: the higher of the two Cook named Mount Pitt, after the prime minister. Cook set sail after the second day, noting the absence of a safe anchorage or natural harbour. On his return to London, Cook's report of the island's flax and pines was passed on to the government, who quickly saw the island's usefulness for ships' masts. When Arthur Phillip arrived with the First Fleet in Botany Bay in 1788, he immediately dispatched his trusty 34-year-old second lieutenant, Philip Gidley King, to take over the island, not least to prevent it falling into the hands of the French.

King took with him twenty-two companions in the *Supply*, seven staff and nine male and six female convicts, each chosen for their skills. Nathaniel Lucas was a carpenter from London, transported for theft of clothing, John Rice, a rope-maker from Exeter, sent away 'for burglariously breaking and entering', Edward Westlake, also from the west of England for 'stealing a wether sheep valued 12s and forty pounds of mutton value 10s' and Edward Garth, another Londoner, 'for feloniously stealing 2 live cows value £17'. The youngest of the nine was Charles McLellan from Sunderland, fourteen years old when sentenced in 1785 to seven years' transportation for 'stealing 1 Bladder purse, value one penny, a gold half-guinea, one halfcrown, one silver shilling and six pennies in halfpence, the contents of the purse', while the oldest was Richard Widdicombe, aged seventy-two, given seven years' for 'stealing 1 wooden winch value 2s and other goods value forty-one shillings and four pence, the property of Vincente Juanez y Echelar'.

The female convicts were nearly all in their twenties. The oldest, at thirty, was Ann Inett, a 'mantua maker', or qualified dressmaker, from Worcester, sent away for stealing '1 dimity petticoat, 1 muslin apron, 1 pair stuff shoes, 3 muslin handkerchiefs' and sundry other pieces of wearing apparel, 'the property of Jane Brookes'. Sentenced to death by hanging, she was reprieved and given seven years' transportation. King, himself a draper's son from Cornwall, took to Inett and made her his mistress. On Norfolk Island they had two sons, suitably named Norfolk and Sydney, the first children to be born on the island, who were later sent off to be educated in Britain. Other female convicts were Elizabeth Hipsley a needlewoman from London, Olivia Gaskin, also from Worcester and Elizabeth Colley, another Londoner, aged twenty-two, sent down for fourteen years for 'feloniously receiving at the hour of 10 in the night, 1 linen gown and 1 silk cloak knowing them to have been stolen'. King promised the women they would not be overworked on the island and would be able to return to Britain once their sentence had expired. He further promised that any 'partiality or reciprocal affection' between male and female convicts on the island would be tolerated.

King took enough provisions to last six months, including tents, farm implements and flax-dressing tools and a four-oared boat. The first days were spent tree-felling, cultivating the soil and planting grain and vegetable seeds. True to King's expectations, convicts started pairing off – Olivia Gaskin with Nat Lucas, Susannah Gough with Edward Garth, and King himself with Ann Inett – and children were born, six within two years. King began to feel he ought to start up a school. The group slept out in the open to begin with, and this frightened the convicts, who woke in terror at the strange sounds made by the owls in the wooded valley behind and at the whistles and long drawn-out moans of the sea ebbing back and forth through narrow gaps in the rocks. The island was a place of outstanding beauty, with its green sloping hills, white rolling surf and coastline of near vertical cliffs and its spectacular variety of birds, including brilliantly coloured parrots that whistled as they flew by in small flocks; but it was tough and unremitting to live upon. The warm south-west wind soon scorched the tender growing plants, and rats discovered and attacked the newly sown grain. Empty ship's casks were then fitted up as rat traps, and 'upwards of 1000' were caught, by King's reckoning. Grubs and caterpillars had to be hand-picked off by the women convicts, a laborious task as 'within two hours they were as thick as ever'.

King set out some house rules. The first was that 'no person is to absent himself from public worship which will begin every Sunday morning at eleven o'clock, in the commandant's house, when every one will come clean and orderly, and behave themselves devoutly.' Work was to begin at daylight, and go on until half past seven in the morning, when they had a break, and continue from half past eight until half past eleven, and then from two until sunset. On Saturdays they could cultivate gardens for themselves with seeds given to any of them who had cleared away sufficient garden ground. Female convicts were to sweep round the houses or tents every morning, and to cook the victuals for the men, 'and every person is strictly forbid cleaning any fish or fowls in or near the houses but to go to the sea-side for that purpose.' The women had to collect the dirty linen belonging to the men every Friday, 'and to return each man his proper linen, washed and mended, on the Sunday morning'. Exchanging or selling clothes by the convicts was strictly forbidden as their clothing was the property of the Crown. King wanted his discipline to be firm but friendly, and hoped his convicts would be 'honest and obliging towards each other'. He warned them that the 'dishonest or idle may not only assure themselves of being totally excluded from any present or future indulgences, but also that they will be chastised, either by corporal punishment on the island, or be sent to Port Jackson, to be tried by a criminal court there'.

Although flax grew plentifully on the island, none of the group knew how to 'cure' it. King then remembered that Sir Joseph Banks had told him about Maoris weaving linen in New Zealand, so he sent a ship over there to bring back weavers. Two struggling and resentful tribesmen were kidnapped and brought back to Norfolk Island. One turned out to be a young chief named Woodoo; the other, Tooke, was a priest's son. Neither had the slightest idea how to prepare flax, for in New Zealand such work was done by women. Tooke and Woodoo, both aged twenty-four, were forced to remain on Norfolk Island for six months, and almost every evening at sunset they lamented their separation by 'crying or singing a song expressive of their grief, which is at times very affecting'. After six months King returned them to New Zealand. Flax production then had to proceed by trial and error. Eventually about 100 yards of coarse canvas were made, but the process was so slow that gradually the project lapsed.

Despite his rules, not all those on Norfolk Island behaved well. King found John Batchelor, one of his marine guards, stealing rum from his tent. 'In the afternoon I assembled the settlement and punished the offender with 36 lashes, causing him to be led by a halter to the place of punishment.' Three days later the young convict Charles McLellan was found robbing Surgeon Jamison's tent of rum. 'This boy is not more than 15 years old,' wrote King, 'I ordered him to be punished with 100 lashes which I hope will have a good effect,' a harsh punishment by modern standards but normal for the time. Other convicts were getting restless. One tried to stir up trouble by saying they were all 'fools' to put up with a fish diet instead of their habitual convict ration of salt pork, that 'the convicts will soon be the strongest, and then it will be seen who is the Master'. King refused to stand for this and had him flogged with forty lashes, warning the others that 'a very severe punishment will be inflicted on anyone who presumed to excite sedition or behave improperly on that account'.

In June and August unexpected disasters occurred. Batchelor, the rum thief, fell into the surf when returning from a fishing trip and was drowned. In August the *Supply* anchored in the bay with provisions, but her boat – carrying James Cunningham, her midshipman, William Westbrook, the sawyer, John Williams, a convict, and Tomlinson, a seaman from the *Supply* – was driven onto the rocks when it was suddenly swamped by a heavy wave and all four men drowned. These four deaths from a total work-force of twenty-three were a serious loss. Then the *Golden Grove* arrived in October 1788 with more convicts, male and female, bringing the population up to sixty-four. Food became more plentiful and King reported back favourably to Phillip, so more convicts arrived. The settlement now became a township, named at first Sydney, then King's Town to avoid confusion and finally Kingston, as it is still called.

King, ill with gout, left for Britain and was replaced by Major Ross, who until recently had been Lieutenant-Governor of New South Wales, who arrived with 200 more convicts in the *Sirius*. Then on 19th March 1790 the *Sirius* strayed from her anchor close to the coral reef and was wrecked in shallow water. No lives were lost, but her crew of eighty had to remain on the island for eleven months before being rescued, which increased the demand for food. Survival depended on retrieving supplies from the wrecked *Sirius* as Norfolk Island had only thirty acres under cultivation at the time. Ross was a cantankerous man and many in New South Wales had been relieved to see him go. On Norfolk Island he proclaimed martial law and made plundering the public stores a capital offence. He told settlers to ease their hunger by hunting the local petrel bird (*Pterodroma melanopus*), which nested on Mount Pitt. Nightly excursions using torches made of pine knots were made up the mountain to procure these birds and their eggs. The petrels 'had a strong fishy taste', as Captain Hunter of the *Sirius* noted, 'but our keen appetites relished them very well; the eggs were excellent'. Between April and August an estimated 170,000 birds were killed.

King returned but as the convict population grew the atmosphere changed. The Botany Bay Rangers, brought in to guard the convicts, became 'very intimate with the convicts, living in their huts, eating, drinking and gambling with them, and perpetually enticing the women to leave the men they were married to'. Friction increased and fights soon broke out, mostly over women, but where a very strong-minded character was needed to control the situation, King alternated between action and passivity, misreading the mood of his soldiers. They were bored and pugnacious and felt less allegiance to King, as a naval officer, than they would have done to a military man. King heard that a mutiny was being plotted and had ten of them arrested and sent back to Sydney.

After five years King left to become Governor of New South Wales. The next commandant was Major Joseph Foveaux (1765–1846), the son of a French cook who worked for the Earl of Cork and Orrery in an English country house. Foveaux had risen rapidly within the New South Wales Corps and had a passion for military correctness – 'necessary rigour', as he called it. Norfolk Island suited him perfectly as it allowed an outlet for his latent sadism. On arriving there in 1800, he found morale low, skilled labour short and buildings falling down. The settlement was also awash with illegitimate children, over 200 of them (nearly a fifth of the island's population), mostly illiterate and wild. The schoolmaster had been put in gaol for debt, and the missionary on the island was thought by one and all to be 'very unfit for a minister'. Foveaux quickly stamped his mark on the island. His methods have best been described by his head gaoler, a transported highwayman named Robert Jones (*alias* Robert Buckey, *alias* George Abrahams), conditionally pardoned in 1795, but who had chosen to stay on Norfolk Island. 'Major Foveaux', Jones remarked, 'was one of them hard and determined men who believe in the lash more than the Bible'. Flogging was Foveaux's speciality and as flogger he used a very powerful County Clare Irishman who took real pleasure in inflicting as much bodily pain as possible, using such expressions as 'another half pound, mate, off the beggar's ribs'. Foveaux liked watching his flogger at work, smiling to encourage him, and the

Flogging at the 'Triangle' on Norfolk Island

victim would be brought before Foveaux after the flogging. 'Hulloa you damn'd scoundrel how do you like it?' he would be asked and then made to put his coat back on and immediately go back to work. A sentence of 200 lashes was called a 'feeler', as the memory of it stayed. Medical treatment for flogging was non-existent, though a bucket of sea water was thrown over the victim's back, an operation known as 'getting salty back'. Other punishments Foveaux introduced were a dark isolation cell and a water pit below ground where prisoners would be locked, alone, naked and unable to sleep for fear of drowning, for forty-eight hours at a time. Death was consequently seen by many prisoners as a welcome relief. Indeed many committed offences specifically to be sent away to Sydney, 'heaven' as it was known in convict slang, for trial.

Some tried to stand up to Foveaux, especially the Irish polit-ical prisoners transported to Australia for their part in the Irish rebellion of 1798. Having been flogged repeatedly on the main-land for supposed complicity in an uprising at Parramatta, near Sydney, in 1800, which never took place, they were sent across to Norfolk Island for life. They joined other Irish convicts there and together a spirit of mutiny formed. The two ringleaders were John Wolloghan, twenty-four years old, from Munster, and Peter McClean, forty, from Ulster, who were first put under close arrest and then summarily hanged by Foveaux without trial from the gallows by the landing pier. Foveaux had warned his officers of 'the fatal consequences that were likely to ensue if such daring & wicked designs were not checked in their earliest appearance'. In his dispatch to King, Foveaux justified himself. 'The nature of this Place is so widely different from any other part of the World, the prisoners sent here, are of the worse Character & in general only those who have committed some fresh crime since their transportation to Port Jackson, in short most of them are a disgrace to human Nature ... [a]fter consid-ering these circumstances, the very little support I receive from the Judge-Advocate and the situation of the Island, your grace will [I am persuaded] perceive that different Examples however vigorous if not exactly conformable to Law are on occasions indispensably necessary.' Norfolk Island was quickly becoming a law unto itself.

The Irish, always seen as a threat, were expected to form a political alliance with the French. An expedition from Tahiti or New Caledonia to take over Norfolk Island was feared and nearly came to fruition in 1804, when a convoy of trading ships appeared off Norfolk Island, escorted by a French warship, *L'Athénienne*. The island garrison thought they were an invasion fleet and prepared to do battle. Soldiers stuck broken rum bottles into the island's two six-pounders, hoping these fragments of glass would 'cut the French to pieces'. Foveaux was away at the time and the island was under the command of his deputy, Captain John Piper. Foveaux had left him instructions how to deal with the Irish convicts in the event of an invasion. Thus, when the ships were sighted, they were herded, some sixty-five of them, into the settlement gaol, its doors barred and windows closed, for fear they could make a signal to the French. Pine brushwood was placed against the gaol walls ready to set them on fire should the invasion take place, but the trading ships sailed by.

During Foveaux's rule in Norfolk Island female convicts were treated worst of all. Their life was in any case a misery since they had to defend themselves against both guards and male prisoners. In the hierarchy women were very much at the bottom of the pile, and some even became prisoners of prisoners. Foveaux took his own convict mistress, Ann Sherwin, by putting her convict partner, an overseer, into gaol on a trumped-up charge. 'The poor fellow, seeing the danger he was in, thought it better to save his life, and lose his wife, than to lose both', as a fellow prisoner, the Irish rebel leader Joseph Holt, put it in his memoirs. Foveaux allowed the island's beadle, Potter, to sell off female convicts. These sales – using rum as currency – were held in an old provisions store and Foveaux watched as the women were made to strip naked and 'race around the room' while Potter kept up his running commentary, selling the unfortunate women to the highest bidder. The same woman might be resold several times during her stay on the island until she was considered to be 'of little or no further use'. In the soldiers' barracks on Thursday evenings a dance took place, known as the 'dances of the Mermaids', where women convicts were made to dance naked with numbers painted on their backs. Admirers would clap their hands on seeing their favourite number perform some grotesque action. Rum was liberally supplied and such amusements became the talk of the soldiers for days on end. The women were so degraded that they lost all self-respect and competed among themselves to find favour with the guards.

Women were also flogged on Norfolk Island, although this never happened on the mainland. Foveaux watched this ceremony as well, driven, as Jones wrote, by 'his love for watching women in their agony while receiving a punishment on the Triangle', the wooden stand to which the convict was secured for flogging, feet bound and arms outstretched. Male convicts were summoned to watch and stood in a semicircle as the 'skinner' or 'backscratcher' (Norfolk Island terminology for the flogger) started. The usual sentence was twenty-five lashes, the so-called 'Botany Bay dozen', but it could go up to many more. Female convicts needed to be particularly strong to put up with their constant abuse. Language was used to debase and vilify them. A female convict was termed a 'bat', a 'crack', a 'case for cattle' or a 'convenient'. If she had a partner, she was his 'natural' or 'peculiar'. This deliberate debasing was intended to diminish the men's sense of guilt at the women's ill-treatment – a strategy found elsewhere with prisoners in wartime. During World War II, for instance, the Japanese called their prisoners 'logs'. Yet many of the women convicts had been transported for crimes no greater than prostitution, and three of those on Norfolk Island at the time had been sent there for abortion.

Accounts of Foveaux's sadism never appeared in official reports as he censored all letters. 'No person', Jones noted, 'was allowed to write any information about the place or the work done here, they were only to write in reference to the state of our good conduct and friends.' Norfolk Island thus became a sealed universe, but its usefulness was diminishing. Sydney's need of the island as a food producer was less now that the town had developed rapidly and spread out into its surrounding country-side and had become nearly self-sufficient in terms of food pro-duction. Norfolk Island thus seemed to lose its way. Flax production on the island decreased and the navy decided against using Norfolk Island pines; gradually, fewer convicts were sent there. By March 1810 the population was down to 117 and Lachlan Macquarie, the new Governor of New South Wales, decided the island should be abandoned. Wooden buildings were torn down, their timber burnt, stone houses demolished and all animals, except a few pigs who were living wild, were destroyed. Nothing was to be left on the island to attract a passing ship as the British did not want the French to think of settling there. Dogs were deliberately left behind to run wild and breed into hunting packs which would also discourage any visitors from landing. The island reverted to the same empty state it had been in when Cook found it and remained abandoned for a decade.

It suddenly began to be used again when a subsequent Governor of New South Wales, Sir Thomas Brisbane, was told by the British government to revive it as a penal settlement. Panic had set in and the authorities needed somewhere to deter increasing mainland crime by 'sheer terror'. Norfolk Island was to become 'the *ne plus ultra* of convict degradation' and was to house the absolute worst of the system, those doubly convicted men who had committed further serious offences since transpor-tation to Australia. The ethos of the place was to be explicit. 'The felon, who is sent there, is forever excluded from all hope of return', Brisbane wrote. Convicts on Norfolk Island will 'have forfeited all claim to the protection of the law' and could not expect to have their legal rights respected. Indeed Brisbane urged that 'if it were not too repugnant to the Laws of England, I should consider it very fitting to have Norfolk Island com-pletely under Martial Law, which would not only form part of the punishment in itself, but save the complicated machinery of

Civil Courts, or sending people for trial [to Sydney] ... My
experience convinces me that there is nothing so effectual in
dealing with convicts as Summary Proceedings.' The regime was
therefore to be inflexible. Prisoners would have 'no hopes of any
mitigation of their sentences' held out to them. Their stay on the
island would be for a minimum of ten years, and they would be
released only if they had behaved perfectly for the first five.
Many subsequent visitors were shocked by what they saw on the
island. It reminded them of Dante's inscription above the gates
of Hell, 'Abandon hope all ye who enter here'. Sir Ralph
Darling, Brisbane's successor as Governor of New South Wales,
endorsed this: 'My object was to hold out that Settlement as a
place of the extremest punishment, short of death', he wrote in
1827.

The first new wave of convicts, fifty-seven of them, each with
some skill as an artisan, landed in June 1825. New living quarters were constructed out of the remains of the old settlement at
Kingston. A succession of short-term commandants, all military
officers, followed before James Morisset arrived in 1829 on a
salary of £600 a year, and with a formidable reputation.

Morisset was now aged forty-nine and was another profes-
sional soldier. During the Napoleonic Wars a mine had exploded
close to his face and seriously damaged it. His cheekbone and
jaw were broken on one side and they formed a swollen mass
'like a large yellow over-ripe melon', as his military colleague
Foster Fyans put it. His mouth ran diagonally upwards and this
meant he made peculiar whistling noises whenever he spoke. He
had one normal eye, while the other protruded like a pebble and
never moved. In conversation he would thrust his cheek
forward, daring the other person to look away. Morisset was
married; his young bride and two children arrived with him in
May 1829. No female convicts were to be on Norfolk Island
during the second settlement, only military and staff wives and
daughters.

Morisset imposed himself as a stern disciplinarian. He cut
down the orange trees on the island, to remove any temptation

to convicts to pick the fruit. He asked Darling for a treadmill – 'grinding air' as convicts called it – but this was disallowed on grounds of expense. Convicts soon suffered from his unrestrained sadism. The fullest first-hand convict account of this was written by Laurence Frayne, who arrived on the island in 1830. Convicted of theft in Dublin in October 1825, Frayne had arrived in Sydney at the end of 1826 on the transport *Regalia* with 129 other Irish convicts. He repeatedly absconded and in 1828 was sent to the penal settlement at Moreton Bay and then on to Norfolk Island, where he arrived in October 1830 with his back in tatters from repeated floggings. Maggots crawled all over it: 'My shoulders were actually in a state of decomposition the stench of which I could not bear myself, how offensive then must I appear and smell to my companions in misery.' He landed at Kingston, and immediately after landing was sent to carry salt beef on his back, its salt brine as well as the pressure 'stinging my mutilated & mortified flesh. I really longed for instant death'.

Under Morisset work on the island went on from sunrise to sunset, with an hour off for the midday meal. All the buildings for the new settlement, including the sentry boxes and the high stone security walls around the main compounds in Kingston, had to be convict-built. Prisoners made bricks, burnt coral to make lime for the mortar and hewed Norfolk Island pines into timber frames. The hardest tasks were performed by the gaol gang, thirty-five multiple offenders who lived in the old gaol near the jetty and cut stone in the quarry while wearing double, or even triple, irons. As extra punishment, they were made to work in the 'wet quarry', a reef partly covered by the sea, where they had to cut stone under water. Convicts were never trusted and at dinner the superintendent issued a mess kit of knife, fork, spoon and pannikin, which they used in rotation and handed back. But there were never enough utensils to go round, so many had to eat with their hands.

Morisset's regime was run with military thoroughness and he relied heavily on informers, creating an atmosphere of mutual suspicion. He always feared insurrection, understandably since

Norfolk Island convicts at the wet quarry

the convicts easily outnumbered the staff and the hundred or so soldiers and officers on the island. Informing, therefore, was given the highest priority and brought with it corruption. Hardly a week passed without a plot being disclosed or convicts denouncing one another. Morisset or his officers always rewarded them. 'Indulgence', Frayne noted, 'was only got by such traffic in human blood', and informers were 'capable of any act of purfidy or blood no matter how Black or horrifying such a deed might be'. On the merest suspicion convicts were summarily tried by tribunal and flogged, the aim being, as always, to instil and maintain terror. Frayne himself was brought before Morisset for breaking a flagstone in the quarry. 'As usual I found my defence useless.' He was sentenced to a hundred lashes:

> After the sentence I plainly told the Commander in the Court that he was a tyrant. He replied that no man had ever said that about him before. I said they knew the consequences too well to tell him so. But I tell you in stark naked blunt English that you are as great a tyrant as Nero ever was. The moment I expressed these words I was sentenced to an additional 100 and to be kept ironed down in a cell for life and never to see daylight again.

Morisset sadistically made sure Frayne's extra floggings were spaced out. He got fifty lashes on his back straight away and then another fifty four days later, when the cuts were only partly scabbed over. Another fifty were given on the buttocks four days later, and on the twelfth day he received the last fifty. Morisset supervised all of these beatings

> specially to see the infliction ... given as severe as the scourgers could possibly inflict it, so that new and heavier cats were procured purposely for my punishment, & the flagellator threatened to be flogged himself if he did not give it me more severe. He replied that he did his utmost and really could do no more ... The Superintendent who witnessed the punishment swore when I was taken down that I was a brickmaker, meaning that I was like an iron man past all feelings of the punishment. Alas, delusive idea! – I felt too acutely the full weight scourge & sting of every lash but I had resolution enough accompanied by inflexible obstinacy not to give any satisfaction ... I knew my real innocence and bore up against it.

Frayne's articulacy is remarkable for a convict.

Morisset, enraged by Frayne's insulting attitude, tried other ways to break his spirit. Ten weeks later Frayne appeared before him again, charged with assaulting a convict informer named Harper. 'What have you to say for yourself?' Morisset asked. Frayne played for time and replied that he would leave it to Morisset to judge whether he was guilty or innocent, 'you know the character & conduct of the informer; you also know mine. It is useless for me to gainsay anything ... If you actually knew my innocence yourself I well know that you would punish me ... If you acquit me for the assault you will flog me for what I have said to you, but I disregard both you and all the punishment you can give me.' Morisset was incensed. 'I will give you 300 at three different whippings, you damned scoundrel.' Frayne replied, 'I am no scoundrel no more than yourself.'

Frayne stayed in gaol for a week until his back had partially healed. He got his second hundred and was put in solitary confinement without any further medical treatment. To alleviate the pain, he poured water on the stone floor of his cell, urinated on it and then lay down in it, 'with my sore shoulders on the exact spot where the water lay . . . I was literally alive with maggots and vermin, nor could I keep them down; to such a wretched and truly miserable state was I reduced, that I even hated the look & appearance of myself . . . The trifle of soap allowed me to wash our persons & shirts was stopped from me, as I thought to spur me to abuse the gaol authorities and thereby again subject myself to more cruelty . . . knowing as they all did my hasty temper.'

Frayne was reprieved before he was given the third part of his flogging, when the Colonial Secretary in Sydney issued a general order limiting the floggings to a hundred lashes. Morisset put Frayne in the 'dumb cell', a dark, soundless stone isolation chamber where he remained for two months. No sooner did he come out than he got into trouble again. Two Irish women from the same town as him were working as assigned servants at Government House, and had been briefly jailed for a minor offence. 'Strange to say (and equally true as strange) I purposely got into gaol if possible to get to them, and while they were walking in the yard for air I shewed myself through the bars . . . I told them they might expect me to pay them a visit at all hazard, I would put up with the consequences if it was 300.' That night he got into the women's cell and hid under their bedding. 'They knew too well the Colonel's feelings towards me . . . They were equally as anxious as myself to annoy the Colonel.' Frayne enjoyed his night of sexual intimacy with the women, but he was found out and brought before Morisset once more. Morisset ordered a hundred lashes in slow time to pay for 'your creeping into the women's cell'. Frayne's lament against Morisset continued: 'I am an oppressed convict, oppressed by your tyranny and sacrificed by your base informers and blood hunters, and my hunger and your cruel torture gives you the greatest pleasure and gratification.' There was almost a symmetry about this dance of the oppressor and oppressed, which Frayne, by his constant defiance, seemed prepared to continue. His punishment this time was three years 'loaded with French or exceedingly heavy irons' in the gaol gang, reefed to a chain cable each night.

On Norfolk Island authority was vested almost entirely in the hands of the Commandant. This was laid down by the regulations. As the Commandant had absolute sway, he could countermand any order, and equally he could indulge in brutality if he so wished. Such a situation was likely to foment sadism. Frayne realized that he was being used by Morisset as a scapegoat, but the harshness of the regime got even to him. He began to sink into despair. 'I began to think that the Almighty had decreed that my life should be made a life of infamy and turmoil and degradation, a life to be perpetually harrowed up and goaded with such inhuman, barbarous and algerine brutality. I began to question in my own then-perverted mind the infinite mercy, nay the justice, of Deity itself.' Frayne never lost his faith, however, but saw God as 'shewing me as forcibly as possible the truth of holy writ'. He resorted to the Bible, particularly the 88th Psalm, which he learnt by heart and recited over and over again in his cell: 'I am counted with them that go down into the pit: I am as a man that hath no help: Cast off among the dead, Like the slain that lie in the grave, Whom thou rememberest no more.' For many convicts, more isolated than ever on this island, their only private refuge was within themselves, within their bodies, an inner sanctum where they became unreachable. Defiance, as long-term prisoners have traditionally found, was a way of maintaining self-respect and dignity. Their defiance became known as the silence of the 'pebble'.

Suicide was tempting. 'If ever it once had entered my mind that a self-murderer could obtain salvation I would not have seen a 10th part of the misery I underwent.' But suicide was forbidden to Frayne and the other Irish Catholics, as it was a mortal sin. Instead, they thought up a variant. A group of convicts would select two men to die by drawing straws: one of them was to die, the other to kill him. Others in the group would stand by as witnesses. This meant that the culprit could seek absolution for the killing at the confessional, whereas suicide was explicitly forbidden. As there was no judge to try capital offences on Norfolk Island, the killer and witnesses would then have to be sent to Sydney for their trial, and this was part of their real aim, as convicts would do anything to get away from their 'ocean hell', even if it meant a gallows on the mainland. Under the rules of their suicide 'game', no person could offer himself up. All members of the group had to be equally ready to die.

Failing this, open rebellion became the convicts' answer to Morisset's oppressive regime. Indeed Frayne saw no alternative: 'I should certainly have taken his life ... and many a time I prayed, if I knew what prayer was, that the heaviest curses that ever Almighty God let fall on blighted man might reach him.' Through the summer of 1833–4 rumours circulated of an outbreak being planned by the convicts. Morisset thought of flogging the convicts to get them to admit this, but was dissuaded by the commander of the garrison, Captain Charles Sturt, later to become famous as an explorer of the Australian hinterland. Sturt was respected by the convicts, and Morisset at the time was suffering from ill-health, both from his old head wound and from the strain of his job, which was bringing him close to a nervous breakdown. He took to his bed and command of the island passed to his second-in-command, Captain Foster Fyans. Fyans sensed something was afoot. An anonymous note had been dropped into the soldiers' barracks warning them to 'beware of poison'.

On 15th January 1834 a mutiny started. At dawn muster an unusually large number of prisoners, thirty-eight in all, reported sick in the prisoners' barracks and so were marched off to the hospital by a warder. Once inside the hospital, the men turned on the warder, overpowered him and locked him in a sickroom. The prisoners then armed themselves with whatever weapons they could find, from chair legs to scalpels and axes, and formed themselves up in the entrance of the hospital, ready to jump on the gaol guard as it passed. A hundred yards away the gaol gang were being mustered by their guard and ordered to march off to work. They stood their ground rattling their chains, an agreed signal. Convicts from the sawpits now came down yelling and the prisoners waiting in the hospital entrance came out and attacked the gaol gang guards. The guards began shooting, and the sound of their shots alerted the military barracks not far away. Soldiers poured down in numbers. The actual combat between the two sides lasted only a few minutes before the hospital convicts, disorganized, retreated towards the gaol yard. The convicts from the sawpits were driven back up again, and as the soldiers fired on them, they ran off into the sugar cane fields alongside the road. 'The men were very keen after these ruffians', Fyans later recalled with some relish. 'It was really game and sport to these soldiers . . . "Come on out, my Honey" – with a prick of the bayonet through both thighs or a little above'. Soon all the rebels were caught and bound together in line with a rope and marched into the penal settlement.

Fyans kept all the mutineers inside the main prison barracks – 'nearly one thousand ruffians', he wrote later, although it was more like two hundred. The final casualty list was five rebels dead and about fifty injured. None of the military had been killed. Fyans recounted to Morisset, still unwell in bed, what had happened. Morisset's orders were, as Fyans remembered, 'Glad I am that I am not responsible. Do as you like.' Fyans and his solders of the 4th Regiment took their revenge slowly over the new few months. New punishments were devised. Blacksmiths cast irons of double or triple weight, with the inside deliberately jagged to lacerate the flesh. Mutineers were kept naked in the gaol yard which was so crowded that only a third of them could sit down. One of the soldiers' amusements, encouraged by Fyans, was to choose a prisoner at random and then thrust a stick into the cord that bound his arms, twisting it round and round until blood burst from the fingertips. Fyans soon earned his nickname of 'Flogger Fyans' as so many lashes were inflicted that the government cat-o'-nine-tails kept unravelling. The prisoners took pride in defying his efforts, becoming 'stone men' again, enduring the triangles in silence. Fyans tried new, specially made cats to strike terror into them – 'prisoners of this description cannot be treated as a Gentleman's Servant in Sydney' – but it made little difference.

A judge arrived from Sydney to try the mutineers. One hundred and thirty-seven men in all were charged but in the end only fifty-five came to trial, as the only evidence was supplied by informers. The judge, a decent Anglican, William Burton, was puzzled, as many previous visitors had been, by the discrepancy between the island's extraordinary beauty and its hellish practices. Why, he wrote, did its 'soft beauty not have its effect on hearts not wholly hardened by the searing effects of Vice?' The convicts seemed 'to gather no heartening effect from the beauties of the Creation around them, but to make a Hell of that which else might be a Heaven'. Burton, once he saw the mutineers, was moved by their evident honesty. They came before him 'grey, wizened and shrunken, their eyes dull and unseeing, the skin stretched taut on the cheeks; they spoke in whispers and were awful to behold'. When they spoke of Norfolk Island, they said, 'it was no mercy to send us to this place. I do not ask for life, I do not want to be spared . . . [L]ife is not worth living on such terms.' Robert Douglas, one of the mutineers, uttered the words that remained indelibly imprinted in Burton's mind. 'Let a man's heart be what it will when he comes here, his man's heart is taken from him, and he is given the heart of a beast.'

The mutiny finished Morisset off. He went back to the mainland a broken man, leaving his wife, Emily, and their young children in the care of her brother Vaux, who was in charge of the commissary store on the island. Vaux died shortly afterwards while fishing off Rocky Point, where he was 'seen struggling for a time, then . . . turned and went down as though seized by a shark'. Emily rejoined her husband, who rashly sold his army commission and invested the proceeds in the newly formed Bank of Australia, when then collapsed, taking his money with it. To pay back his debt he became a police magistrate in Bathurst and died in 1852, leaving ten children and his wife, still struggling to make ends meet. Morisset's successor was another Peninsular War veteran, Major Joseph Anderson, of the 50th

Regiment, a large Scotsman with bushy white whiskers, always known as 'Potato Joe' from his attempts to foist a potato diet on the prisoners.

At the trial twenty-nine of the mutineers were finally found guilty, but sixteen had their sentences commuted to hard labour for life. With the remaining thirteen due to hang, two clergymen – one Catholic, the other Anglican – were sent across to minister to them. The Catholic priest was William Ullathorne, who later testified to the Molesworth Committee in London. On arriving in September, Ullathorne went straight to the gaol, where he met with 'the most heartrending scene that I ever witnessed. The prison was in the form of a square, on one side of which stood a row of low cells, covered with a roof of shingles. The turnkey unlocked the first door and said: "Stand aside, Sir." Then came forth a yellow exhalation, the produce of the bodies of the men confined therein. The exhalation cleared off, and I entered and found five men chained to a traversing-bar.' Ullathorne then stated the names of the men due to die in five days time, 'and it is a remarkable fact, that as I mentioned the names of those men who were to die, they one after the other, as their names were pronounced, dropped on their knees and thanked God that they were to be delivered from that horrible place, whilst the others remained standing mute; it was the most horrible scene I ever witnessed. Those who were condemned to death appeared to be rejoiced.'

Three of the condemned men were Catholics, but four of the others asked to put themselves under Ullathorne's care. He began his duties with them at six o'clock the next morning, and got 'an intelligent Catholic overseer appointed to read at certain times under my direction for those who could not read, whilst I was engaged with the others'. After his day's work he proceeded to Government House, where he found 'a brilliant assembly, in strange contrast with the human miseries in which my soul had just been steeped'. Ullathorne found the convicts on Norfolk Island to be 'a desperate body of men, made more desperate by their isolation from the outer world and by being deprived of access to all stimulants; by the absence of hope; by the habitual prospect of the encircling sea that isolated them from other lands by the distance of a thousand miles and by the absence of all religious or other instruction or consolation. The day of the executions came. 'The Commandant had received orders that all the convicts, to the number of two thousand, should witness them. As he had only three companies of infantry, some contrivance was required to prevent a rush of the convicts on the troops, as well as to conceal their number. Several small but strong stockades were erected and lined with soldiers, between the scaffold and the standing ground of the convicts, whilst the rest of the force was kept in reserve close by, but out of sight.' The executions took place on the gallows by the gaol entrance, half one day and half the next, with a thousand convicts watching each day. The convict who acted as hangman was rewarded by being sent to Van Diemen's Land once his job was done.

Ullathorne had his men put together in one cell and the Protestants were in another, one set to be executed each day.

My men asked as a special favour, the night before, to be allowed some tobacco, as with that they could watch and pray all night. This indulgence was granted. When the irons were struck off and the death warrant read, they knelt down to receive it as the will of God; and next, by a spontaneous act, they humbly kissed the feet of him who brought them peace. After the executioner had pinioned their arms they thanked the jailers for all their kindness, and ascended the ladders with light steps, being almost excitedly cheerful. I had a method of preparing men for their last moments, by associating all that I wished them to think and feel with the prayer, 'Into Thy hands I commend my spirit; Lord Jesus, receive my soul'. I advised them when on the scaffold to think of nothing else and to say nothing else. The Catholics had a practice of sewing large black crosses on their white caps shirts. These men had done so. As soon as they were on the scaffold, to my surprise, they all repeated the prayer I had taught them, aloud in a kind of chorus together until the ropes stopped their voices for ever. This made a great impression on all present, and was much talked of afterwards.

Ullathorne returned from 'this awful scene, wending my
way between the masses of convicts and the military, all in dead
silence. I barely caught a glance of their suspended bodies. I
could not bring myself to look at them. Poor fellows. They
had given me their whole hearts, and were fervently penitent.
They had known little of good or of their souls before that
time. Yet all of them had either father or mother, sisters or
brothers, to whom they had last words and affections to send,
which had been dictated to me the day before.' Then came the
funerals. A selected number of the convicts followed each
coffin to

> the most beautiful cemetery that the eye of man could possibly con-
> template, at some distance from the settlement, in a ravine that
> opens upon the sea, being encircled on the land side with dark
> thickets of manchineel, backed by the bright-leaved forest trees . . .
> Arrived at the graves, I mounted a little eminence, with the coffins
> before me and the convicts around me; and being extraordinarily
> moved, I poured out the most awful, mixed with the most tender,
> conjurations to these unfortunate men, to think of their immortal
> souls, and the God above them, Who waited their repentance.
> Then followed the funeral rites. So healthful was the climate, that
> all who lay in the cemetery had been executed, except one child,
> the son of a Highland officer, over whose tomb was the touching
> inscription: 'far from the land of his fathers.' After the executions I
> devoted the rest of the time to the convicts, instructed all who came
> together for the purpose, and got a man to read to them, whilst I
> heard about one hundred confessions. Many of them had not seen
> a priest for some twenty years, others since they had left their native
> country.

So grateful were the prisoners to Ullathorne – a sign that their
deep-felt spiritual needs were being at last met – that they con-
fided their secrets to him. After the executions were over
Ullathorne drew Major Anderson aside and told him that the
men had authorized him to let Anderson know that there had
been a plan for escape. 'That they had got a piece of a watch-

spring concealed in the heel of one of them, had passed it by all agency from cell to cell, and had sawn all the fetters ready for snapping; and that their plan was to mount one on the back of another, to tear the shingles off the roof, and so escape in the night to the thick bush, hoping in time to get a boat into their power.' Anderson did not believe him, but it was true, as his officials found out when they checked.

Ullathorne felt his last act before leaving the island was worth recording as an example that the 'most desperate men ought not to be despaired of'. Anderson had told him at breakfast of a case that gave him a great deal of solicitude, a convict who was 'always in a round of crime or punishment'. He was one of those who had been reprieved, and yet was already again under punishment. Ullathorne found the man chained in a cell with three others, and he asked him to come out as he wanted to speak with him. He was a tall, strong-built man

and I saw he was one of those proud spirits that would not seem to cave in before his comrades. I told him the turnkey would take off his fetters if he would only come out. He replied: 'Sir, you are a kind gentleman, and have been good to them that suffered, but I'd rather not.' I turned to the others and said, 'Now, men, isn't he a big fool? You would give anything to get out of this hot place; but because I am a priest, he thinks you will take him for a softy, and chaff him, if he talks to me. I have got something to tell him, and then he can do as he likes. He knows I can't eat him. What do you say?' 'Why, Sir, you are such a gentleman, he ought to go out when you ask him.' 'And you won't jeer him as a softy because he talks with me?' 'Oh no, Sir.' 'Well, take off his irons.' I wanted to get him into a private room, but he would not go out of eyeshot of the other men, and nothing could induce him. I did not like to shut the door on them, lest it might be for a trick. I said: 'Let's go into the turnkey's room.' No, he would not. So we walked up and down, with a sentry on each side a short distance off. I found he was a Catholic, made an earnest appeal to his soul; but he held himself still, and I seemed to make no way. A sailor came up: 'Anchor short hove, Sir, Governor waiting in the boat.' I felt bitter: it was the first time I had found a soul inaccessible. I threw up my arms, looked him full in the face, and poured out the most terrible denunciations upon him for neglecting the one opportunity of saving his soul; for I never expected that he would have a chance of seeing a priest there again. But though I did not know it until fifteen months afterwards, his heart was changed. As soon as I left he asked to be put in a cell by himself, got a turnkey, who was a Catholic, to lend him books, and became a new man. In going on board I said to the Commandant: 'You must not mistake that man. There is nothing mean about him. He would not tell a lie. Under other circumstances he would be a hero. But if he says he will thrash an overseer, he will do it. And if the man resists he will kill him.' The hint was taken. After a time one chain was taken off him, then the other. And on my return, after fifteen months, I met him smiling as he worked among the flowers in the Government garden; and he proved most useful among his fellow-convicts. He ultimately got his liberty, and became a respectable man.

Morisset's successor, Joseph Anderson, was a firm disciplinarian and a flogger. He once gave five men 1,500 lashes before breakfast. The punishment record of William Riley, in heavy irons for two years after the mutiny, tells its own tale:

100 lashes	For saying 'O My God' while on the Chain
100 lashes	Smiling while on the Chain
50 lashes	Getting a light to smoke
200 lashes	Insolence to a soldier
100 lashes	Striking an overseer who pushed him
8 months' solitary confinement, on the chain	Refusing to work
3 months' ditto	Disobedience of Orders
3 months' Gaol	Being a short distance from the Settlement
100 lashes before all hands in the Gaol	Insolence to the Sentry
100 lashes	Singing a Song
50 lashes	Asking Gaoler for a Chew of Tobacco
100 lashes	Neglect of work

Another prisoner, Michael Burns, got even more – 2,000 lashes in less than three years. His crimes, like Riley's, included 'singing a song', probably one of the Irish 'treason songs'. Anderson worked convicts hard all day. When they were laboriously hoeing a field, he made sure the strongest workers were placed at either end so that when the weaker ones in the middle sagged they would be forced to catch up and continue working until they dropped. Many resorted to the 'government stroke': working as little and as slowly as possible. The harder the overseers and guards urged them, the more they malingered or feigned sickness. Some poisoned themselves with nightshade berries, others got friends to slice their toes off with a hoe to avoid work, and others even blinded themselves in the belief that they would now be left alone. Anderson tried flogging malingerers, but some were genuinely sick and died as a result.

Frayne summed up this convict attitude: 'If you endeavour to take out of [a prisoner] that manly confidence which ought to be cherished in every civilized human being, you then begin the work of demoralisation; and it will end in the very dregs of debasement & an insensibility to every species of integrity & decency, and eradicate every right feeling in the human breast.'

James Backhouse, the Quaker missionary, visited in 1835, a year after the mutiny, and noticed how many convicts were now obsessed with escape. 'Their passions, severed from their usual objects, centred in one intense thirst for liberty, to be gained at whatever cost.' He said 'their faces were like those of demons'. Some gave him letters to be sent back home to their families. One such read:

Norfolk Island, April 1835.

My dear Wife and beloved Children,

I never had a task so painful . . . as the present one, of addressing you from this doleful spot – my sea-girt prison, on the beach of which I stand, a monument of destruction; driven by the adverse winds of fate, to the confines of black despair . . . I am wearing the garb of degradation and the badge or brand of infamy, N.I. which being interpreted is Norfolk Island, the 'Villain's Home'. My present circumstances and picture, you will find truly drawn, in the 88th Psalm, and the 102nd commencing with the 3rd verse to the 11th inclusive; which you and my dear children I request will read attentively . . . I am exceedingly anxious that my dear children should have the cause of my present privations and humiliating and degrading situation constantly pressed upon their attention, that they may never be exposed to the same fate as that which has over-taken me.

Anderson and his officers, however, enjoyed life on the island. The *Journal of Ensign Best*, written by one of Anderson's officers, describes a seamless existence of shooting, riding and excursions, with hardly a mention of convicts. Anderson wrote of similar outings in his own *Recollections,* in which he describes 'a pretty spot beyond the settlement with a nice bower with tables and seats for our accommodation; and in one or other of these paradises we used to pass many hours. We had also frequent dinner-parties and dances, and as I had then finished building the new military barracks and hospital, the latter (for we had no sick) made a most excellent and commodious ballroom. In a word, we all agreed well together.' He described the soldiers' other amusements, fishing and shooting on Philip Island, which abounded with wild pigs, wild fowl, and a variety of birds. 'Whenever any of the officers wished for a day's sport there, they had a boat at their command for the day . . . and generally brought back with them some half-dozen or more pigs, besides other game.' By this time Anderson had an open carriage built on the island for himself and as there were government horses 'doing nothing' he used them 'as much as I liked . . . and from that time we had our carriage and a first-rate (convict) coachman'.

Anderson's regime came to an end in February 1839. He was succeeded by Major Bunbury of the 80th Regiment and then by Major Ryan of the 50th (formerly Arthur's Military Commandant on Van Diemen's Land), both short-term replace-

Major 'Potato Joe' Anderson

ments. They were less severe in their methods – Bunbury replaced the hoe with the plough and quickly doubled farm production. But Norfolk Island was still seen principally as a deterrent to mainland crime, the unseen dark shadow of Australian convict life.

7

Tour of Inspection

MACONOCHIE AND HIS family finally left Sydney on 23rd February 1840, travelling on the convict ship *Nautilus*, a 400 ton barque that had left Dublin four months earlier with 178 male convicts on board, most of them Irish. Over the next few months a further 439 new convicts were to arrive on Norfolk Island aboard the *Augusta Jessie*, the *Woodbridge* and the *Mangles*. In 1841 a further 62 arrived from New South Wales after it had ceased to be a penal colony.

When Maconochie arrived on Norfolk Island on 6th March this was the first time he had actually set eyes on the island, and his first impression confirmed what Ullathorne had written: 'one of the most beautiful spots in the universe. Rising abruptly on all sides but one from the sea, clustering columns of basalt spring out of the water, securing at intervals its endurance with the strong architecture of God . . . The land consists of a series of hills and valleys, curiously interfolded, the green ridges rising above one another, until they reach the shaggy sides and crown-ing summit of Mount Pitt, at the height of 1,000 feet above the level of the sea.' These valleys were full of 'wild shrubs, wild flowers, and wild grapery', while 'from the deep gloom of the forest, glades and openings lie on each side, where among many plants and trees the guava and lemon prevail' and then 'in other places the parasite creepers and climbers rise up in columns, shoot over arch after arch, and again descend in every variety of

Gothic fantasy'. Ullathorne's prose is mesmerizing, but it conveys the lushness and richness of the island.

As the *Nautilus* passed the uninhabited Philip Island, five miles off Norfolk Island, Maconochie glimpsed Kingston and the principal buildings of the settlement standing close to the shore for the first time. To his right stood the prisoners' barracks eighty yards back, where convicts lodged and slept. Three storeys high, with protruding side wings, it covered about three acres and was surrounded by a protective wall 16 feet high. Alongside it ran the road to Quality Row, a quarter of a mile back, where staff and military officers' houses stood. To the right, halfway between the two and on a slight bluff, was Government House, where he and his family were going to live. This was a substantial single-storey mansion built in 1829, its thick walls made of local coral stone, roughcast on the outside to keep out the damp sea air. Outside on its terrace stood two defensive cannon and there was always a pacing sentry. A large veranda with iron trelliswork encircled the house. Its commanding position meant it overlooked both the prisoners' barracks and the military barracks at the end of

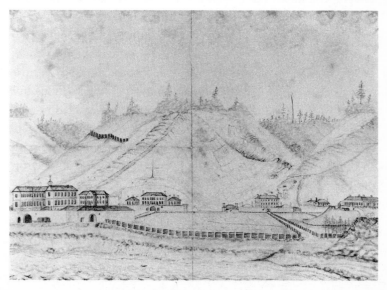

The settlement at Norfolk Island, 1838

Quality Row and so everything that was going on in the settlement could be seen.

The island administration comprised about twenty civil salaried staff and a military garrison numbering about 200. The civil staff included a superintendent of convicts, a commissariat officer, a chief constable, a clerk of works, a gaoler, a principal overseer, two surgeons, three clergymen (two Catholic and one Protestant), a postmaster and, at the Longridge Agricultural Station, a superintendent of agriculture with two assistants. The military were from a regiment doing a tour of duty on the island (during Maconochie's time it was the 96th), who did guard duties, provided sentries and quelled any thought of insurrection. Ancillary to the civil staff were convict overseers and convict police, drawn from among the ranks of the prisoners and paid in marks.

Once installed in Government House, Maconochie, keen to make an impression, carried out a more detailed personal inspection of the settlement. He started with the prisoners' barracks. Inside he found twenty-two wards, or sleeping areas, the largest capable of holding about a hundred men, the smallest about fifteen. The main wards ran the whole length of the building and were 18 feet wide, and had stone floors and windows at either end, giving welcome ventilation in summer but cold in winter. Each prisoner had his own canvas hammock and these extended in two tiers and two lines the whole length of the wards, with a passage about 4 feet wide between them. Prisoners' 'lights out' was at 8 p.m. A wardsman elected by the prisoners was responsible for the upkeep of the wards and stayed behind during the day while they went off to work, sluicing down the wards and emptying the night tubs into the sea near by, fourteen tubs from the largest ward. These sleeping areas were dangerous places, as one of the clergymen had pointed out: 'in a single ward were placed for at least 10 hours every night, persons of all ages from 16 to 60, and of every conceivable degree of depravity. Through the heat of the climate, the violence of unbridled passion and the absence of women, unnatural crimes were of common occurrence.' Maconochie sensed this from his own inspection –

hence his plan for a new prison, and his idea of bringing women and families of convicts to the island.

The prisoners' day began at 5 a.m. – or 6 a.m. in winter – when a bell was rung at the guard post on the high boundary wall. The men had five minutes to get ready and to muster in the barrack square before the second bell was rung for roll call. Ullathorne had witnessed one of these morning calls in Anderson's time. 'There each man carries every little thing he has in the world about his person, lest it be stolen the next moment. "Do give me a pair of old shoes of any sort to show at muster", said one, a hard, brown-visaged man, to me, not without a tear, having escaped a moment for the purpose, "for mine have been stolen, and I am sure to be flogged." ' On the barrack square Ullathorne heard the 'hoarse loud brawlings of the imperative overseer' and saw the 'gory triangle incessantly being erected for the infliction of punishment'.

On the other side of the road to the barracks stood the shoe-makers', sailors', carpenters' and wheelwrights' workshops inside the lumber yard, which Maconochie inspected next. All had a functional chill about them, a cold and impersonal severity which Maconochie felt he needed to humanize. The mess-sheds provided eating areas for up to 600 prisoners, some under cover, others not, so that, as one observer put it, 'I have seen numbers of men on stormy days crouching down for shelter under the wall next to the sea with their clothes drenched and their pan-nikins half filled with rain.' Closer to the landing pier were the gaol, where men who had committed serious crimes on the island were put, and the crankmill, used for grinding corn and – more often – for punishment, as described by one visitor, David Burn, a retired naval officer in Van Diemen's Land:

I have read and listened to descriptions of the gun decks of line of battleships during the heat of action, but such pictures are faint to that of the working room at Norfolk Island's Crank Mill. The labour appears to be dreadfully severe and the loss of power excessive, and the yells and screams of the unfortunate criminals as they heave at the cumbersome engine almost induces a belief that the spectator has suddenly been wafted to pandemonium where he is listening to the cries and scanning the gesture of lost souls. Some begrimed with dirt and perspiration glare at you with tiger like ferocity of aspect, some half naked jumping madly to impel the unwilling crank, show every fibre and muscle strained to their severest tension, some dash fiercely at their work as if in the bodily struggle they found vent to the throes of the mind, some toil in sullen silence, some in abject despondence, but ever and anon a shout will rend the air whilst the mill whirls under the influence of the rigorous but momentary influence. Occasionally a song will be heard, but is not the cheerful warblings with which the mariner seeks to lighten duty. To my thinking, it sounded far like the orgies of the damned.

Deliberate sabotage of the crankmill was frequent. A convict would suddenly jerk on one section of the machinery, while others made no effort at all. This would strain the machinery excessively and it would be forced to stop.

Maconochie next went up to the new military barracks, built in 1834 by Major Anderson, whose name was proudly displayed on its façade. Adjoining this building was the officers' quarters, where five or six officers lived. Some were married, but others were not and used to hold riotous parties, as this account indicates: 'Towards four in the morning some of the party waxed boisterous and chairs flew like flies about the room.' The military barracks were at one end of Quality Row, and at the other the road led on to the cemetery, a forlorn spot close to the ocean where graves lay scattered in haphazard fashion, mute testimony to lives ended so far from home. Ullathorne had described it as 'closed in on three sides, . . . whilst the fourth is open to the restless sea. The graves are numerous and recent. Their lives were brief, and as agitated and restless as the waves which now break at their feet, and whose dying sound is their only requiem.'

The following day Maconochie went up to Longridge Agricultural Station, about a mile and a half higher up, from where any produce surplus to island requirements was exported to Sydney. His 'new' prisoners were already installed here in their

The cemetery on Norfolk Island

newly built but still incomplete accommodation. Convicts on Norfolk Island usually wore a long, yellow cutaway loose frock-coat in summer and each had a straw hat. In winter their uniform was a coarse woollen jacket. Maconochie changed the colour for his new prisoners' clothing to grey, and also put his newly appointed convict overseers, convict police and other 'special' prisoners into blue. He wanted everyone to see that his regime was going to be different.

It had been a salutary tour of inspection and, taking stock afterwards, Maconochie found things 'in some respects even rather worse' than he had expected. Inside the prisoners' barracks had been the 'old hands', 1,242 doubly convicted prisoners, 'the refuse of both penal colonies'. He could see that until now they had been 'rigorously coerced all day', and 'cooped up' at night in barracks too small for them. Their feelings, he soon noticed, were 'habitually outraged', and 'their self-respect destroyed'. Previously they had been required to doff their cap to each soldier they met, and even the empty sentry-boxes whenever they passed them. If they met an officer, they had to take off their hats and stand aside, bare-headed, in the ditch if necessary, until he had passed. All this was demeaning. He tried to find out how the staff already there were treating these old hands. Punishments, he discovered, were frequent and often meaningless. 'For the merest trifles they were flogged, ironed, or confined in gaol for successive days on bread and water.' Staff seemed concerned only with disciplinary matters, and had little interest in the prisoners' moral welfare. Maconochie related how the 'most horrid vices, with acts of brutal violence, or dexterity in theft and robbery, were detailed to me by the officers, with little direct censure, rather as anecdotes calculated to astonish and amuse a new-comer'. By contrast, the possession of any unintended extras such as a 'pipe, a newspaper, a little tea, some article of clothing not furnished by the Government, or the omission of some mark of respect, or a saucy look, or word, or even an imputation of sullenness' were deemed 'unpardonable crimes'. Maconochie could see he needed to change the priorities of the staff.

He watched the prisoners at meal times. The old hands were fed 'more like hogs than men', with neither knives, nor forks, nor other conveniences allowed at their tables. They had to tear their food with their fingers and teeth, and had to drink for the most part out of a bucket. Two-thirds were able to eat inside the mess-shed, while the rest ate outside, in an 'open shed beside a large privy'. Maconochie could see signs of this neglect etched on the men's faces and how men's countenances 'reflected faithfully this description of treatment'. He noticed that not a single place of worship had been erected in the past fifteen years, and no residential clergyman – other than one, who lasted a mere three months – had been there until recently. There were no schools, and no books. Maconochie felt his first task should be to address these 'old hands' as a group in a more humane way. He described how 'a more demoniacal looking assemblage could not be imagined, and nearly the most formidable sight I ever beheld was the sea of faces up-turned to me when I first addressed them.' Ullathorne remembered the same thing: 'Well also', he wrote, 'do I recall that almost inhuman expression in a thousand faces massed together.'

A witness to this first address was Thomas Cook, already on the island for three years as a prisoner, who eventually wrote his memoirs after he left Norfolk Island. Cook had been born in Whitchurch, a market town in Shropshire, one of eight children. At the age of fourteen he joined a local solicitor's office as a clerk. In the early 1830s rural unrest was rife in the area. An economic slump at the end of the 1820s had left many agricultural workers below the poverty line. They had then rallied to the figurehead of 'Captain Swing', a legendary character used as a bogeyman by such workers all over England to intimidate landowners and the propertied classes in general. Threatening letters were posted under doors late at night or stuck on village greens signed 'Captain Swing', and these widespread agricultural riots became known as 'Swing riots', spurred on by the loss of jobs through newly mechanized farm tools, such as steam-driven threshing machines. By 1831 Cook was charged with writing two 'menacing' letters to William Churton, the auctioneer of the town.

There had been recent arson attacks in the Whitchurch area and hayricks and barns had been burnt and machines broken. Churton had been calling for more police protection and for harsher punishments for the culprits. Cook's prankish letter to Churton accused him of getting his property through 'roguery'. The letter went on, 'We men of determination, firm, resolute and undeviating, are now without scruple and determined that your property shall not be of long duration, nor yet your existence', and it was signed: 'Men determined to right the oppressed. Agents to Swing. London.' Cook claimed it was 'done for the sake of sport, the act of a youth bearing no malice', wanting 'to entail alarm upon him without the remotest intention of injuring'. He was, in modern parlance, winding up Churton, whom he saw as a pompous ass. However, the magistrates, because of the local 'Swing' unrest, viewed the case differently. Churton took the letter straight round to the authorities, who saw it as sedition. Cook at first denied complicity but evidence from an older accomplice gave him away. After being sent for trial at Shrewsbury assizes in March 1831 he was given fourteen years' transportation. He wrote, 'My feelings are indescribable. The shrieks of a tender and beloved mother, and the tears gushing from the eyes of a religious and revered Father, from whom I had childishly concealed by guilt, disturbed my individual to an extent approximating madness.' From Shrewsbury he was sent to the convict hulk *Leviathan* in Portsmouth docks and then put on board the convict ship *Surry*, bound for Botany Bay. The surgeon on board, the Revd Colin Arnot Browning, noticed his ability and well-disposed demeanour and made him his clerk and dispenser for the journey. Cook was a mere nineteen years old.

In all, some 481 'Swing' protesters were sent to Australia, their sentences either seven or fourteen years. More than half of them were married men, who never saw their families again. They took with them powerfully written recommendations from their former employers attesting to their skill as carpenters, wheelwrights and blacksmiths. Nearly all conducted themselves well in Australia, and Sir George Arthur called them a 'cut above the rest'. Yet very few returned because they could not afford the passage. Arthur reckoned that out of 102 'Swing' men pardoned by him between 1826 and 1833, only eight managed to get back to Britain. Most, as Arthur told the Molesworth Committee in 1837, felt a 'deep sense of shame and degradation'. Some had even died from despair. It was one of the worst examples of transportation being used for political ends.

On arriving in Sydney in 1832, Cook, as an educated prisoner, was given the post of clerk in the office of the Principal Superintendent of Convicts at the town's Hyde Park barracks. His incipient rebelliousness must have still been with him, as he was soon charged with disrespect to the Superintendent for failing to take his hat off to him. His appearance at this time was recorded in an official document: height 5' 9", ruddy and freckled complexion, dark brown hair, brown eyes. After a second offence of arriving back late at the barracks in the early hours of the morning, he was sent to work on a road gang in the Blue

Mountains above Sydney. Cook hated it. 'The inclemency of the weather, the haggard countenances of the men, the severity of the cold and the want of a second blanket to save half the frozen men from perishing, the cruelty of the overseers who robbed us of our rations; a sheet of bark for my head, the half of a thread-bare blanket for my covering; many a tear did I shed when contemplating my hard fare, and this slight offence for which I had been doomed.'

Cook was now exposed to the full horrors of the convict system. Homosexuality was widespread. 'So far were these wretched men in depravity, that they appeared to have lost the feelings of men, and to have imbibed those that would render them execrable to all mankind.' As he could read and write, he was asked to become book-keeper. Then, falsely accused of being involved in the killing and eating of two young bullocks, Cook was marched off for twenty miles to await trial. He was discharged, but his hostility to the system increased and he next fraudulently added the names of four fellow prisoners, who wanted to go to Sydney, to a list of witnesses due to go there for trial. Again he at first denied his involvement but was eventually sent to a different road gang, whose commandant 'enforced a system of running us to work at the point of a bayonet, at five miles an hour'. He and other prisoners eventually offered resistance 'which led to much traffic in human flesh and blood, by the soldiers with their bayonets and the scourgers with their cat o'nine tails . . . at times, the officer riding past on his horse, would sentence the whole gang to 50 and 100 lashes each'. Cook absconded and ran away into the bush, but was later caught. In May 1836, now a 'doubly convicted' felon, he was sentenced to be sent to Norfolk Island. 'My feelings on landing here, no pen or language can describe. In a state of nudity we were ranked up on the Beach, and after undergoing a minute and most indelicate inspection, our miserable rags were huddled on, and we were marched to the Post Office, and from thence to the Barrack Yard. From this instant all my hope of happiness was to cease. My beloved Parents, my brothers and Sisters for ever lost to me.'

Cook arrived on Norfolk Island during Major Anderson's term as Commandant. He took stock and decided to conform. At the beginning he was employed in one of the hoeing gangs at Longridge and then made clerk in the Royal Engineer office, where he ended up as chief clerk and storekeeper in charge of tools. But his first days on Norfolk Island were a great strain. 'The insupportable labor imposed on me and the harassing and hunger I experienced at Longridge had in this short period so weakened my frame that as I retired to my Hammock at Night, I frequently implored the Almighty in my supplications to take me from the burden under which I then laboured before the rising of the Sun on the following day, and for the space of 5 weeks after my appointment to the Office in question I consumed no more than Two Pounds of Bread to renovate my exhausted frame.' So weak did he become that 'the offices of my nature had almost ceased to perform their functions and I had made up my mind and prepared myself for another World'. However, 'it pleased providence to spare me' and he survived. After Maconochie took over in March 1840, Cook's continued good conduct led to his being sent across to the mainland to finish the unexpired part of his sentence there. His petition was accompanied by favourable testimonials from officials on Norfolk Island, and by a remarkable letter sent out from Britain signed by Sir Robert Hill, late colonel in the Royal Horse Guards, who had been one of the magistrates at Cook's trial at Whitchurch in March 1831. Hill's letter was also countersigned by Churton, the auctioneer to whom Cook had sent his subversive letter back in 1831. Furthermore Churton had got fifteen other townspeople of Whitchurch, including four curates, to co-sign the letter, stating that Cook's original sentence had been excessive. Cook's petition to go to Sydney was granted and he left Norfolk Island on 6th October 1841. Thereafter his whereabouts become less well known. He appears to have absconded, as the Governor's dispatches of New South Wales, dated 22nd May 1844, show a list of convicts who are 'supposed to have escaped from the Colony between 1st January and 31st

December 1843'. The list includes 'Thomas Cook, Attorney's Clerk, absconded from Port Macquarie since 21st August, 1843'. Perhaps he was fed up with waiting for his sentence to finish: he still had another two years to go and at thirty-one was undoubtedly keen to get home. He had met a sailor in his travels who in all likelihood 'showed him the way' to escape, by stowing away on a boat or signing on as crew.

A clue to Cook's eventual whereabouts comes from the manuscript of his memoirs, *The Exile's Lamentations*. A note attached to it is initialled by Maconochie, and reads: 'This narrative was written after its author left Norfolk Island. He shortly after succeeded in absconding, and I rather think is now in France. His connections are respectable – but he was afraid to remain in this country (England)'. Maconochie's own hand-written note goes on: 'Where blank paper is wafered, or pinned, over the Narrative, it is to cover details regarding unnatural offences – the covers can be removed. The writer is a very well purposed man, never was dishonest, and was very useful as an Overseer. AM.' Maconochie saw the manuscript in Britain – hence the prudery of the blank paper wafered over the narrative – after his return there in 1844 and he passed it on to the novelist William Henry Kingston, hoping he might get it published. Cook's text was eventually published by the Library of Australian History in 1978. The manuscript had ended up in the Mitchell Library, Sydney, after being purchased in London in 1929 for £250. Cook, it seems, did in all probability get back to Whitchurch. Baptismal records for 1849 and 1851 show two sons born to Thomas and Margaret Cook, though this cannot be taken as conclusive evidence.

8

Queen Victoria's Birthday

THOMAS COOK WAS present at Maconochie's opening speech to the 'old' prisoners on the island and commented: 'Captain Maconochie in a most Christian-like and eloquent speech, which drew Tears from the Eyes of the most hardened and depraved beings, gave us to understand that it had been the pleasure of our most Gracious Queen to forward him to that Island for the purpose of ascertaining how far the system of discipline by which we had for many years been governed was susceptible of improvement; that our wretched condition and Mutinous proceedings, which had invaded the peace of the island, had given rise to a deal of anxiety on the opposite side of the Globe.'

This was Maconochie's mission statement. Its impact was considerable as it suddenly made isolated island prisoners feel that they were linked again to the far side of the world, to home. This was a shrewd move, a psychological act that would win them over, but, as the notion of mission statement implies, it was also a reflection of his own sense of the importance of the job he was embarking upon. He saw himself as entrusted by the British government to reform the present system, not just on the island, but by implication elsewhere. This sense of mission would permeate his approach and ultimately affect his dealings with authorities such as Gipps and, by extension, the Colonial Office in London.

Cook went on to record Maconochie's claim 'that he did not

enter that island with the intention of torturing the unhappy prisoners whom he was appointed to control. On the contrary he purposed introducing measures by which alone the industrious and otherwise well-conducted could purchase their Freedom.' This was the bait he was offering, the fundamental change of approach that would make prisoners agents of their own welfare. They looked up at him in disbelief at someone who was genuinely offering them a change of regime, convicts who, though many of them were still in their twenties, had become hardened and embittered.

In his new system there would be two distinct stages of treatment – punishment for the past, and training for the future. Prisoners would be expected to meet both in the right way, 'the first with manly penitence and resignation, the second with a manly hope and aspiring after better things'. The preliminary punishment stage was a period of isolation, of confinement for the prisoner to reflect on his past misdeeds before moving on to the next stage.

Maconochie then described how his new system would grant marks according to conduct on a daily basis and these would be added to, or subtracted from, according to their conduct as evaluated by the overseers. 'By this means a minute record will be kept of every man's conduct, from day to day; he will advance from punishment to probation, and from probation to entire release, as he behaves himself. His fate will be entirely in his own hands.' Responsibility would thus be returned to the convict himself and this principle would emulate industry outside and hence be the best preparation for his return to society. Prisoners would now have an interest in their own labour, instead of trying to evade it. His mark system, he explained, for the 'old hands' was still awaiting authorization by the Governor of New South Wales, and by the government at home, but Maconochie was optimistic that this would come through in the near future. The system, which would be put into immediate effect with the 'new' prisoners, would run along these lines: a seven-year sentence would be made commutable to 6,000 marks, a ten-year one to 7,000, and fourteen years and upwards to 8,000. The first 2,000, 3,000 and 4,000 marks respectively would relate to the initial punishment portion of these sentences. During this period the restrictions imposed on the men would be 'most severe', and indulgences granted them few and far between. Ten marks a day, or 60 marks a week, would be granted for ordinary day labour 'well and truly performed'. Sundays were 'idle days'. Anyone in the punishment period would need to gain one half of all his marks before being allowed to exchange any of them for indulgences such as tea, sugar and tobacco.

During the next stage, namely the first half of the probation period, a limited sale of fresh and other provisions could be exchanged for marks, along with extra or superior clothing and better accommodation and supplies, and during the second half of the probation period the sale even of spirits, under suitable regulation, would be sanctioned. He explained that buying goods for marks was meant to be an exercise in self-denial and providing convicts with an experience of thoughtful choice. He did not see it as an indulgence *per se*, more an encouragement towards the use of discretion and judgement. 'Their whole after-life may take its character from the degree in which they avail themselves of the opportunity afforded of acquiring self command.'

In this probation period, 'when the eyes of all are cast exclusively forward', the men would form themselves into messes of six, responsible for each other's conduct and gaining or losing marks according to the behaviour of each. Thus a prisoner could only move from punishment to probation when he had found five others willing to be associated with him. They would not all necessarily be required to labour, or even live together, but had to be responsible for each other and had to exert themselves on each other's behalf, as well as on their own. This was the principle of mutuality that he had used in Quebec.

Maconochie's overall aim was to develop an *esprit de corps* through his system of marks. 'Rewards should be infallibly given, and punishments infallibly imposed.' In this way men would become 'the artisans of their future fortunes'. Once he had explained this to the assembled group, 'the cheers which emanated from the Prisoners were most deafening', as Cook wrote. Cook, admittedly a partisan writer and on Maconochie's side, took up the theme: 'From that instant all crime disappeared. The old hands from that moment were a different race of beings. The erroneous notion of manliness that had been engendered in their minds by a course of harsh and cruel treatment under which they had for many years been compelled to groan, was almost entirely eradicated when they found themselves viewed as men by their Philanthropic Ruler.' This was the first level of response, at the human level. But a deeper one was in store as well. 'No sooner did they rightly comprehend the purport of his message from our most Gracious Queen, that Sovereign who had been forgotten by them as having any Dominion over the land of their Captivity, that land in which so much Blood had been spilt, than Her Majesty reigned in their hearts and they all appeared to labor cheerfully in the one large field of Reformation.' This was the real key, bonding people together as part of one large family, with the young and attractive Queen Victoria as figurehead. Most of the prisoners felt distanced from their homeland, having suffered the indignities of the voyage and subsequent incarceration in Australia, the horrors of the chain gangs and much else. They had long felt cut off and abandoned. Now Maconochie was reminding them of their ties with home, and the relief they felt was almost palpable.

Maconochie could now move on to explaining his system of messes. Cook described it:

> They were allowed to choose their own companions in Messmates or Families of Six, and each man of his respective Mess was responsible for the conduct of the other; or in other words if one man of a mess offended the fine imposed upon him devolved on the others and so procrastinated the Freedom of all, thus making the demeanor – and industry of the one an object of importance to the rest; and in the event of an offender escaping detection in the commission of

any crime, every man under the system would be fined a given number of marks, thus encouraging the suppression of crime by all.

After only a short time on the island Maconochie realized the impracticality of keeping the two groups – the 'old hands' and the new prisoners – under two different systems. Such divisions were creating envy and resentment on one side and were making his new system with the new prisoners less and less enforceable. Within ten days of his arrival Maconochie therefore joined the two groups together. Each group was now under his new mark system.

On 26th March 1840 Maconochie sent Gipps an account of his first few weeks on the island, explaining that he had found the difficulty of maintaining two systems of discipline at the same time on the island 'almost insuperable', and so had joined them up. However 'precipitate' he may have been in doing this, he felt his difficulties would have been greater by delaying. 'The officers under me were confused by conflicting methods; their zeal in favour of the men was only half exerted while it appeared only half introduced.' The old prisoners, too, had had their hopes 'half roused' through the introduction of the new system of rewards elsewhere on the island and this difference in treatment was causing great dissatisfaction and a feeling of injustice among them. He had put his mark system into full operation with both sets of prisoners on the island on Monday 16th March, and had put up a list in their barracks stating their respective sentences, periods of arrival, conduct, and character, and the number of marks which each had to earn. Four free overseers would record marks earned each evening.

Some misdemeanours, he conceded, had already taken place – insubordination mainly, aggravated by indecent language – and had been punished accordingly. His aim, however, as he told Gipps, was to get his men to 'rise from turbulence to order, and from insolence and obscene language to obedience, civility, and decorum' and he had constantly reminded them that 'every gross or brutal act or expression, every falsehood appearing on the face of the police records, will operate to the disadvantage of all, and to no one's disappointment more certainly or grievously than the superintendent's own.' His hope was that his new system would raise everyone 'even from the lowest depth, to renewed hope and manhood'.

Gipps was livid when he heard this. Maconochie had presented him with a *fait accompli*, undermining his authority. Gipps got his Colonial Secretary, E. Deas Thomson, to reply from Sydney on 28th April 1840. 'I am directed by the Governor to inform you that he has read with great attention, but not without some degree of surprise and apprehension, the two public orders issued by you at Norfolk Island, and transmitted with your letter of the 26th ultimo.' He conveyed Gipps's indignation.

> The understanding on which you were sent to Norfolk Island was that the new establishment at Long Ridge should be kept quite distinct from that of the old settlement, and if no positive instructions were given to you in this respect, it was only because such an order was judged by the Governor to be unnecessary, in consequence of the anxious desire constantly expressed by you that it might be so. In the management of the men sent from England you were allowed very great discretionary powers, powers which his Excellency felt disposed to look upon as limited only by the law (as for instance the 2 & 3 Will. 4 c.62), and by the necessity of observing a due degree of economy in the expenditure of the public money, but in respect to the old or doubly convicted prisoners, no powers were, as far as his Excellency recollects, given to you to hold out expectations such as are contained in the second order; expectations which he is reluctantly forced to say he has it not in his power to realise. The Governor cannot promise to bring back to New South Wales all or any number of the prisoners at Norfolk Island as soon as they have accumulated the number of marks allotted to them by you, and the consequences which might result to the colony if he did so are too serious to contemplate. Already his Excellency even fears that the report of what is going on at Norfolk Island will destroy the salutary dread in which transportation to it had always been held among the convict population of New South Wales whilst, for the present at least, he has it not in his power to substitute any other kind of punishment.

Here was the nub of the conflict from Gipps's point of view. He feared Norfolk Island prisoners, once they had accumulated sufficient marks, coming back to New South Wales. Gipps, as Governor, knew his local population would be hostile to this and certainly would not want them there. New South Wales had just given up transportation and was keen to remove the stain of its convict past forever. He insisted that the old prisoners were to be put back on the old system.

Gipps's counter-order was a shock to Maconochie. He had felt he had been given a free hand but now Gipps was invoking all the old statutes again. It showed a fundamental difference in mentality between the two men. Maconochie was a former naval man and taking command of Norfolk Island was like taking over a new ship and bringing the crew together, getting them to act in concert for the good of one and all. Military men such as Gipps operated more by rule and precedent: statutes were there to be obeyed. Nearly all the previous commandants on Norfolk Island had been military men and had held the view that convicts had to be driven hard, disciplined and kept in line: Anderson was the prime example.

To Maconochie, the first test of co-operation with the colonial administration had failed. Gipps was backtracking, sticking to the letter of the law. But Maconochie, always an improviser, was determined not to be done down by Gipps's apparent volte-face. His 'sanguine' temperament came to the fore, and he decided to press ahead with a plan he had formed to celebrate the birthday of the young Queen Victoria, who would be twenty-one on 24th May. He set aside Monday the 25th as a holiday for everyone on the island, both bond and free, the first time the monarch's birthday had been celebrated on Norfolk Island.

The appeal to Queen and Country was to touch a deeper chord. It was a link to home, an antidote to despair. 'I had very early observed, and with great regret, in the penal colonies generally, the hatred existing in most prisoners in them towards their native country and all her institutions. They have for the most part known little of her, but the vicious social combinations which plunge so many of them inevitably into crime, and then the vindictive penal institutions which convert them ultimately into fiends. They thus almost to a man resent their position, rather than acknowledge its justice.' He had seen how their feelings for their motherland had gradually been eroded by her institutions. Maconochie wanted to 'overcome this feeling' and change the nature of his institution. A further reason was a wish to 'stir up the spirit' of his new prisoners, many of whom were 'very low, about their illness, and the severity of our country work, to which they are necessarily chiefly set.'

The necessary preparations were put in hand and on the day itself, 25th May, a new set of signal pennants, which Maconochie had especially brought to the island to signal to ships anchored in the bay, was raised at first light and fluttered from flagpoles near the landing pier, the Royal St George proudly displayed at the top. The old hands and the new convicts up at Longridge got out of bed in the morning and were astonished to find their prison gates open. They could wander as they pleased throughout the island, swim in the sea, play games on the grass, as long as, so Maconochie's proclamation warned them, they showed by 'retiring to their quarters at the sound of the bugle . . . that they might be trusted with safety'. This was quite a risk, as Cook noted: 'These men who had for many years been ruled with the rod of Iron and had received their hundreds at the Triangles for being short distance from their Barracks were on this loyal occasion permitted to range from the Settlement to Ansons Bay, Cascade, or any other part of the Island without the least fear of their committing any depredation.' These were men who had previously been so desperate to escape that they had, as he noted, 'seized Boats under a Fire of Musketry'. Now those same boats lay all day long in the harbour, their oars lying idly in them.

The day began with a ration of fresh pork being issued to each prisoner, to be cooked on barbecue fires during the morning. Flour was issued as well, so that special bread could be baked. Throughout the morning Maconochie wandered among his prisoners, taking his family with him, chatting affably with them, like Henry V before Agincourt. At midday the convicts sat down to an open-air lunch on tables set up on an open patch of ground alongside the prisoners' barracks. Maconochie and his officers sat down with them. Maconochie then gave each man in succession half a tumbler of a mixture of rum and lemonade specially prepared from the island lemons. 'It scarcely smelt of spirits, and went, as was intended, to the hearts, not the heads, of those who drank it.' After the meal it was used to toast their young sovereign. In Cook's words: '"Long Life to Queen Victoria" was echoed from one end of the Island to the other in the most deafening cheers, three times three.'

This toast was followed by the national anthem, played by convict musicians on the instruments Maconochie had brought across from Sydney. As it was played, prisoners uncovered their heads with 'as great a share of decorum observed as could have distinguished a free community'. Then a 21-gun royal salute was fired, answered by musketry from the military garrison. Maconochie then delivered a speech 'most admirably calculated to nourish our feelings of attachment to our beloved Queen in which he traced her from the Breast of her Royal Mother', as Cook commented. After this national games between the Irish, Scots and English took place and prizes were given to the winners.

The highlight of the afternoon's entertainment was a theatre performance. Playbills had been produced announcing the performance at 'The Royal Victoria Theatre, Norfolk Island'. The old hands were taking the leading parts and had been preparing their costumes, scenery and music for the past two weeks in their spare time. The afternoon began with two acts from the comic opera *The Castle of Andalusia*, with James Lawrence, a 35-year-old son of a London diamond broker, retransported to Norfolk Island for fraud on the mainland, playing the lead role of Don Caesar, plus a supporting cast of ten other players and 'the usual *Banditti*' as extras. Lawrence was a talented actor and musician who had been sentenced in Anderson's time to fifty lashes for singing a song in

ROYAL VICTORIA THEATRE.

Norfolk Island

On Monday 25th May in honor of Her

MAJESTY'S BIRTH DAY,

Will be Performed by Permission

Two Acts of the Admired Comic Opera of the

CASTLE of ANDALUSIA.

Don Cæsar	Jno. Lawrence	Sanenova	Jno. Cranston
Scipio	Geo. Wolfe	Rapino	Jno. Potter
Fernando	Jno. Walker	Calvette	Will.m Small
Alphonso	H. Witton	Vasquez	K.r Sanderson
Sparte	Jas. King	Lorenza	Do
Pedrillo	Jno. Monds	With the usual Banditti	

After which a Musical Melange consisting of

Glee "Prithee Brothers speed to the Boat"	Witton Walker Potter Cranston Sanderson Small	Song "Powder Monkey Pete	J. Lawrence
Song "Old England for Ever	H. Witton	Song "Spirit of the Storm	H. Witton
Comic Song "Walker the Vagrancy Postman	J. Monds	Song "The light Irishman	J. Potter
Song "Pound provisto to a Waterman	J. Lawrence	Glee "Some Love to Roam	Witton Walker Potter Cranston Lawrence Small
"The Fisherman's Glee"	Witton Walker Potter Cranston Small	Song "The Old Commodore	J. Lawrence
Song "Paddy from Cork	J. Walker	The Tent Scene in Richard 3rd	H. Witton
Glee "Behold how Brightly	Witton Walker Potter Cranston Small		

Naval Hornpipe — Mich.l Burns. *Dance "Tyrolese Waltz* — The Barry

After which the Musical Entertainment of the

Purse or the Benevolent Tar

The Baron	J. Cranston	Will. Steady	J. Lawrence
Theodore	J. Ralph	Sally	J. Monds
Edmund	H. Yelverton	Page	J. Ker

After which

Paddy Carey in Character — J. Lawrence. *The Banner of War* — J. Witton

The Whole to conclude with the Grand National Anthem of GOD SAVE THE QUEEN

Vivat Regina

Playbill for Queen Victoria's birthday celebrations

the barracks. No doubt he was pleased to get his revenge. Then came a 'musical melange' of comic songs and ballads – 'Prithee, Brothers, Speed to the Boat', 'Paddy from Cork', 'Behold How Brightly'. Then Lawrence gave a further rendition of 'The Old Commander', a veiled reference no doubt to Anderson, who had flogged him so mercilessly. James Porter, one of the Macquarie Harbour convicts who had seized the brig *Frederick* and sailed her across the Pacific to Chile, then sang 'The Light Irishman'. Other sketches followed. A *danse tyrolese* was waltzed by Thomas Barry, and the Sailor's Hornpipe performed by Michael Burns, another prisoner heavily flogged in Anderson's time.

Then there was the moving tent scene from *Richard III*, played by another convict H. Witton, chosen no doubt by Maconochie to encourage thoughts of introspection:

> My conscience hath a thousand several tongues,
> And every tongue brings in a several tale,
> And every tale condemns me for a villain.
> Perjury, perjury in the highest degree,
> Murder, stern murder, in the direst degree –
> All several sins, all us'd in each degree,
> Throng to the bar, crying all, Guilty! Guilty!
> I shall despair. There is no creature loves me,
> And if I die, no soul will pity me:
> Nay, wherefore should they, since that I myself
> Find in my heart no pity to myself?

A further playlet, *Purse, or the Benevolent Tar*, was put on and the entertainment ended with another rendition of the national anthem. Later that afternoon the same show was put on up the hill at Longridge in front of the new prisoners who, after the midday meal, had departed up the hill, being separated from the old hands at Maconochie's request, no doubt as a result of Gipps's recent letter. Maconochie was present at their performance there as well. As the evening drew on, fireworks, paid for, like the rum, by Maconochie himself, were let off down at Kingston beside the prison compounds, and Government House was specially lit up for the occasion. At eight o'clock, as per the terms of his proclamation, the bugle was sounded and the prisoners returned to their respective sleeping wards to answer muster. Not a single man was absent, nor, as Cook observed, 'was there a solitary instance of the most trivial offence being committed'. Maconochie noted this too. By the time they had finished, 'not a single irregularity, or evening anything approaching an irregularity, took place . . . [E]very man quietly returned to his ward; some even anticipated the hour' (a reference to some of the 'old hands' who had even turned in early). As he wrote later, 'not a shadow of disorder occurred when bell and bugle recalled every poor fellow at night to his dungeon, or still more horrid ward, with a precision and punctuality that were to the last degree affecting'. It had been a major achievement.

After the day's events, Maconochie put up this notice for the prisoners:

> Norfolk Island, 26 May 1840.
> The superintendent most heartily congratulates the prisoners on their celebration yesterday of the Queen's birthday. It was a universal holiday, even more agreeable to him to witness, than for them to enjoy . . . It is very seldom that anything half so pleasing rewards the labours or the anxiety of the superintendent of a prison; yet, when it has once occurred, it is not to be doubted that similar means will obtain it again.

It was the invocation again of the queen as a symbol, giving prisoners something to live for. But Maconochie believed strongly that it was important to keep prisoners informed of what was going on – hitherto they had always been kept in the dark – and now he had to tell them some bad news. Gipps had not authorized the joining up of the two groups into one but had insisted on keeping them separate. As Maconochie put it in his notice, 'The moral state of the penal prisoners [the 'old hands'] is, in truth, still regarded with doubt and hesitation in Sydney.' Maconochie told them that he saw it differently and that yesterday's example was a demonstration of this.

This news was bound to be a disappointment to the 'old hands', but Maconochie was here relaying the message of Gipps's dispatch (via Thomson) of 28th April, which had arrived just before the festivities. Maconochie nevertheless begged them to keep up the good work and exhorted them to persevere. The queen's birthday had shown that they could respond to a challenge and be trusted and he had officially recorded this. That should, he hoped, have an effect on the governor. He told them he would apply again and again on their behalf to Gipps to review their position favourably. 'No testimony can be so weighty as that which they have just borne for themselves.'

Maconochie answered Gipps's dispatch of 28th April on 27th May, expressing his 'very great pain' at Gipps's disapproval of what he had done, but still asserting that it was impossible to maintain the distinction between the new and old prisoners. The difficulties of doing so were too great. He explained how the agricultural establishment at Longridge required 600 men to run properly, and that he had only brought 178 with him (these were the *Nautilus* convicts) and that it was the beginning of maize harvest, and all the convicts on the island had to be employed in the same fields performing the same tasks. His overseers for the new hands had been drawn from the old hands as their instructors. They shared the same cooking apparatus, the same places of mustering and worship and it would be impossible to keep them apart. Maconochie reminded Gipps that he had anticipated difficulties of this kind, but they were now proving greater than he had imagined. 'Everything tended to a fusion, even to the interest excited in each body about the other.'

Maconochie also felt that it would be 'morally inexpedient' to keep the two groups apart. 'It enlisted every old prisoner on the island against me.' Early on, in an attempt to keep up the old system with the 'old hands', he had inflicted 'three very moderate corporal punishments' and the Protestant clergyman had come up to him to express a hope that he would never do so again as he had never seen the barrack-yard in so much agitation as on this occasion. Maconochie felt that the whole success of his experiment was at stake, and that it was quite impractical to keep the old hands isolated. 'I might as well have tried to make experiments on steam in an ice-house, as have sought to develop the powers of moral reasoning and persuasion amidst every possible form of moral counteraction.' He accepted that he had left Gipps with the understanding that the old hands were not immediately to be brought under the new system. But once he arrived, things had looked so very different. 'Why (it occurred to me) should these men be excluded from an improving system? They had been, above all others, injured by a deteriorating one; and ought this, their greatest misfortune and for which they were in no degree accountable, to exclude them from the chance of amelioration?'

Maconochie felt he had been authorized to innovate, or at the very least, improvise. He reminded Gipps that the report of the Molesworth Committee, and the minutes of Lord Russell and Lord Howick (Sir George Grey's cousin and another member of the committee) had been in favour of a 'total and complete change being immediately made; and the first of them even makes such change the only and indispensable condition on which it recommends the retaining of transportation in any form as a secondary punishment'. The report had explicitly concluded that 'the mode of governing convicts suggested by Captain Maconochie might in part at least be attempted with advantage.' Maconochie felt he had covered himself by 'again and again, verbally and in writing' stating that his innovations were 'provisional and contingent on the approval of himself [Gipps] and of Her Majesty's Government at home'. He could see it 'is true that they in some measure conflict with the Act quoted by you, 2 & 3 Will. 4. c. 62, but it can scarcely be doubted that this Act will be repealed, if indeed it has not already ceased to be law. Lord Howick in his minute exemplifies the mark system by taking 9,000 marks as his number, and considers that these may be obtained in three years: and Lord John Russell directly speculates on the economy to be derived from shorter punishments.' At the back of his mind Maconochie must have felt that he was moving with the times, that he was in tune with the penal changes and reforms now being made in Britain under Russell's direction. He fully expected the previous rules and regulations on the island to be amended or modified. 'The truth is that I never thought of those rules at all as a guide; I thought them a dead letter. They were issued under General Darling's government; have never, I believe, been revised, and, except as regards the returns prescribed by them, I know of no one here who ever thinks of them.' He had already got 'testimonies of the several officers in this establishment to what has been already done here' and the two surgeons, Drs Stuart and Reid, were very strongly in favour of the changes he had brought about.

This was a strong counter-argument to Gipps's standpoint. Maconochie reminded Gipps that an earlier letter of his was devoted exclusively to the 'exposure of the lamentable state of society which these rules have produced among us here, and which is only one specimen among many of the essentially false and erroneous principles on which they are founded'. It was a fair point. He had, as he said, when he arrived found things 'even worse than he expected'. If he was going to reform the existing form of operation, the old rules would need to be changed or scrapped. 'If I have done wrong in deviating from these rules, I am quite certain that in the same circumstances his Excellency would have done so too; and if any of my other measures seem to him still to deserve censure after this explanation, as having been hasty, premature, or unauthorised, I do not think it possible that he could be displeased by their results, by the willing labour and contented submission to inevitable privations, which reward me every hour for the trouble I take to bring them about.' This was the proof he was looking for, and the prisoners were clearly responding.

This letter shows Maconochie's pragmatic approach, his willingness to adapt to the circumstances he found on the island and his slight irritation at having to deal with the hidebound Thomson rather than with 'his Excellency', Gipps himself. As an innovator, it was the spirit of the law, rather than the letter, that counted. He was clearly hoping now that Gipps would take his side. But it was not to be. Thomson wrote again from the Colonial Secretary's office in Sydney on 26th June 1840. 'I am directed by the Governor to acknowledge the receipt of your letter of the 27th ultimo, relative to the changes you have made in the discipline of the penal prisoners at Norfolk Island, and to inform you in reply that his Excellency regrets he feels forced to say that the arguments contained in your letter have produced no alteration whatever in his opinion of the impropriety of the changes introduced by you in the management of the men on the old establishment at the island.' Thomson went on:

> It was stated in your former letter, that you found (although after the experience of a single week) it was impossible to carry on two distinct systems of discipline: his Excellency, without inquiring whether the experience of a week was sufficient to justify such a conclusion instructs me to remark that allowing the impossibility to exist, it would have been more proper for you to have suspended the execution of the system over which you had entire control, than to alter that with respect to which you had been entrusted with no discretionary power whatever. His Excellency cannot admit, as you appear to suppose, that the penal regulations of Norfolk Island had become obsolete, or that they had ever been considered so either by this government or by any of your predecessors.

This was a contradiction in terms as far as Maconochie was concerned, as he had been specifically authorized to try a new system. He could not simply have stopped after a week and reverted to the old system, or 'suspended' his new one.

Maconochie had transgressed and was now being brought sharply into line.

> Sir George Gipps will not enter into an examination of any of the arguments adduced by you to prove that your system is working well at Norfolk Island, such an examination is quite unnecessary, because his Excellency's objections to your proceedings have reference to the

effects which they are calculated to produce, not in Norfolk Island, but in New South Wales and his Excellency directs me to say, that whether the system of punishment heretofore pursued at Norfolk Island was good or bad is not the question; it was a system which caused transportation to that settlement to be held in great and salutary dread by the convict population of New South Wales, and to destroy that dread before even any substitute for transportation to Norfolk Island has been devised, would be to expose this colony to risks for which he cannot make himself responsible. I am therefore desired to inform you, that the instructions contained in my letter of the 28th April are now repeated, and that his Excellency considers nothing short of an apprehension for the safety of the island will justify you in acting in contravention of them.

Here was the crux of the difficulties between Gipps and Maconochie. Gipps was backtracking on his earlier assurance of giving Maconochie a 'fair trial'. He had changed his tune, through the fear of the early return of its prisoners to New South Wales and the fear of the contagion of what he saw as a loose, disruptive regime at Norfolk Island. Gipps was wearing his colonial governor's hat, tilted definitely towards Whitehall this time.

Gipps had also been shocked to hear of the Queen Victoria birthday celebrations, and he was not the only one: adverse reactions proliferated in newspapers. Gipps's letter of 26th June also rebuked Maconochie for this:

It is scarcely possible for his Excellency to conceive anything more calculated to produce mischievous effects amongst the large convict population of this colony, whether in private assignment, or the service of the Government, than to learn that men of their own class, who have been transported to Norfolk Island for crimes of the most atrocious nature, are there entertained with the performance of plays, and regaled with punch, and he considers it his duty not to allow the reports of such proceedings to reach them, without causing them at the time to learn that they have met with his marked disapprobation. As his Excellency has ever expressed a desire to give to you the utmost discretion in the management of the men who were sent to Norfolk Island, expressly to be at your disposal, he will, as far as they are concerned, only remark, that the issue to them of spirits appears to him to have been highly objectionable, and the propriety of granting to them marks, in the way of wages, for a day on which they did not work, very questionable, even on your own principles.

On 27th June 1840 Gipps wrote to Russell reporting on the 'voluminous correspondence which I have had with Capt Maconochie, on the subject of the proceedings at Norfolk Island':

> Your Lordship will . . . I am sure, readily imagine what must have been my surprise when I learned that Captain Maconochie had, within a week after his arrival in Norfolk Island abolished all distinctions between the two classes [of prisoners]; that he had extended equally to all a system of extreme indulgence, and held out hopes, almost indiscriminately to them of being speedily restored to freedom; that he had entirely overlooked that passage in Lord Normanby's dispatch, which, even in respect to prisoners from England, directed 'that a fixed period of imprisonment should in the first instance be allotted for the punishment of the crime of which the prisoner has been convicted', and disregarded equally the effects which so great a change of discipline at Norfolk Island was calculated to produce on the large convict population of this colony, and the feelings of dissatisfaction and alarm with which the colonists of New South Wales could contemplate the speedy return to the colony of more than a thousand persons of the most reckless character, who had been sent from it for the commission of crimes, for the most part of the deepest dye.

Gipps wanted Russell to be in no doubt about Maconochie's high-handed treatment of him. 'Your Lordship will perceive by the correspondence which is enclosed, that though my disapproval of Captain Maconochie's proceedings was notified to him on the 28th of April 1840, and received by him on the 20th of May, no attention whatever was paid by him to my communications, but that, on the contrary, within a few days after the receipt of them, the whole convict population of the island was, on the occasion of Her Majesty's birthday, regaled with punch, and entertained with the performance of a play.' This played straight into Victorian prejudices against excesses being given to prisoners.

The response from Russell ran as follows:

> I have received your despatch of the 27th of June last, enclosing copies of a correspondence which you have had with Captain Maconochie, relative to the system of convict discipline with he had been pursuing at Norfolk Island. I regret that the experiment which was entrusted to the management of Captain Maconochie should have been so materially injured in its execution by the manner in which he has attempted to work it out. Under the circumstances which appear in the correspondence now before me, I see no alternative but to direct, that Captain Maconochie should not be entrusted with the management of any convicts who have more than three years time to serve, before, under the ordinary regulations, they may obtain a ticket of leave. The rest of the convicts at Norfolk Island should be gradually removed from under his control. You will, therefore, make the necessary arrangements with Sir John Franklin for the reception of such convicts in Tasman's Peninsula.

Panic had set in at the Colonial Office, with either Russell or Stephen behind this, and they were now ready to abandon the whole experiment. Russell went on: 'I have already authorised you to remove Captain Maconochie from Norfolk Island, if you should consider it necessary. The correspondence now before me convinces me of the necessity of leaving you full discretion to supersede that officer, if it should appear to you that the good of the public service required such a measure.' Russell was taking no chances. But he was passing the buck to Gipps, as his own mind was now more preoccupied with penal changes at home, such as building 'modern' penitentiaries such as Pentonville.

Maconochie remained unrepentant. Writing later, he wondered:

> Would it have been better to have undone the whole effect of the day by showing jealousy and suspicion at night? Or to have omitted the

celebration altogether? I am still of the fixed opinion that, circumstanced as I was, dragging up two thousand of my fellow men almost
by the hair of the head from perdition, sent expressly to the Island for
this purpose, with the highest of all moral objects thus in view, possessed of the requisite authority, the requisite means, a clear perception of the object, and of its importance, even had the result proved
unfavourable I could not have been justly or severely censured.

He recalled the effect the birthday celebration had had on the
prisoners. 'Ten out of the number have since declared to me
that it chiefly contributed to win them. It inspired confidence,
affection, and many collateral feelings. It revived the memory
of home, and home festivals, which had long been forgotten.'
The evidence of Cook's account certainly bears this out.

Maconochie never afterwards 'repeated the punch or the
plays', but he did continue to celebrate the queen's birthday each
year. In future years he also gave half holidays on St George's, St
Patrick's and St Andrew's days, and he gave a half holiday on the
anniversaries of Waterloo and Trafalgar since he had about two
dozen Waterloo veterans and Trafalgar men among his convicts.
However, he subsequently felt that the initial Queen Victoria
celebration had probably caused more long-term damage to his
reputation than anything else.

The 'old hands' therefore went back on the old system on 18th
July. Maconochie put up a handbill explaining this. 'The Old
hands are informed that Orders have been received to remove
them from under the New System of Discipline and replace
them under the Old.' This meant that piece or task work for
which marks could be granted would have to be discontinued,
and that the 'old hands' would go back to working government-
regulated hours. Secondly, the duration of their sentences would
again be measured strictly by time, 'as fixed by the Original
Judgement, or by the Conditions of remission specified by the
Act of Council Ist. Victoria Cap: 2 & 3.'

Despite these backward steps, Maconochie tried to reassure
them that he still had their best interests at heart. He explained

his objection to time-related sentences. 'Men are led to consider their only object to be to get over this time as easily as possible. A great stimulus to exertion is thus taken away, for no exertion can destroy time: good conduct comes to be regarded as of little importance; rewards become low, animal, temporary, and even childish, as Tea, Sugar, Tobacco or an occasional Holiday; while punishments are made equally temporary affecting only the immediate comforts of the Body, and without bearing on the general condition.' He wanted a higher level of functioning from them. 'When men's minds are raised to the idea that their daily or even hourly conduct may have an influence on their ultimate liberation, they are in a much more improvable state – they have a stronger motive to resist temptation, and stronger inducements to regular exertion.'

Now he was being forced to revert to the old system, Maconochie urged the old hands to resist these small temptations, 'small offences, small deceit, a little evasion, a little swearing or foul language, a little Theft or other enormity'. In compensation he was going to offer them a system of limited rewards for 'extra labour performed, or good conduct exhibited'. Reinstating the old system meant using punishment as before, whether this was bread and water, working in chains or the lash. He would also use the punishment of delaying recommendations to Sydney for prisoners' removal from the island, a known hardship. However, he wanted to let the 'old hands' know how well they had done in such a short space of time, and praised their attitudes. 'They have equalled the new in most respects, and even surpassed them in some.' They had made 'strong resolutions against foul speaking, they have overcome much Theft, they have been in the whole very orderly and subordinate towards their superiors and generally have behaved far beyond anything the Superintendent expected.' He urged them to go on: 'They must continue it, or the good effect of what they have thus done will be much lost both on his own mind and that of others.' He explained to them why he was telling them so much. Change was more likely to be brought about if they knew his reasons for acting rather than by remaining ignorant of them. This way they might feel things were for their benefit and therefore they were more likely to make 'some sacrifice of present ease'. Otherwise it would be like with 'every previous Commandant'.

Cook explained the importance of being sent to Sydney.

> The very idea of his delaying their recommendations to Sydney for a month or two was more severely felt or cared for by the quarter number than would be the infliction of 300 Lashes at the Triangle. This fact might appear incredible, but I can assure my Readers without fear of contradiction that the bare contemplation of the lash may act as a check to the commission of many offences with men who have never received it, whereas the more frequently it is inflicted, the more hardened grows its Victim in iniquity, and ultimately braves the utmost severity it is in the power of a summary court to inflict upon him.

The lash might deter offenders 'but its Victims at length entirely forget themselves as Men, and as a consequence they indulge in everything that is odious and execrable'. The greater hardship was always the loss of liberty, as was implied by the delay in being sent to Sydney.

Maconochie's concession, or reward, to the 'old hands' was a reduced version of the mark system. If they worked each day above the full government hours and this at the end of each week proved satisfactory to their head of department, they would get half a day off to work in their own gardens. 'He will thus, he hopes, give industry a double encouragement making its exercise in the service of Government during the week, earn a power of exercising it in each man's own Service at the end of it.' This modification of his mark system would, he hoped, still give them some incentive.

Maconochie now sent Gipps an account of his first five months on the island. Its mood was upbeat. He was clear that he had 'no remaining doubts as to the adequacy of the general principles of the new system for every purpose contemplated in it'.

His mark system had transformed people, as had the 'principle of mutual responsibility'. The results were 'even stronger than I expected, and in many cases strongest precisely where there had been formerly most contumacy', namely among those previously most resistant to change. The buoyant tone of this report indicates Maconochie's growing sureness in feeling his system was working and would continue to work. It was, in fact, a notable achievement in a short space of time to turn round a recalcitrant group of prisoners into such willing workhorses.

He admitted he had made 'several mistakes', but he had learnt from them. On the credit side, he had adapted his system of mutual responsibility to offenders by putting them not into separate cells but joining them up with others. 'When men have been kept separate, and on the usual prison fare here, a straw mat to sleep or otherwise rest on, bread and water diet, and a single blanket at night, they have merely got irritated. But when two or three have been together, the result has been opposite in all cases. They have always preferred one reading, and the others listening, to each reading to himself; and whether with or without moderate bodily comforts, they have taken an interest in what was thus brought under their notice.' This was part of his educational approach, his 'social imprisonment'. And to provide for the prisoners' spiritual welfare, he had already started building separate Protestant and Catholic chapels adjacent to the prisoners' barracks.

Nearly half of the new population were Irish Catholics, and many were 'political' rather than criminal prisoners: Ribbonmen or Whiteboys transported for minor affrays or trumped-up charges such as being out at night. Seven years' transportation was meted out simply for belonging to one of these secret societies or for having 'papers found on the person'. The 1820s and 1830s had been times of economic hardship in Ireland and many had joined the Whiteboys after running into difficulties with the rent due to their absentee, usually English, landlords. Forced evictions had taken place from cottages. A typical case was Patrick Carey, a thirty-year-old house carpenter from Galway, sentenced to transportation for life at Galway assizes in 1832 for having joined the Whiteboys, whose crime had been to demand an 'increasing of hire wages and decreasing of the rent of land'. At his trial Carey had been strongly supported by a petition signed by half a dozen prominent local people who, while deploring the excesses of 'misguided peasantry', had insisted on Carey's 'gentle character and peaceful non-violent disposition' and on his 'irreproachable character'. The jury too had entered a recommendation of mercy and even the prosecutor had added his name to the petition, but to no effect, and Carey was sent off on the *Eliza* in 1832, before ending up on Norfolk Island.

Maconochie had been impressed by the zeal of the Catholic clergymen on Norfolk Island. They had 'fully concurred in my views' and 'actively assisted' in the new system, especially with the new Irish prisoners, 'who resemble wild colts rather than rational men', but who nevertheless were responding to religious exhortation and had a 'craving rather than disrelish, in the absence of all other excitement, for any description of rational address'. But his greatest satisfaction came from the old hands on the island. They had greatly exceeded his expectations. 'As a body they have shown themselves more sensible to the promises of the new system, and steadier against temptation under their influence, even than the new hands.' Maconochie was having problems with his old staff, though. The 'old' ones still abided by former regulations, 'looking only to coercion, and disregarding individual improvement'. Maconochie spoke of their 'collateral action', and how they loved to turn each 'breach in petty matters' into a joke. He repeated his wish for one or two 'intelligent assistants to help him, able to reason with him on general principles, and superintend minute details'.

The hardest prisoners to deal with were the invalids and the exempt. 'It is a painful fact to record, but almost without exception the old and infirm are here the worst characters, and the most inaccessible to any form of moral excitement. The hoary ruffians, who are necessarily drawing towards the end of their career, are far more obdurate than the young and vigorous; and their presence in the common barrack is most injurious; they scoff at newly-formed good resolutions, they scheme to overcome or expose them, they perpetuate offensive language otherwise going out of repute; they thus set themselves almost systematically against all improvement, and there is no punishing them, for they can earn no marks, and their health and strength neither admit of whipping or punishment.' But Maconochie's optimism was undimmed. 'My estimate of the capabilities of human nature, when properly acted on, has been raised, not lowered, by my recent close contact with the so deemed most worthless of their species. I have found a desire to improve and recover themselves in all.' If his system went on in this way, he felt quite confident that he would 'incalculably diminish and not encourage crime in the adjoining colonies' and furthermore that crimes as such might progressively disappear altogether as a class from all the Australian colonies, thereby freeing society in these from the unspeakable evils which arise from their presence'. This was Maconochie's deepest hope, the focus of his idealism as a reformer.

A few months later Maconochie was writing again to Gipps over where prisoners would go from Norfolk Island on discharge, a key issue.

> No minimum of time appears yet to be fixed for men to be with me; and I am thus still at a loss what expectations to hold out to my new hands. There are some who, on my own provisional regulation, will probably be eligible for discharge in five or six months that is to say, if they behave as well, and hoard their marks as carefully, with the power of purchasing present indulgences with them, as they have without. But would your Excellency then sanction their removal to Van Diemen's Land or not? They are all very anxious on this head.

Also some of the 'new' prisoners wanted to have their wives and families sent to join them. Maconochie gave an example. 'One of my men, William Paterson (per *Mangles*), was transported at the same time with his wife, a Mary Paterson (per *Mary Anne*) and for the same offence (receiving). She is now in New South Wales, and he is here. I strongly recommend that she be sent to him, on a charge, say of 1,000 marks, and that they be allowed to work out their joint sentence together.' Having wives and families together had always been one of Maconochie's improving proposals.

Maconochie ended by listing some of the achievements so far.

Among other institutions at Longridge we have an evening adult school, which above 200 attend voluntarily, after all the heat and toil of the day, paying 12 marks a month each man for the privilege, which I double on the part of the government; and on the last day I divide the produce into salaries to masters, prizes for attention, proficiency, and so forth, and the effect is most excellent. On Sunday evenings I have also sacred music played and sung, at which the attendance is equally voluntary, but always numerous. For extra marks I can at all times (as at present, in harvest) obtain extra exertion without a murmur, and a mere holiday, without marks, is no longer prized. In a word, the wages principle seems invincible, and it is only necessary now more and more extensively to apply it. And it calls out every form of social virtue, as well as industry, which I am sure will much interest and gratify your Excellency. I want them much to walk by themselves, and not lean currently on public crutches.

Gipps replied via Thomson on 27th January 1841, standing his ground. 'His Excellency desires me to remind you that he has no more power to fix a minimum than you have; that the law in fact has fixed a minimum, which is four years for a seven years man, six years for a 14 years man, and eight years for a man transported for life. These enactments have often been complained of, but they are still unrepealed.' What was Maconochie meant to do? If these 'enactments' were not going to be reviewed or repealed, then Maconochie should never have been appointed. How did Gipps expect Maconochie to work his mark system with the new prisoners if their length of sentence remained unaltered? Gipps still seemed to be in a state of shock after Maconochie's double transgression of joining the two groups together and celebrating Queen Victoria's birthday so extensively. Gipps did, however, make some sort of concession. 'There is, perhaps, a power (although on this head there is some doubt) of transferring men from Norfolk Island to Van Diemen's Land before the expiration of their respective periods; but even then they can only be sent there in the condition of ordinary convicts, and will be there treated as such.' Maconochie of course wanted his system to run through its full course on Norfolk Island so that he could then discharge prisoners as free and reformed men at the end of it, preferably to a new setting far from the taint of convict status.

On Maconochie's other point Gipps was just as adamant.

With respect to the wives and families of convicts being sent to Norfolk Island, as proposed in your eighth paragraph, his Excellency remarks, that whether women are to be sent or not to the settlement is a question which must be settled by Her Majesty's Government. The objections to it, and especially those which have been urged on the ground of the temptations which it would hold out to soldiers, are so great, that his Excellency cannot undertake to sanction the measure without the knowledge of the Secretary of State. If only the wives and children of convicts on the island were sent there, and no women who are themselves convicts, there would be less danger perhaps in the measure; but according to the existing regulations, the wives and families of convicts are only allowed to join them when they obtain tickets of leave and before the men at Norfolk Island are eligible for tickets of leave, they are, according to the latest instructions from the Secretary of State, to be sent to Van Diemen's Land.

It was a rigmarole. Existing regulations were being invoked again: Gipps was giving little away.

The following month, February 1841, Gipps acknowledged in a dispatch to Russell that reports had come through, 'unofficial as well as official', that Maconochie's system was working well as far as the behaviour of the convicts was concerned, and that it 'promises to produce good effects also as a reformatory system'. But, mindful to whom he was writing, he also pointed out that it was 'a system of extreme indulgence and whether as such it will answer all the ends that are sought for by the punishment of transportation, is the first and most important question that I consider to be at issue'. Gipps never states how he was hoping to reconcile the two uses of Norfolk Island as a place of terror and as a place of reform. The confusion and equivocation remained. Maconochie understandably pressed ahead with his system. He had embarked on it and for him there was no turning back, and he could see evidence of its success in the general transformation of his men on the island, their willingness now to go about their daily tasks in a co-operative manner both with each other and with the staff.

9

Maconochie's First Year

CHARLES ANDERSON WAS an orphan from a workhouse. At the age of nine he was sent to sea as an apprentice in a coal ship and then joined the Royal Navy. At the Battle of Navarino in 1827 he was badly wounded in the head and afterwards, whenever angered or drunk, he picked fights. He met some drunken sailors at an English port and in the ensuing fight several shops were damaged and broken into. Anderson was sentenced to seven years' transportation. At the age of eighteen he was alone in the world, and soon gained a reputation as a difficult and cussed prisoner. On arriving in New South Wales he was put on Goat Island in the middle of Sydney harbour. He absconded but was recaptured and taken to Hyde Park barracks in Sydney, where he was given 100 lashes. He was then sent back to Goat Island, where he got a further 100 lashes and was put in irons for twelve months. During this year 1,200 lashes in all were meted out to him, mostly for trivial offences such as looking around while working, or watching a steamer in the river. He managed to abscond again, was caught and taken back and given another 200 lashes. This time the authorities decided to attach him to a rock with a chain 26 feet long fastened to his waist. Trumpet irons were put on his legs and he had the skimpiest clothing to cover him. This lasted for two years. A hollow was scooped out of the rock shaped like a chair where he had to sleep at night, covered by a wooden lid perforated with holes which was locked and removed in the morning.

He was fed by pushing his food towards him with a pole. None of his fellow prisoners was allowed to approach or speak to him, under penalty of 100 lashes. Regarded as a wild beast, he became one of the sights of Sydney harbour and visitors would pass by in boats and throw bits of bread to him. Exposed to all weathers, his back and shoulders were covered in sores from his repeated floggings. Maggots fed on his flesh. He was denied water to bathe his wounds, 'such denial being not an unusual portion of the punishment to which he had been condemned'. When rain fell, he would lie and roll in it in agony.

Sir Richard Bourke, Governor of New South Wales, started investigating Anderson's case in the mid-1830s and ordered his release. Anderson was sent instead to the penal settlement at Port Macquarie, where he worked in the lime kilns, carrying lime in baskets down to the water's edge to the barges. Every time the lime came into contact with sea water the skin burnt off his back. He escaped and joined a group of Aborigines. Recaptured, he was flogged again, before being returned to Port Macquarie. His only wish now was to die and so he killed an overseer with a spade, but his death sentence was commuted and he was sent to Norfolk Island for life. There his behaviour was as bad as ever and he committed further violent assaults. He was there when Maconochie arrived. The contemporary account in the journal *Meliora* continues:

Though then only twenty-four, he looked forty years old. The Captain was told he was 'cranky', and he found that his fellow prisoners amused themselves with teasing and making him vicious. This was at once forbidden. Anderson being one of the colonial convicts, the prohibition from Government to place that class under the mark system, precluded him from its influence. Casting about, therefore, for any means of reclaiming the unhappy creature now sunk deep in wickedness, Captain Maconochie thought some unruly bullocks which had to be kept in bounds would usefully exercise his superfluous energies, and would, besides, separate him for a time from his fellows. Many thought 'Bony', as he was nicknamed, and his bullocks would come to grief. But strict orders were given that none should interfere with him, and very soon a marked change was apparent in the man. He became less wild, felt himself of some value, and won praise for this good conduct and successful management of his bullocks. He and they grew tractable together. He knew instinctively that high and strong tempers will not bend to the lash; and often were the anxious watchers of the experiment amused by the just insight into criminal discipline which Anderson displayed in the treatment of his charge.

It was an inspired move, a pathway for him back to normal life.

Indeed Anderson's improvement was so great that Maconochie next put him in charge of the signal station up on Mount Pitt, the highest point on the island. So well did he perform his duties that Maconochie next gave him use of a garden, which he kept well tended and fruitful. When Gipps later visited the island in 1843 he was astounded to have Anderson pointed out to him, now trimly dressed in a sailor's garb and going about his business, as the same man who had been chained to a rock in Sydney harbour. Eventually Anderson's head wound got worse, however, and he ended his days in an asylum, having lost his reason. Even during his madness, his attachment to Maconochie and his family remained.

Maconochie's use of a form of occupational therapy showed his intuitive understanding of the plight of desperate individuals. He believed it was important to reach back into an individual's life 'when he was yet comparatively innocent, and thus endeavour to revive in him impulses which then guided his conduct, before he became corrupted by the scenes he had subsequently gone through'.

Maconochie's first year report on Norfolk Island was sent to Gipps on 20th March 1841. He was 'still perfectly satisfied with the working of the mark or wages system', though it was still 'imperfectly tried'. He was still waiting for authorization to implement it fully, but this was delayed by the cumbersome system of communication: Maconochie to Gipps in Sydney (one month); Gipps to London (four to five months); London to

Gipps (four to five months); and a reply from Gipps (another month). It would be a year before any official decision could be made. His system and the motivation it provided seemed to be working, as it gave the prisoners more power and self-control. Putting the men into messes, and making them responsible for each other, had created an atmosphere of 'mutual watch, check, and self-command' that seemed to be valued by the inmates. Some were still unco-operative but Maconochie felt there would always be 'rogues and fools' present who would prefer the advantages of crime to steady exertion. His system hoped to marginalize and discredit these few, to make them no longer admired as they had been previously. As with any innovative and newly evolving system, Maconochie knew that 'some little pliancy in applying it is unavoidable'.

New barracks had been constructed up at Longridge of twenty-four mess rooms, each 16 feet by 12, and each sleeping six mess men in hammocks. Each had a fireplace for cooking, a table, stools, shelves and two chests for clothing. Lights, which the men paid for in marks, had to be out by nine. The rooms were furnished with books and the men could buy pens, ink and paper out of their extra marks. At Longridge a small punishment prison for offenders had also been erected. Over each cell was a trapdoor leading to the floor or gallery above, which was divided into two rooms, one Catholic, the other Protestant. This meant there were six cells, three on either side. Whenever divine service was performed at stated intervals by the respective clergymen the trapdoor could be opened for the inmate to listen. At other times a man was kept there to read aloud to the prisoners beneath, who, by opening a small square aperture in their respective hatches, could hear distinctly what was being read. If they were otherwise engaged or did not wish to be disturbed, they could, by drawing a sliding panel across the trapdoor, seclude themselves. This option, outlined to Gipps before Maconochie set off for Norfolk Island, was a clear innovation, designed to give prisoners the chance to improve their minds and moral welfare if they so chose. From Maconochie's point of view the choice was the important thing. The scheme for the punishment cells was partly educational, and partly born out of his principle that a convict's time should be put to good use.

Maconochie still had doubts about the suitability of Norfolk Island, its remoteness, its difficult of access, 'so tropical in character and productions, so entirely out of the way of general communication, so unfitted consequently for inspection by impartial eyes in the course of our proceedings'. It did not provide a particularly good preparation for freedom, as island life was so different from mainland life. However, there were advantages. 'Its building materials (with some exceptions as iron, glass; brick, &c., all of which would require to be imported) are, I think, abundant for almost any demand', and there was likely to be no shortage of building timber or fuel in the immediate future. Maconochie was also hopeful that agriculture could be improved so as to yield a much larger return than hitherto. The only disadvantage was that it was 'furrowed into steep hills and gullies, its native vegetation is very rank, and its tillage is thus generally very laborious'.

He was able to report 'most favourably' on the general conduct of the 617 new prisoners, who had now been encamped for nearly a year in wooden barracks at Longridge two miles above the military station down at Kingston, and in all that time 'nothing even remotely approaching to insubordination has appeared among them'. With the penal prisoners (the 'old hands') his relaxation of severity had produced less crime than with his predecessors, Majors Anderson and Bunbury. Maconochie had backed this up by showing the greatest confidence in them, walking familiarly among them, taking his wife and family with him without protection, removing the iron bars from his house windows and even leaving the defensive cannons formerly outside Government House up on Flagstaff Hill after the Queen Victoria celebration. Furthermore he had allowed those who worked as woodcutters and others who had previously been required to walk out from the barracks and return home there every evening, a distance of two to three miles, to camp out as bush gangs instead.

Kingston, 1848. The prisoners' barracks are by the shore, convict overseers' houses behind, the military barracks and Norfolk Island pines in the foreground.

These were risks, but taking such risks in an imaginative way was the core of Maconochie's approach. He had changed the system of excessive deference and had relieved the men of the 'slavish marks of respect' previously required to be paid to every free person on the island, and even to private soldiers. 'I bade them stand up like men, whomsoever they addressed.' An even greater innovation was to allow them a 'reasonable freedom of representation' while defending themselves in court for local offences. Previously prisoners never dared to contradict witnesses against them and were punished for doing this, for their insolence as well for any offence they were meant to have committed. Trials now took place in the open barrack yard, with other prisoners acting as jurors. This was a bold move, almost unheard of at the time, which allowed convicts to act as jury at their fellow convicts' trials. Yet it was a crucial step in getting them involved, and Maconochie knew that the administration of justice was a key area if prisoners were to shift their attitudes towards the new regime. 'Their sole object on all occasions before had been to defeat it, but now they began to sympathise with it, because themselves frequently engaged in its investigations.' Maconochie, 'unwearied in my endeavour to do justice in court', frequently acquitted them, preferring to err on the side of leniency rather than punish out of hand, although this leniency was subsequently held against him. He also refused to use informers as previously. 'I rejected anonymous informations, previously much in practice: or, if I brought them forward at all, it was to hold them up to scorn.' But he welcomed men who came forward 'boldly' and pointed out real offences. 'I anxiously sought, however, to ascertain if there were any private motives for their doing so; if I found such, I disappointed them.' This reform of the justice system on the island was important in giving prisoners hope and a sense of being involved in their futures.

Maconochie's system relied heavily on his overseers, mostly ex-convicts who had 'graduated' to these positions of responsibility. He had built ten special houses for them just behind the prisoners' barracks. 'I told the overseers that two things were requisite to recommend them to me, that they should get work done, and without making many complaints, for any man could force work through punishment, but my wish was to obtain it through persuasion.' His fundamental aim was to 'raise the men's respect for themselves and for each other'. Prisoners had responded to this and shortly after his arrival had formed among themselves an 'association for mutual reform and putting down of bad language and other crime and this I also encouraged'. Maconochie repeatedly reminded them that he could 'work no miracles with them', that he had come to be not their gaoler but their reformer, that he would do as much as he could if they assisted him and that nothing could be done without this.

Language was important, as previously convicts had used it as a private refuge, subverting it in ways that made sense to them. Ullathorne had also noticed this: 'So corrupt was their most ordinary language . . . that, in their dialect, evil was literally called good, and good, evil – the well-disposed man was branded wicked, whilst the leader in monstrous vice was styled virtuous. The human heart seemed inverted, and the very conscience reversed.'

In his report Maconochie also discussed the convicts' sexual habits. 'Nameless offences are equally under ban; I fear that they are still committed, but it is in silence and secrecy, whereas formerly they were boasted of.' Petty theft still went on and he threatened to put up a 'thieves' list', but he hoped stealing would lessen if the 'old hands' were under his mark system. He took this up more fully. Why, he asked, should the penal prisoners 'be considered hopeless and fit only for punishment?' He felt they had been 'directly injured, to an extent almost beyond belief, by the ordeal through which they have passed but they are not beyond the reach of a curative process'. He wanted Gipps to realize the significance of this, to see how this experiment was still working with 'every possible disadvantage' against it, how he had come with 'undefined powers, and no instructions. The promises by which I sought to sway the men were thus necessarily vague; many have been already falsified, and none as yet been confirmed.' Having two systems at work in a confined locality where one party were considered 'irreclaimable ruffians, and really were hardened by a long previous course of vice and crime' was too difficult. His staff did not know where they stood, especially his old staff, who had been mostly unconvinced of the merits of his new system. 'Their previous notions of prison discipline were shocked by my proceedings and both their tempers and those of the men under them were soured and hardened by the long previous prevalence of others.' Their attitudes had remained unchanged and Maconochie had more and more to rely on his own efforts. He believed in the Victorian principle of the 'power of the Human will'. For him, exercise of the will was 'very nearly the alpha and omega of all improvement in prison discipline'. Persuasion was his method, and the long-term aim was to make prisons into 'moral hospitals, with the almost exclusive purpose of discharging cured patients'. Here he was anticipating a later approach, the combined therapeutic and custodial function for hospitals, of which Philippe Pinel had been the forerunner in France at the turn of the nineteenth century, though Maconochie is unlikely to have heard of him.

Maconochie's view of the criminal disposition and of the causes of crime was evolving out of his experience of Norfolk Island.

> Men are not generally cautious, but enterprising. Profligate men are especially so; they usually live from hand to mouth, and are supported by the commission of small offences before they venture on great ones. The danger to which the latter expose them becomes thus familiar; and growing necessity, as well as impunity, urges them on, for when men take to crime as a means of indulgence they usually give up steady application to every other source of livelihood. To suppose that in this onward career they will be stayed by the dread of severe punishment is to reason in opposition to all past experience, and all theory correctly based on it. The hope of impunity in such minds will always overcome the fear of punishment; and the true way of reducing crime is to weed out these persons, if possible, at an early period of their career, and then, by due training, gain or remove them.

This would 'deter young or hesitating offenders'. This again is a key statement, and ahead of its time, and Maconochie was more and more convinced of its truth. 'Like animals whose passions are excited, yet who know themselves to be overmatched, men hardened in crime, and thus, as it were, challenged, shut their eyes and rush in. It is on this principle that "crime thrives on severe punishments"; nor will it ever, I am persuaded, be materially checked in society till the fact is recognized, and a higher object than mere example be thus pursued as the first in prison discipline. My experience here throws much light on this.' It was to prove a real bone of contention with Whitehall and Gipps, however, who both still believed that the main purpose of Norfolk Island was as a place of 'ultimate terror', a deterrent.

The new prisoners, as Maconochie explained to Gipps, had been an 'undisciplined bunch on their arrival; and he regretted that he had not been able to 'sober their minds to a sense of their penal condition by a short preliminary imprisonment'. Circumstances had not permitted this intended first stage of his mark system. They had had to go out to work immediately, for instance on the maize harvest. Nor had they been easy to handle: 'their spirits were elated on first landing from on board ship; their irregularities were thus many' and since they were inexperienced, they were in the beginning 'more easily led off by evil counsel, if offered them by the penal prisoners'. They were a mixed group of English and Irish, Protestants and Catholics, and they had to live in the 'extremely defective construction and distribution of their barracks', which had only three large rooms, each of which held more than 200 men. Things were now better and their offending rate was 'much lower'. As regards serious offences among them, 'about ten men monopolize to themselves alone nearly all the serious charges and are proportionally in debt on our books, going back instead of forward, and two of them more remote from their liberty now than the day they landed.'

The composition of nationalities among the 617 new prisoners was as follows:

234	English	14	Welsh
346	Irish	1	American
21	Scottish	1	Polish

Of these, 312 were Protestants (24 of them Presbyterians 'who have objected strongly to attending the church of England service'), and 304 were Catholics. There was also one Jew.

Among these new convicts Maconochie had observed different characteristics within each national group. 'I have been struck by the general want of mechanical skill and contrivance among the

Irish. They make good tailors and shoemakers, but little besides, which is probably owing to the low state of domestic accommodation in their native districts. They do not excel either in anything requiring long consecutive effort. Many have good ears and voices and enjoy music but though several have tried, only one has succeeded in acquiring command of an instrument. On the other hand, they seem to have hardier bodily constitutions, more elastic spirits, and more frugal habits, than either English or Scotch.' The Irish spent less on food than their counterparts, especially the English: 'The excess in our ration accounts is almost entirely among the English messes; and, on the contrary, some of the best Irish ones are in credit.' But the English gained in other respects: 'In cleanliness and comfort, in domestic accommodation, though not always in person, the English surpass both Irish and Scotch; and they are almost invariably superior to them also in activity of mind, and alert in taking up of new pursuit.'

Some of the Irish were 'as wild and untutored as I ever saw'. The English, on the other hand, were 'above the usual par of their class that I have seen in these colonies, and many of them are among the best and most serviceable men I have ever known. The Scotch also are a very favourable specimen. I could select 100 men from the two, with some Irish, for discharge now, with perfect confidence that they would not again fall. It is precisely such men as they who are most affected by kind, confiding treatment, and who, fully appreciating my desire to reform them, meet it with their whole hearts.'

The English prisoners had taken up his offer of music. 'Every Sunday evening we are enabled, in consequence of it, to have meetings for Sacred music, partly vocal, partly instrumental, which are numerously attended by all the men. On Thursday evenings after work we have similar meetings for general music, in which I especially seek to encourage patriotic, national, naval, and other music, calculated to keep up affectionate recollections of home.' Maconochie felt that 'much of the general softening of manners among us' could be attributed to this. Education had started well. 'Above 100 men have learned to read, who did not before know a letter and the desire among as many more to improve in reading, writing, and arithmetic, generally is very strong.' But they still needed more books and slates and a school-master, ideally someone 'who shall have no other charge, and who is not, invested with any clerical character'.

Maconochie praised the work of his clergy. As he wrote earlier, 'the zeal of the Catholic clergy here is without bounds'. Five Protestants had been converted to Catholicism, and ten more conversions were in progress. The exertions of the Catholic clergymen had reduced bad language, which within the last six months had almost disappeared among the Irish, 'and though the same cannot be said of the English, it has yet with them also much abated'. Maconochie was against such language as it upheld a criminal subculture. 'The Irish are mostly ignorant of it, or at least, theirs is not the same, nor so extensive, nor in the same repute; they also more readily abandon it.' This was because many of the Irish were from rural backgrounds: 'of the Irish prisoners two thirds could, on landing, neither read nor write.'

Education was still a priority. Besides the men who had learnt to read and write, others had acquired 'the rudiments of seden-tary trades' and some had chosen to stay and work on the island after completing their sentence. He gave an example, Joseph Barnes, originally transported per *Woodbridge*, then subsequently sentenced to twelve months for a brutal assault while on Norfolk Island.

> He went in little better than a wild beast, daring the worst that could be inflicted on him. In less than a month he asked for employment, and received instruction. In six months he had much improved his reading, had learned straw hat plaiting, and become so submissive and well-behaved that six of our best men, chiefly policemen, and one the man he had assaulted, offered to go bail for him, in 1,000 marks each that he should keep the peace during the remainder of his sentence. On this he was released about two months ago, and behaves unexceptionably. All the vindictive punishment in the world would not have produced the same effect, or the same improving example.

Overall, despite his 'equivocal position', Maconochie considered that his success was 'astonishing' and that he had been able to become the prisoner's best friend, 'the friend of his moral recovery'. He believed that the better feelings of the men were 'with very few exceptions touched; that their impulse is, consequently, for the time upward; that their manners are softened, their habit and language improved.' But he had no illusions about the struggle ahead. 'But the majority are not of this character. They require also to have their selfish feelings engaged and confirmed in a right direction by long habitual exercise.'

Maconochie included his returns of crime and punishment for the year, adding that in almost two years he had never had to call for help from the military and had only to use force in two or three cases. The help of his Prisoner Police (convicts he had selected to act as policemen) had been invaluable, with instructions to 'soothe, not to irritate, to persuade, not to coerce, except in the utmost extremity'. These convict police had been selected chiefly from the 'old hands' on the island, as being more reliable and with greater influence over the newer prisoners.

His comments about the two sets of prisoners were illuminating. He had found the 'old hands' to be more staid than the new prisoners, less subject to 'fits of caprice or petulance'. Their characters were more robust, more manly. Since they had previously long been treated with excessive suspicion, they now responded well to Maconochie's confidence in them, and were touched by his solicitude about them. He found that individually they were more independent. They were 'fonder of dress, and generally more cleanly in their habits, than I have as yet succeeded in making the others; their long confinement to a degraded dress, and only recent emancipation from the necessity of wearing it (for in old times it was a punishable offence even to be possessed of any other), probably contributes to this'. Many of them were expert handicraftsmen, able to turn themselves to a greater variety of occupations. They were stronger, with stouter bodily constitutions, and less likely to fall into 'incidental temptations' than the new prisoners.

Maconochie began to feel that prolonged imprisonment, as in the case of the penal prisoners, made individuals long for liberty all the more and that, given a chance to seek that liberty, they would respond. Essentially his view was that the yearning for freedom was stronger in the minds of the prisoners than the fear of punishment. He was worried about them being sent to Van Diemen's Land on tickets-of-leave, as he felt almost certain that this would lead to their 'second fall'. He compared it to 'dropping, as it were, from the clouds, without friends or experience', and being thrust again into 'the habits of evasion and suspicion which in existing circumstances must and do characterize the mass of the convict population there, likely to be regarded with dislike by the inferior authorities as having been trained on different maxims from their own, indifferently supported thus by their superiors when they do get into difficulty and jeered and tempted, if but for the fun of it, by their equals'. He would much prefer to see them discharged to New Zealand, where there was a demand for labour and where there was no taint of a convict past. Maconochie clearly hoped Gipps would take notice of this. Maconochie felt strongly that his new system, to succeed fully, needed somewhere suitable afterwards where his 'reformed' prisoners could put into practice all they had learnt. 'If they may only be made to pass under the new discipline, and when discharged from it may go away quite free (by way of New Zealand, or in any other direction than the old Penal Colonies) I am confident of their eventual recovery, and of the perfect safety of such a destination for them.'

Maconochie's use of corporal punishment had increased this year. He had used it for the following offences: 'One was for gross perjury, another for malicious prevarication in evidence (intended to screen guilt by fixing a theft of leather from the tan-pits on innocent parties), two were for indecency, two for gross insolence by comparative boys, intended to provoke a breach of the peace, and one was a nominal sentence on a sick patient in hospital, who assaulted the surgeon, and was sentenced to 300 lashes, but received only fifteen.' But he added, 'the more I see of this form of punishment, however, I must add, the less I like it; I doubt much if benefit is derived from it in any case, even in present circumstances here; and I'd say the same of working in chains. I reserve this exclusively for men repeatedly guilty of leaving their stations without passes, and whom I thus profess only to secure. Yet even so restricted, the operation of the punishment is bad, both as regards sufferers and spectators; it hardens rather than subdues.'

His purpose in pointing out these facts was to try and discredit the system of punishment for its own sake. 'I wish it were possible, by giving details like these, that I could bring minutely under the notice of the advocates for the infliction of vindictive punishment for the sake of example, the mischief wrought by it. If they could see its handiwork as I see it here they could not abide by its principles.' Maconochie was using his report as a form of work in progress, reporting back to the authorities in New South Wales and London his own discoveries about the prisoners. It was as if he was using the same sort of research skills here as he had done as professor of geography at London University. He only wished those authorities 'could realize to themselves the superior interest of prison management when its subjects are regarded as food for instruction and reform not for vindictive punishment'. Maconochie felt it was only through the experience and study that could be obtained in a place such as Norfolk Island that he could 'individualise the mischief done to each of almost 4,000 victims who have been annually sacrificed for years to a mistake'.

He had also been much helped by the Protestant chaplain, the Revd Mr Naylor, recently appointed. 'He is much with his men, and takes a warm interest in all their concerns and in existing circumstances (I do not say it in their praise) prisoners are much swayed by this.' It was an important point, Maconochie felt, 'for it is a great mistake to think that generally prisoners want feeling, it is quite the reverse. They have too much.' It was often this excess of feeling that got them into trouble. They felt things too keenly, too sensitively, and sometimes this prompted them to act

in an impetuous way. 'They thus never balance distant considerations against near ones, but fling themselves head foremost in
any direction the latter prompt.' He aimed to instil deferred
gratification in them, 'the long consistent following of a distant
object through present self-denial'.

At a more practical level, 1840 had been a difficult year, as he
told Gipps, mainly because of the deficiency of the recent crop
of wheat. 'Up to October it was impossible for any crop to be
better or more promising.' Then a severe drought had set in just
when it was in flower. 'The crop never filled and rust showed
itself on it in various places. All that was left now was inferior
wheat, of indifferent quality. This had led to difficulties with
Charles Ormsby, the Superintendent of Agriculture, with whom
trouble had been brewing for some time. 'Ormsby's opposition
to me arose from his desire to obtain more work from the men
under his immediate superintendence than he could get under
my system.' For Maconochie the problem was that Ormsby never
could understand his system, 'much less get work done upon its
principles'. This went back to the first days on the island, when
Ormsby had been appointed by Gipps as Maconochie's deputy,
in charge of the old prisoners on the island. Then just before his
arrival, the then Superintendent of Agriculture, McLean, had
been drowned in the bay and Ormsby had been hurriedly put in
his place at Longridge. Ormsby and Maconochie had never got
along. 'He told me once expressly that the best part of my system
was his returns [i.e. his statistics re crops, livestock and so on]; and
in this very expression was embodied a large proportion of the
false principle which gave a wrong direction to his originally
well-intentioned zeal and energy.'

Maconochie felt that Ormsby was now undermining his
regime. 'His habitual language to the men was shameful; he was
thus constantly irritating them. They dared not oppose him
openly, but they did it covertly and passively. He thus had them
frequently to court, and exclaimed against me if they were not
punished with the old severity.' He became 'even in his good
temper, an incessant thorn in my side'. And he had other faults.

'He was always behind in his work. He never cleaned his crops till the weeds were three or four feet high, and in seed; he thus made his operations doubly laborious and the men felt this, and murmured accordingly.' The conflict had come out into the open and Ormsby had left somewhat acrimoniously in the middle of 1841. Maconochie felt the prisoners' temper and purpose were better now that Ormsby had gone. 'Instead of being in a constant fret under his explosions of temper, or gross partiality for some to the injury of others, they are content and steadily industrious.'

Maconochie ended his report with his old hobby-horse. 'Had I the old hands under the mark system, as well as the new, much of the necessity of thus stimulating them to willing exertion would vanish.' The different treatment of these two groups was still 'very striking', but, as he notified Gipps, for all his supposed indulgence, Norfolk Island was not the 'Felons' Paradise' that people seemed to think. Evidence of this had been the escape attempts recently made.

The first had taken place in 1840. A shooting party from Norfolk Island, consisting of the commissariat officer, the store-keeper and three or four officers of the 96th Regiment, had gone across to Philip Island for a week's leave to hunt the wild pigs, goats, hares and rabbits that lived there. They stayed in a hut on the island with a convict servant to look after them. After their week's leave expired, a boat was sent across to collect them. The first thing they did was to put all their game in the boat and then handed over their guns to be put in the stern of the boat. As soon as the convicts saw this and once the firearms were aboard, they grabbed them and turned on the leave party, driving them back up on to the island, where they tied their arms behind their backs and put them inside the hut. They then stripped them of their hats, coats, vests, trousers and took their watches, pocket compasses and anything else they took a fancy to. One convict kept guard while the others made a sail out of one of the tents and they found large flat stones to cook on inside the boat. Then the five convicts sailed away, having first asked the convict servant whether he wanted to escape with them; he declined.

As soon as the boat was away the convict servant managed to release himself and then freed the others. They then made a large fire as a signal to those on Norfolk Island. A boat was sent across and they were brought back, 'and such a sight you never saw, and so crestfallen, I can tell you. It was great fun for us chaps', as a soldier witness, Richard Pelvin, stationed on the island in the 96th Regiment, later described:

It was no use sending another boat after the escaped convicts, as we had no sails, and they got clear away. This occurred in the latter end of 1840. The nearest land was New Zealand, and I often wondered whatever became of them until I was recruiting in the West of England at Bridgwater, after being in India, when I accidentally came across a soldier who was out here [New Zealand] at the time. He told me they made the Bay of Islands in safety, and gave themselves out as shipwrecked seamen to some captains of whaling ships lying there, but suspicion was aroused and the captains put their heads together, and invited them on board one of the ships, when they were seized and made prisoners. The Governor, Sir George Gipps, was made acquainted with it, and sent a vessel to fetch them to Sydney. This information I received about 1855 or early in 1856, some 15 or 16 years after the occurrence, and I do not doubt it.

Replying to his report, Gipps thanked Maconochie in a letter written by his Colonial Secretary, Thomson. 'His Excellency is extremely unwilling to take any step that may have the effect of prematurely declaring your system of management to have been a failure; and believing as he does that much of your theory is founded on sound principles, he has resolved to take on himself the responsibility of remaining inactive for a time sufficient to allow of his receiving a further communication from you; and he accordingly has to request that you will, without loss of time, report to him what prospects there may be, in your own opinion, of your henceforth carrying on your system at Norfolk Island with success.' It was the usual mix from Gipps, half approving, half critical. The letter ended:

His Excellency is induced to press in a particular manner these points on your consideration, because it seems to him that, the difficulties and embarrassments with which the Government is now beset have arisen out of your failing to give due attention to the position in which you were placed when you first went to Norfolk Island. Had you duly considered the position in which you then stood you would have seen the necessity of maintaining the distinction which you were so plainly directed to observe, between the old establishment and the new one; and if you had only looked to the Act of Parliament above referred to, and to the instructions of the Secretary of State, you would have been cautious of raising expectations which it was doubtful (to say the very least) whether it would ever be in your power to fulfil. The errors which you thus committed appear to his Excellency to have been the consequence of your own too sanguine temperament, and of your looking too lightly on the difficulties which were before you. Deeply impressed with the truth of your own principles, and elated, it is not unreasonable to suppose, with the notice which your writings had attracted in England, you appear to his Excellency to have set to work with the idea that every thing was to give way before you. Deep-rooted feelings or convictions, especially those of the inhabitants of this colony, were to be set aside as idle prejudices, and even the safety of New South Wales endangered; old established regulations, whether of this Government, of the Ordnance, or of the Treasury were to be over-ruled, as well as the orders of the Secretary of State; and Acts of the Imperial Parliament, no less than those of the legislature of New South Wales, altered or repealed in order to make way for your system.

This was Gipps playing safe again, invoking precedent and due process of law. No flexibility was being shown. Yet it had been clear from Maconochie's own dispatches that a flexible approach, adapted to local circumstances, was called for. Much was being made of Maconochie's 'too sanguine temperament', now seen as a fault, although it had been this very aspect of his temperament that had encouraged Gipps to ratify his experiment initially. As a colonial governor, Gipps was always in fear of losing administrative control. What was happening on Norfolk Island was highlighting the struggle between an experimental outpost and central bureaucracy, the one relying on imagination and initiative, the other on well-established practice.

On 1st August 1841, however, Russell replied to Gipps's dispatch of February. Russell now seemed to perform a volte-face and stated: 'I agree with Captain Maconochie, that it is impossible to keep up two different systems in Norfolk Island at the same time. The removal of the old convicts from that island should properly have been directed before the new system was put in force.' This is what Maconochie had argued all along. Russell felt the 'old hands' deserved some recompense. 'It is clear, that the convicts ought not to have their merits unrewarded and their expectations disappointed, although it may be difficult wholly to fulfil them. Perhaps the best mode will be to grant conditional pardons to those who have gained all their marks and kept them when indulgence was within their reach. I would leave it to you to recommend the periods at which such remissions of punishment should in each case be granted.' This was buck-passing again.

Russell ended his note with this observation: 'The system appears hitherto to promise well, and to deserve a continuance of it but will not be completely tried until the men have been for some time at liberty.' Here was more muddled thinking. Suddenly Russell was looking ahead to the time when Maconochie's men would be at liberty, even though their means of getting there had not yet been worked out. Whitehall seemed to oscillate between panic and unprocessed hope. Hope had always been fundamental to the transportation idea, even if it was based on nothing more than a blind faith that a solution would somehow be magically found 'over there'.

The tone of this August 1841 communication from Russell was much more approving and conciliatory, even friendly. What had happened to cause this? Was this the liberal Russell speaking rather than the critical Stephen? Or was it an example again of the haphazard nature of Whitehall's attitude towards penal reform, based on the mood of the moment rather than forethought and planning?

In September 1841, however, Russell's tenure as Secretary of State for the Colonies, which had begun when he left the Home Office in 1839, came to an end with the change of government. Australia had become a secondary issue for him now that he was pushing ahead with building Pentonville Prison as the first of the new model penitentiaries along American lines. When it opened in 1842 its Separate System of solitary confinement meant that each prisoner worked a twelve-hour day cobbling or weaving. Each time he left his cell, he had to put on a woollen mask with slits for the eyes so that no one else could see or recognize him. In chapel each day he stood in an upright box, able to see only the preacher ahead of him in the pulpit. Such a dispiriting regime contrasted sharply with Maconochie's more enlightened approach being tried simultaneously on Norfolk Island.

10

Unfavourable Reports

RUSSELL'S SUCCESSOR WAS Edward Stanley, a Tory MP and son of the thirteenth Earl of Derby. A former Colonial Secretary in 1833-4, with James Stephen then as his under-secretary, Stanley now wanted to introduce different arrangements for convict administration in Australia, his 'Probation System'. Stanley was conservative by temperament and politics, with 'force, energy and vivacity', as a Colonial Office junior wrote, 'an effective speaker, always clear and strong, sometimes commonplace, but not seldom brilliant'. He had 'the gifts of a party politician, playing the game of politics with more of party than public spirit'. His autocratic nature led him even to disregard Stephen at times. His predominant view of the colonies was to avoid unnecessary expenditure and so his arrival at the Colonial Office boded ill for Maconochie.

Stephen sent Maconochie's first annual report on to Stanley on 7th February 1842, commenting that the report seemed to be the production of a man 'much less fitted for active than for contemplative life, and who had very much to learn even in the way of thinking and composition before he could become of much use in that way'. Stephen, now as later, seems never to have tried to understand Maconochie. Perhaps he was put off by the report's prolixity, as he added that he felt Maconochie's mind was 'enveloped in a sort of fog which distorts the objects brought before him and perplexes his account of them', orotund language from a dyed-in-the-wool civil servant.

Lord Stanley

Gipps had added a few, rather hesitant observations of his own in his covering letter to Stanley. 'I must confess myself unable to offer them with any degree of confidence.' Stanley was his new boss and he did not want to alienate him. Gipps was worried about the eventual destination of Maconochie's reformed convicts once they were released. He passed Maconochie's New Zealand suggestion across to London and wrote to Stanley: 'I, therefore, venture to submit that the question of their ultimate destination should be settled before any alteration be sanctioned in the management to which they are now subject.' Gipps also mentioned he was planning to visit Norfolk Island himself, 'if I possibly can absent myself for a sufficient period from my other and more immediate duties'.

Stanley agreed that Gipps should visit Norfolk Island to see for himself the 'alleged defects and assumed merits of Captain Maconochie's system'. He went on, and here Stephen's voice can be heard: 'The extreme doubt attaching to it, the long period which elapses between the receipt of communications, and the events to which they refer, and the inconvenience attending the disturbance of an experiment in progress on so large a scale, have made me hesitate in at once sending out to you any definite instructions on the subject.' He continued, 'I should place much greater confidence in the reports which I am led to expect from you after a personal inspection of the place than in those of Captain Maconochie, however faithfully he may endeavour to describe the operation of his system', and he reminded Gipps 'the whole question of convict discipline, will receive, during the approaching recess, the very serious consideration of myself and the Secretary of State for the Home Department.'

Gipps sent more documents to Stanley on 15th August 1842. In one of them Maconochie was asking for a freer hand, more 'discretionary power regarding the whole arrangements here', and in particular regarding the ticket-of-leave system on the island. At the moment he had twenty-seven small farms of four to six men each, in an areas of nearly 300 acres. This was all new land, not previously under cultivation, but dug out of the bush. Prisoners liked growing their own food. On Norfolk Island they dreamt of food as much as of sex. Maconochie's problem was that thirteen of the new farmers had already asked to be released 'and the whole body is much disheartened'. This was because of the feeling that their surplus marks were to be of no value to them. He assured Gipps that the government was gaining from this new arrangement, since the men were clearing land for cultivation which before were scrub or sheep-run, and that they were held to paying a fixed rent for the land of twelve bushels an acre of maize, or the entire crop of one acre out of three. But unless the men felt that the marks they earned had some ulterior value, they would not go on working.

Cultivating the land was an intrinsic part of Maconochie's system. It gave prisoners a sense of involvement and a tangible result for their efforts. They would leave their barracks early in the morning willingly and keenly, their faces uplifted, morale high. Gipps was worried about the cost of this, but Maconochie argued against him, not wanting economy to be a concern at this stage, 'for if we spare the seed-corn in it how can we look for the harvest?' Gipps got Thomson, his Colonial Secretary, to reply and asked him to remind Maconochie that there were limits in expenditure, 'beyond which he cannot go'; nor could he 'lay the public purse open to your hands'. Gipps was mindful, as always, of the Treasury's reaction. Gipps was clearly getting irritated by Maconochie's incessant demands, and told him he knew his system well enough not to need 'any discussion of the first principles of it'. Furthermore he could not help remarking, 'although he does it with great reluctance', that Maconochie's frequent practice of introducing theoretical reasoning into his dispatches was causing their correspondence to be 'both tedious and unsatisfactory'. Gipps's frustration was clear. Maconochie's restless temperament was working against him.

Meanwhile on the island a disagreement had sprung up between Maconochie and his Commissariat Officer Smith. Smith had told Gipps about it first, without telling Maconochie, in a letter that was full of serious allegations. Gipps, in his present mood, appeared to take Smith's side. Smith was an officer, he reported to Stanley, 'who bears a high character in his Department for regularity and discretion, and he did not go to Norfolk Island in any greater degree prejudiced against Captain Maconochie's system than persons living in this community usually are'. Smith alleged that Maconochie had allowed a man who had robbed the commissariat store to go unpunished and then that

> the most unaccountable case is that of a man named James McGregor, who was formerly a domestic servant of Captain Maconochie's, and who has already commenced a General Store upon the Island with the articles of trade brought down with him in the Brig. He is not in any way connected with the establishment here, yet he has been permitted to occupy two apartments in the convict barracks, where he has had a shop fitted up for him with counter, shelves, and drawers; and he has moreover been allowed a convict servant, who is victualled and clothed at the public expense. How this man could get permission to come here under these circumstances is to me a mystery, for the Secretary of State, in one of his late dispatches, states, that 'no free settlers are to be allowed at Norfolk Island.'

Smith went on: 'The principal part of the goods belonging to this man were, I believe, actually shipped in the name of Captain Maconochie, who, however, it is to be hoped, was not aware of it. Indeed the manner in which these people are allowed to act appears to me very absurd, and calculated to upset all those notions of prudence and economy which my experience has hitherto taught me to entertain with regard to the Public Service.' Smith represented the old school of staff on the island, as his notions of 'prudence and economy' indicate. He had got his facts wrong. McGregor had been Maconochie's butler and had recently married the sister of the postmaster on the island; he then moved out of Maconochie's employ to set up with his new wife on their own.

Smith also claimed that government boats and government servants were being used for private means. 'Such a glaring sacrifice of the public service to private interests I never could have conceived possible till I came here; and the only conclusion at which I can arrive is, that the World will be turned upside down, and that this is the beginning of it.' He continued in the same vein:

On the Queen's Birthday, three head of cattle, one a fine young heifer, were slaughtered to supply the convicts with a ration of fresh meat; a proceeding which need not have been resorted to if the pigs had been retained for the purpose. I knew nothing about it until the beef reached the stores. In short, Captain Maconochie fancies himself supreme, and that all the public property here is disposable at his will and pleasure. He has contended for absolute power in most of his official dispatches, and has stated that the success of the system is almost dependent upon having everyone entirely under his own control. He will find himself in this, however, mistaken with regard to the Commissariat, for if such power should by any accident be vested in him the sooner our Department is removed from the Island the better.

Smith was now into his stride and advocating strong remedies.

A most radical change is wanted here immediately. The place bears no more resemblance to what a Penal Settlement should be than a playhouse does to a church. Idleness and insubordination prevail to a shameful extent amongst the prisoners, or they employ themselves for their own benefit. The beautiful timber of the Island is recklessly wasted, and it is expected that there will soon be a great scarcity both for the public works and for fuel. Ticket of Leave men are building huts all over the Island, and occupying ground apparently to no good purpose, which should be used either for pasture, or for the Government agricultural operations. You may think that I am prejudiced against Captain Maconochie, and that I have thus given an exaggerated picture of the present state of affairs; but this is not the case. I pledge myself to the accuracy of these facts, in which I should be borne out by every one who is not afraid to speak boldly, and who has had similar opportunities with myself of ascertaining them.

This was a powerful denunciation of Maconochie's system. The fact that Gipps sent it through to Stanley without comment or qualification will have had an effect.

Smith claimed that Maconochie's system of marks was 'a most unwarrantable expense upon the British Treasury', and he listed cases of what he saw as the wrongful use of marks.

One man in particular, the Band Master, obtained through favouritism upwards of 30,000 marks, with the surplus of which could
either have helped several of his friends to their Tickets of Leave, or
have turned them into valuable property. Another man, an overseer,
is, I am told, now getting 130 marks a day; and it would appear that
a prisoner named John Martin, who, not having marks enough
himself, borrowed from a friend who did not want them, a
sufficiency to entitle him to a Ticket of Leave before he had been
ten months on the Island; and this is not the only case of the kind,
but it will serve to show the principle upon which the mark system
is carried out. But, what is worse than all, Captain Maconochie who
is certainly not infallible, holds in his hands the destiny of every prisoner placed under his charge. He can, either by a lavish gift of marks
procure the immediate freedom of a man, or by constantly fining
him for imaginary offences (supposing an extreme case) keep him
in bondage all the days of his life; even though his sentence were
firstly only for seven years. Such a power as this is wholly incompatible with the spirit of the British constitution, and more than even
the Sovereign herself possesses. To delegate it to any one individual
appears to be at variance with every principle of justice, and I often
wonder why it was not viewed by the Government as an insuperable objection to the whole affair.

Smith was clearly gunning for Maconochie, misrepresenting
the operation of the mark system. He wanted a traditional, well-
oiled hierarchical structure – 'It is a well ascertained fact that
when once a man has lost his character in Society he requires the
very reverse of Captain Maconochie's treatment to keep him in
proper subjection, and deter him from a repetition of the crimes
for which he was transported' – and he regretted the loss of deference as formerly practised. Smith added as a final backhander
an account of Maconochie's weak method of dealing with the
case of two convicts, Bolger and Hamilton.

Before I conclude, I cannot but advert to the case of a man named
Bolger, who was convicted, at my instance, of the double crime of
betraying his Trust as porter at the Commissariat Gate, and of being
an accomplice with Hamilton in robbing the stores. This man has

never been punished, further than being deprived of his office; indeed he has not received any sentence, but is at large about the settlement as if he had been the innocent. Hamilton is also at large; but you will recollect that his punishment was remitted, on condition of his showing how the stores had been entered. But it was not so with regard to Bolger; nor, in fact, was it necessary that any such stipulation should be made in his case. I have remonstrated with Captain Maconochie on the subject, and he states that Bolger was included in the immunity; but I most distinctly deny the assertion, and could refer even to the man Hamilton himself, who merely claimed it on his own account when the discovery was made.

Once he had heard about Smith's allegations from Gipps, Maconochie refuted them point by point. The case of the two robbers of the store who had supposedly escaped with impunity was incorrect.

On the 27th March last a prisoner named Hamilton was found drunk in a summer house in one of the officer's gardens, and with a small quantity of rum about him in a tin flask. He was immediately apprehended, and the rum, when compared with that in the Commissariat Stores, was found of the same quality. Being employed about the Stores it was thus clear that he had robbed them; but had he any accomplices? His habitual companions were inquired into, and one of the porters at the Commissariat Gate, a man named Bolger, was found to be his messmate, and to have been seen walking with him on the very afternoon on which he was thus detected. He accordingly was also taken up; and on the circumstantial evidence of Hamilton's undoubted guilt, and the habitual intimacy and recent companionship of the two men, I convicted both; the impression on all our minds at the time being that the Stores, when robbed, were entered in the daytime, by false keys or otherwise, and that the liquor was removed from them, at least by the collusion of Bolger, if not his more active participation; and their sentence, under this impression was, Hamilton twelve months imprisonment, Bolger to be remanded till further examination of the Stores was made, and the case against him thus made a little clearer. A few days after their conviction, however, Hamilton offered to make a full confession, and show us how the Stores had been entered, on condition of absolute impunity both to himself and Bolger. He strongly asserted even the latter's entire innocence, and said that he would show us that he did not require his assistance for the Stores had been and were still open to him without any aid at all; if his terms were not accepted, he would bear his punishment, and there was an end of it; the Stores would still continue open, but, if accepted, he would show how to secure them so that they never could be again entered, at least in that way. I was most unwilling indeed to lend myself to any such arrangement. Before agreeing to it, I had the Stores most minutely examined, both by the foreman of works, and all our most zealous and intelligent Police. The drains were looked to; every place we could think of was sounded, but to no effect; and I even sent for Mr. Smith expressly to consult him before I agreed, and received his specific advice in the circumstances to accept the man's terms, 'the future security of the public property,' he expressly said, 'being in his eyes a consideration worthy of the compromise' and on this, and all the other circumstances combined, I acted. Hamilton was brought to the Stores in Mr. Smith's presence, and showed us that two of the bars in the spirit room window were so tampered that they would bend and straighten again with little effort. They had been originally put in so, whether intentionally on the part of the workmen, or accidentally, I cannot tell; and by the means afforded by them, in five minutes, before our eyes, he passed in. Could I then recede from the bargain made with this Man? Mr. Smith admits that he so purchased his own impunity; but Bolger was equally stipulated for, and in fact the circumstances on which he had been convicted were totally changed by this discovery. No Liquor had been found on him, nor had he been observed drunk. He had been convicted only through his intimacy with Hamilton, and the supposed impossibility of the latter's getting Spirits out of the Store in daytime without collusion with the Porter. But Hamilton's real robberies were committed at night. It seemed to us all impossible that they could have been effected without collusion with the military sentries habitually on guard over the Stores; but Bolger could not have aided then, he being then shut up in barracks. When the whole thing was explained I did not thus even think him guilty, unless possibly of occasionally sharing in the booty, though even of this I had no proof and, apart from all promise to Hamilton, I think in the circumstances I should have released him. As it was, I had not the least hesitation, nor could I have.

Smith then was more involved in this than he cared to make out. As regards Smith's other accusation, about the bandmaster, Maconochie reminded Gipps that this man was one of the most useful on the island: bandmaster, principal attendant in the hospital and headmaster in the adult school, all at the same time. His remuneration was eighteen marks a day, four more than an ordinary overseer, plus a monthly allowance of 100 marks out of the school funds. Besides this, after January 1841 he had, in common with all the others, an allowance of eight marks a day for his ration, with the offer of the value of his slop clothing in marks when he did not draw it, and he earned more from private teaching, and so for the most part fed and clothed himself without drawing his allowances. This was why his marks rapidly accumulated, and there were 15,004 to his credit when he got his ticket-of-leave.

Maconochie sent Smith a copy of his letter to Gipps at the same time. 'I thus court his disproof, on the spot, of any of my statements, and at the same time I desire to express to him the strong sense that I entertain of the unfairness of his conduct in not giving me the same advantage. Had he done so, this whole correspondence might have been spared and certain feelings between us, which are now unavoidable and must more or less affect the discharge of our respective duties here, with the pain which they must at the same time cause, would all have been spared us.'

Maconochie was happy for his official conduct to be rigorously scrutinized and had already stated that one of his greatest objections to Norfolk Island as a field for his experiment had always been 'the want of impartial spectators', something he had 'repeatedly expressed to his Excellency'. No officer in his position, he went on, 'can stand the transmission of pure fables and gossip as authentic intelligence, unless he has the opportunity afforded him at the same time of showing their incorrectness', and he added: 'I trust that in appreciating my conduct, not only in relation to the matters specified, but also any others which have been or may yet be similarly, brought before you, you will not fail to observe the disadvantage at which I am taken when they are not transmitted through myself, or otherwise communicated to me.'

Smith's main complaint was summed up in the patriotic cry: 'Would the population of the Mother Country have submitted quietly to be taxed for supporting an establishment where their very outcasts, the violators of their laws, were maintained in comparative luxury and idleness?' He was missing the point of Maconochie's system, and could only see what he wanted to see. 'What I have to complain of with regard to these men is their extreme indolence. This is palpably evident to the commonest observer. Industry has never been enforced amongst them, but, according to the system, it has been left in great measure to themselves.' He was referring to the fact that prisoners were making furniture, working in their own gardens and engaging in other pursuits, which were, as he put it, 'chiefly for their own individual benefit'. But that was just the point. Maconochie wanted them to branch out in this way. Most tellingly, Smith claimed he was 'influenced alone by an anxious wish to relieve the British Treasury, whose interests I represent on this island, from what I conceive to be a wasteful and injudicious expenditure'. He knew his complaints would go down well in Whitehall.

11

Scandalous Allegations

By FAR THE worst of Maconochie's worries in 1842, however, was a family one. His elder daughter, Mary Ann, now aged nineteen, had formed a romantic liaison with the assistant surgeon on the island, Dr James Reid, whom Maconochie had brought across with him from Sydney. Besides being a doctor, Reid was a keen musician and Maconochie had met him when he bought Ellard's musical stock in Sydney before leaving for Norfolk Island. Once on the island, Reid became a family friend and taught Maconochie's children music. He gave Mary Ann violin lessons in the secluded library of Government House. The couple grew fonder of each other and letters were secretly exchanged, written in French. Their attachment grew stronger and was soon noticed by others. Reid later claimed that though 'our guilt is equal' she was the more responsible – 'her portion of it far exceeds mine'. Once the Maconochies heard of it, they called Reid before them and banished him from Government House, but he was allowed to stay on the island. A replacement tutor took over. This was Charles Packer, a young well-educated convict with known musical ability, transported from London for forgery. He was already tutoring two of Maconochie's sons and was later to make a name for himself in musical circles in Tasmania and Sydney. He continued giving Mary Ann music lessons in the library as before and, perhaps not surprisingly, the same thing happened. She fell for him. When news of this leaked out to her parents, they were furious. She must leave the island forthwith.

News of this scandal reached Sydney, and in Van Diemen's Land Lady Franklin also heard about it. She wrote to her sister:

Sir John received yesterday some very interesting and confidential letters from Sir George Gipps – that wretched girl Mary Ann Maconochie was at that moment in his house – she was brought to Sydney from Norfolk Island by the first opportunity, attended by Sion, Mrs Maconochie's most faithful servant and his, Sion's brother. Sir George and Lady Gipps with the most noble and generous kindness, for such it assuredly is, took her into Government House till the ship (*Jubilee*) sailed which was to be in first week of September. She was of course in the utmost seclusion, had not been seen by Sir George but was frequently visited by Lady Gipps – Sir George says the affair was one of notoriety at Norfolk Island – how it was first discovered . . . not exactly known – but all of a sudden the man who had been living in the house as tutor to the boys and music master to Mary Ann, was thrown into prison and she was shut up in her room – the man had been a musician and composed in England and was transported for life forgery – he is of good address and handsome person – all these details, most of which I knew before were given to us by Sir George who at the close of his letter says Lady Gipps begs that what he has said on her authority be kept secret. I have omitted but little except the name of the villain. The girl is to be sent to her aunt Mrs Oldham, Captain Maconochie's illegitimate sister whom you may recollect having seen and she lives at Cheltenham and is, I believe, rich and liberal of her gifts to her brother's children, which does not prevent her, if I judge correctly, from being somewhat despised by her brother.

Why did Mary Ann choose to transgress in this way so openly? Was it a misguided attempt to help her father? The children often mixed with the convicts. Maconochie's eldest son, Alexander, then fifteen, was involved in this and had, as his father put it, 'taken much to the object of reforming the prisoners, and used frequently to attend the gaol, and read the Bible to them'. So perhaps Mary Ann's involvement was part of a family pattern.

Government House, 1841, drawn by Mary Ann Maconochie

Or was she caught up in an island 'madness' that made her heedless of consequence? Was she bored by her social horizons? She had an artistic temperament, as her skilful sketches of the island, now in the Mitchell Library, show. Perhaps she was upset by her younger sister, Catherine, who had got married to Captain Hill, serving with the 96th Regiment on the island, in the spring of the same year. Sibling rivalry can destabilize.

Lady Franklin was always critical of the Maconochie children's upbringing, as her letter to her sister shows. 'They were all badly brought up. Their parents had a certain outrageous liberality of principle in education which left unchecked their children's greatest faults. They did not see them even, nor could they put faith in anything but their own notions. This was peculiarly the case with Captain M. How often have I disputed with him on that licentiousness of principle which made him assert that anything that ever was written was fit for children to read. They were allowed to read whatever they could lay their hands on, except the Bible; this alone were they forbidden, not I believe from his respect of it, but perhaps the contrary.' She then commented on Norfolk Island. 'Norfolk Island by the recent accounts is stated to be in a very disorganised and disorderly condition. Perhaps this domestic calamity working on Sir George Gipps' compassion may induce him to retain Capt. M. longer there than under such circumstances he might otherwise have done. But of this I know nothing. Evils are magnified by distance and they may not be so bad at Norfolk Island as is represented. I have long owed Captain Maconochie a letter, how can I write to him now? Yet I think I must write to him and that sympathy and tenderness and the existing ties of friendship require it.' Mary Ann soon left Sydney for Britain, where she stayed with her aunt.

But this was not the only piece of scandal to disturb Maconochie in 1842. That same year Father McEnroe, the Catholic priest on the island, sent Gipps letters alleging increased homosexuality on the island, always an emotive subject. McEnroe had been on Norfolk Island since 1838. A Tipperary man, he had first come out to Sydney in 1832. Rumours indicated that he was a drinker, a binger, and a possible reason for his then being sent to Norfolk Island by Bishop Polding was to help him dry out. William Ullathorne had written of him as being from time to time 'overcast with a terrible melancholy, accompanied by a great internal heat and a peculiar twitching of the corners of the mouth; and then came an intense longing for drink on this really otherwise very sober man. If then I took his shoes and his hat and locked his door to save him from sallying forth, he so far lost his senses as to get out of the window as he was and cross the park to some Catholic house, where he would implore the people for the love of God to put the light wine used in the country down his throat.' Now McEnroe was returning to Sydney and so he wrote a series of letters to Gipps describing his time on Norfolk Island. Initially he had been strongly in favour of Maconochie, and this was reciprocated by Maconochie, but recently differences had grown up between them. McEnroe had liked the previous commandant, Major Ryan, a fellow Irishman. He also felt that under Maconochie's regime the Irish were not filling the same important posts as before. But fundamentally McEnroe disapproved of Maconochie's approach. 'As a *Penal* settlement, with its present relaxed discipline, it is rather a *Gymnasium* for spoiled children, to work or play nearly as much as they please, than a station for the "correction" of criminals.' Maconochie, he went on, 'does not seem to pay proper attention to the constituent parts of the dregs of human nature on which he is experimenting. A great part of those placed in his crucible are persons who spent their days in idleness and dissipation and their nights in thieving.' McEnroe's contacts with the prisoners were largely influenced, of course, by his religious duties: he saw them when they got into trouble, or in the confessional.

What particularly upset McEnroe was that his 'new' prisoners, the Irishmen especially, were involved in homosexuality.

> Some have sunk into that most dreadful crime, a crime they never even so much as heard of until they arrived on this degraded Island, the horrid crime that called down the fire of Heaven on the guilty cities of Sodom and Gomorrah. Several of the old prisoners were infected with this most iniquitous vice, and sought every opportunity of infecting the newly arrived, in which, alas, they have too fatally succeeded; so that this crime is now common, especially among the English first convicted prisoners. I have now one request to make, and I make it with the utmost and most earnest solicitude; and it is that no more 'first' convicted prisoners be sent to this focus of corruption. I would rather see every one of them transported to the wilds of Siberia, and myself with them, than have them come here and be contaminated with this detestable vice.

McEnroe's letter goes on, 'One of these miserable beings, who was touched with remorse told me ...', but then the official record notes: 'HERE THE TEXT BECOMES FOR TWO LINES ASTERISKED AS THIS SECTION HAS BEEN DELETED FOR ITS IMPURITY'. This deletion came about because Gipps later sent McEnroe's letters to Stanley and they thus entered the public record; but Victorian sensibilities would not allow such impurities to be put down in print, any more than they would with the manuscript of the prisoner Thomas Cook.

McEnroe concluded:

> I fear the Captain will have to give rigorous account on the day of Judgment for not attempting at least to put down these crimes that cry to heaven for vengeance. These miscreants are as well-known among the prisoners, by their dress, carriage and conversation, as the most notorious prostitutes on the streets of Sydney, and strange to say several of these have wormed their way to confidence and to places of ease and trust! This has disgusted many of the well-disposed prisoners and so it ought! One miserable being who was not long since notorious for these vile propensities and who is still so, in the opinion of many of his fellow prisoners, is a principal over-seer and man of all works to Captain Maconochie, and to his manoeuvres and mis-statements I attribute the Captain's omission in not acting on His Excellency's recommendation in this matter. I shall dwell here no longer on this disgusting subject.

This tirade played to the worst fears of Maconochie's critics and to the widespread fears held by society at large at that time about homosexuality.

In fact, homosexuality had existed on Norfolk Island for some time. No sooner had the second settlement started in 1825 than the island became known as 'Sodom Island' according to the Sydney *Monitor*. 'Marriages' between Norfolk Island convicts and their being given women's names were described by witnesses to the Molesworth Committee. Ullathorne knew of this in 1834: 'Soon after my return to Sydney I placed the state of the convicts at Norfolk Island before Sir Richard Bourke, and strongly represented the great evil of their being locked up at night in the dark, without any division between the men or any watchman to control their conduct. I earnestly pointed out the necessity of partitions, lights, and watchmen under proper superintendence.' Ullathorne's pamphlet *The Catholic Mission in Australia* charts such 'displays of malignant passions' as 'another class of crimes too frightful even for the imagination of other lands, which St. Paul, in detailing the vices of the heathens, has not contemplated, which were unknown to the savage, until taught by the convict – crimes which are notorious – crimes that, dare I describe them, would make your blood to freeze, and your hair to rise erect in horror upon the pale flesh. Let them be enfolded in eternal darkness.' Ullathorne feared sodomy would corrupt the Aborigines. 'The naked savage, who wanders through those endless forests, knew of nothing monstrous in crime, except cannibalism, until England schooled him in horrors through her prisoners. The removal of such a plague from the earth concerns the whole human race.' Ullathorne's fear of sodomy echoed that of his age. For the Victorians it was still the 'unmentionable crime'.

The Molesworth Committee had in fact used the existence of homosexuality in Australia as one of its strongest arguments against transportation. It heard lurid details of sexual malpractice in Sydney, where a homosexual *demi-monde* existed at Hyde Park barracks, with fresh young arrivals off convict ships being thrown together with old lags and becoming their 'punks', passive homosexuals to be safeguarded by dominant males. Few of these new arrivals had had homosexual inclinations before. Ullathorne, to his evident distress, learnt this from his confessional. One young Irishman, newly arrived, told him 'such things no one knows in Ireland'.

Double standards over homosexuality occurred in Britain at that time too. Homosexual behaviour went on at all levels of society, despite the apparent public disapproval. Byron was known to be homosexual, or bisexual, and the Anglican Bishop of Clogher in Ireland in a notorious case had been caught *in flagrante delicto* with a guardsman in 1822, while General Sir Eyre

Coote was found canoodling with boys from Christ's Hospital School. Lower-class homosexuals fared badly, however, and many were executed, as sodomy still remained a capital offence in the early part of the nineteenth century. Indeed hangings were proportionately higher for sodomy than for any other crime.

The post-Napoleonic era was a particularly homophobic time in England as the English press sought to portray England as superior to the effete French and the decadent Italians. In Australia, with four men to one woman in towns and twenty to one in the bush, homosexuality thrived, though at first it was treated with disdain. Arthur Phillip, the first governor, condemned it, together with murder. 'For either of these crimes I would wish to confine the criminal until an opportunity offered of delivering him to the natives of New Zealand, and let them eat him'. Thomas Cook mentioned widespread homosexuality in his accounts of convict life. As part of a road gang above Sydney, he had watched men bed down together in twos and threes, displaying mutual 'demonstrations of brutal regard'. Cook reckoned he met only two overseers who were not homosexual.

Against this background it might seem surprising that homosexuality on Norfolk Island in Maconochie's time created such a stir, but by now evidence was being sought to show Maconochie's regime as unsuccessful. That Maconochie was prepared to discuss so precarious a subject openly was probably a mistake. He discussed it because he felt something should be done about it. In his next report he wrote: 'With unnatural offences I have been peculiarly embarrassed. The proof of them is seldom complete; the very investigation into them is degrading to the men subjected to it. If innocent, they are deeply injured by it; and if acquitted, though guilty, they are known to be so by their companions, who are thus injured by their impunity, while the wretches themselves become only the more impudent and abandoned through their escape. It is all most vexatious.' Maconochie had tried to lessen it.

Where I have been able to convict, I have punished corporally, and with great severity. I have leant also to conviction where the probability seemed considerable. I have made even the loss of character in this way, though without detected offence, a ground for temporary imprisonment; and I have set aside eight separate cells in which the most notorious, or considered such, are made to sleep at night alone. All this, however, I am sensible, rather gratifies my own feelings on the subject than improves the men's. The evil lies far deeper than I can now reach. It is inseparable from the circumstances in which my men are and have been placed. I can apply palliatives, but not remedies.

He went on, however, to suggest one solution:

The true, the only remedy for that addiction to unnatural offences, now so grievously common among prisoners, is a total revision and improvement of our whole arrangements concerning them. While men are lodged, as my home prisoners here were universally during the first year, and many are so yet, in rooms calculated to hold 200 together, in a warm climate, where the clothing is light, and frequently thrown aside and where night tubs in the same room are in common use among them all, being the only conveniences within their reach for the relief of the ordinary wants of Nature, we cannot expect but that their feelings of personal reserve and delicacy must be speedily destroyed. While we further sequester them from the very sight of women (whose mere presence is with Englishmen imposing in this respect), we cannot be surprised that their passions should take a different direction.

His recommendations were clear. 'Women must be present, with the strictest precautions to prevent illicit intercourse, and very heavy fines where it is obtained; but with a fair prospect and every encouragement given on both sides, to form or to renew lawful connexions at a given period of their several probations.' He felt that wives and families of prisoners could be allowed to join them there, but not to live with them

till they had, in like manner, earned the privilege. A wing in the women's barracks, with a different entrance, might be assigned them. A charge in marks might be made against the husbands for their maintenance, which would stimulate the husbands to industry, yet could be reduced for work done by the wives, and this would in like manner stimulate them. The accommodation allowed must from the first be more decent; and, in a word, the whole treatment must be made social and improving, not merely coercive and deteriorating. When this shall be effected there is no doubt that a vice, the most revolting to Englishmen, the most degrading, the most injurious, (destructive of health and looks as well as of moral feeling, and in this last particular injuring the lookers-on as well as the guilty parties) will speedily disappear.

It was a brave suggestion, too far-reaching and unsettling for his contemporaries to take seriously.

Gipps sent copies of McEnroe's letters to Stanley in October 1842. But Gipps had already expressed his own views on the overall situation on Norfolk Island in an earlier dispatch to Stanley sent in August that year. 'In my dispatches I have brought before your Lordship numerous details respecting Norfolk Island, which collectively, I think, must lead to the conclusion that the time is nearly arrived when it will be proper to remove from the island the prisoners who during the last two years and a half have been there placed under the experimental system introduced by Captain Maconochie.' This was sounding like the death knell of Maconochie's experiment, as removing the 'new' prisoners would effectively be the end of it as originally planned.

Gipps had been hearing contrasting accounts of what was happening on the island from officers or soldiers coming back from Norfolk Island once their tour of duty had finished. The military were mostly hostile to Maconochie's regime. Other sources were the hearsay of traders or casual visitors to the island. However, Gipps had to admit that from what he had heard 'the men are all (or nearly all) personally attached to Captain Maconochie', although sometimes 'the least deserving men are most in his confidence'. He went on: 'Punishment is rare on the island, and hardly ever severe. Attempts are frequently made to produce striking effects on even the worst men, by unexpected acts of leniency, forgiveness, or confidence, calculated to awaken and call into play the good feeling implanted in them by nature, but which may long have lain dormant; and such attempts are not infrequently successful' – an acknowledgement of some merit in Maconochie's system. Gipps continued: 'Petty crimes, however, abound; and perhaps are even on the increase. Acts of overt or combined violence seldom occur; and heinous acts of atrocity, such as the unprovoked infliction on each other of bodily injuries, are less frequent than they formerly were.' This was surely a good sign: that prisoners respected each other. But he went on: 'Unnatural offences it is to be feared are on the increase.' This set alarm bells ringing. Gipps was also worried that the produce of the island was falling off, which meant that the cost of supplying provisions from Sydney was rapidly increasing. This was probably true, as under Maconochie's scheme, ticket-of-leave prisoners were often working on their own farms and gardens to earn marks to complete their sentences rather than contributing to the island's export earnings. Gipps had probably also been influenced by the adverse reports from critics such as Smith and Ormsby.

Gipps was now coming to a conclusion, which he outlined to Stanley.

> When Captain Maconochie was sent to Norfolk Island (now two and a half years ago), it was intended by Her Majesty's Government that large additional numbers of prisoners should be dispatched from England to join this establishment; but none such have hitherto been sent, a fact which of itself would seem to indicate that Her Majesty's Government entertain some doubt of the propriety of keeping up his establishment; and such doubt must indeed have been suggested by the general tenor of my despatches. Moreover, Captain Maconochie himself neither seems to desire nor to expect to be continued at Norfolk Island, but, on the contrary, constantly expresses a hope and expectation of being removed to some other locality.

This was true. Maconochie had begun to wonder whether he would not be better off, given all the opposition he was receiv-

ing, starting somewhere else. Gipps acknowledged some of
Maconochie's difficulties. 'In Sydney and indeed throughout
New South Wales, with very few exceptions, every man was
against him, every man derided his system, and clearly every one
dreaded the effects of the evil example which it was supposed
would be presented by it to our own convict population.' Gipps
conceded that this sort of hostility reminded him of 'that which,
a dozen years ago, manifested itself in the West Indies against any
attempt to ameliorate the condition of slavery'. Gipps had been
there at the time and this may have helped Gipps empathize at
times with Maconochie's problems, and led him to support him.
'So long as the remonstrances of these officers were directed only
against Captain Maconochie's habitual disregard of forms, regulations, or what may be styled departmental observances, I
thought it my duty, in a very great degree, to overrule them,
considering that in the very novel and difficult position in which
he was placed, all impediments should as far as possible be moved
out of his way.' But now things had changed. 'The evidence
lately brought by the same officers before me, of a rapidly
increasing expenditure, has become so convincing (the good to
be derived from it being still as problematic as ever), that the
point seems to me to be attained at which I ought to take a
responsibility in another direction on myself.'

The plan was to remove the new prisoners to Van Diemen's
Land the following March or April. Gipps was still smarting from
Maconochie's early transgressions. 'I see no reason to change the
opinion I long ago entertained, that the error committed by
Captain Maconochie in putting the two establishments under
the same system of management (reported in my despatch of the
27th June 1840), was a fatal one, as far as regarded the trial of his
system at Norfolk Island, or in any place within the Government
of New South Wales.' Fatal was certainly the operative word. As
regards the future of Norfolk Island, Gipps felt that 'on this
subject the only decided opinion I can offer is, that whilst the
island is admirably adapted to the purposes of a strictly penal
station, it is scarcely adapted to any other' and he concluded

'these considerations lead me, I must avow, to the opinion, that the best thing to do with Norfolk Island will be to let it revert to what it was prior to the year 1840'. This was written in August 1842 and appeared to be the final nail in Maconochie's coffin.

Gipps now heard of a recent escape attempt. On 20th June 1842 the *Governor Phillip*, the government brig that plied regularly between Sydney and Norfolk Island, was unloading stores in the bay off Kingston. Work had stopped for the night and the ship lay offshore with its crew of eighteen on board as well as twelve convicts there to unload the vessel. They had stayed overnight on board, guarded by twelve armed soldiers of the 96th Regiment. Shortly after dawn the convicts noticed that the two sentries guarding their hatchway were half asleep. They were attacked and their guns seized and one was thrown overboard while the other sentry surrendered. Two other unarmed guards were also on deck and tried to wrest the guns from the convicts unsuccessfully. One of these guards then escaped down the main anchor chain into the brig's launch, while the other one tried to swim ashore but was drowned. The sergeant of the guard was now aroused and came up on deck, immediately shooting the nearest mutineer, but was then knocked over himself by a blow to his head from another mutineer. The crew on board had hidden themselves in their forecastle and battened down the hatches. Unable to work the vessel, the convicts summoned two of them up to assist them. As this was going on, other guards from below broke through into the captain's cabin and started firing at the mutineers through the window gratings, wounding several of them. The captain of the ship was asked to surrender but he refused and fired a shot at them, killing their leader. The remaining convicts now panicked, ran below and the vessel was quickly retaken. One of the soldiers who had set off swimming for the shore, now swam back and was being pulled on board with the help of a mutineer when he was mistakenly shot by his own sergeant. After their surrender the convicts were brought up on deck; one was shot in the thigh and another, who raised his arms and cried out 'Spare me', was also shot, either by mistake or in revenge. The mutineers had controlled the ship for half an hour and now the deck lay covered with the dying and the dead. Once ashore, the seven surviving convicts were put in irons in the gaol.

Gipps, in describing these events to Stanley, took the view that it was the guard's fault for being slipshod. He wrote: 'The late attempt to take the Government brig was, I believe, only a solitary act of desperation. The original intention of the parties engaged in it was to seize a small schooner, called the *"Coquette"*, which visited the island for the purpose of delivering some Commissariat stores or provisions from Sydney; and it was only in a fit of rage or despair at seeing themselves disappointed of the prey, which they had expected would prove an easy one, that they turned upon an object altogether beyond their strength.'

Maconochie visited the prisoners straight away and on learning who they were decided to use this situation to apply his social system to the guilty men. His version of the incident ran as follows:

> Five of the mutineers were English, two Irish; all had been prisoners from a very early age, the leading mutineer from the age of eleven, four of the others from fourteen, another eighteen, another twenty-two, and all were in the first instance transported for very slight offences. All had led hard and reckless lives in the colony, the leading mutineer and two others having been before capitally convicted for piracy and robbery in Van Diemen's Land, and sent here on a commuted sentence; another of them had been capitally convicted before for mutiny in this Island in 1834, but reprieved. None of them were educated men; but the leading mutineer, John Jones per 'Asia', had very considerable natural ability, could read well and write tolerably; two others of his companions could read. Two of the mutineers, not the leader, were tradesmen, which usually involves some greater degree of cultivation than common labour. Their ages ranged from twenty-four to thirty five; three of the mutineers, the leader and two others, had even served long and well in our Police.

At first they were sullen and impatient. Maconochie then introduced a form of 'mutual responsibility' with them by keeping the seven together. 'The season being winter, I placed them in a room with a fireplace in it, which was thus kept always comfortably warm. I gave them all comfortable stretchers and bedding; and I permitted a subscription to be made among the men outside, which in less than a day exceeded £5, to purchase them tea and sugar, luxuries much prized by their class, and which they could not otherwise have had. I also from time to time sent them a meal of fresh meat myself, and authorized others to do the same; in our prison, from the indifferent state of the men's stomachs through long confinement to salt meat and the want of usual exercise, a very bad form of dyspepsia is very prevalent; and I wished to keep these men right in body, that the means taken with their minds might have fair play.'

This was Maconochie's 'holistic' approach, mind and body addressed at the same time. 'I visited them almost daily myself, and Mr. Naylor, the Protestant Chaplain, was with them some hours every day.' After a few interviews with them, Naylor

perceived their minds were softening and joined with them in the penitential confession of sin, and instructed them in such truths as were most applicable to their state. At length they were brought to a deep sense of their guilt, and from that moment till they were launched into eternity, they maintained a humble, penitent, and submissive deportment, and most carefully refrained from any act of impropriety. Doubtless the kindness manifested towards them during their imprisonment, and the judicious treatment which they received, had a great effect in the first instance, in softening their hearts, and preparing them for the reception of religious truth. Two of them, being Catholic threatened for some time to curtail his usefulness, and even perhaps break up the whole plan; but one was compelled to be removed to hospital; and the other man insisted rather on turning Protestant than being separated from his companions.

Every Sunday afternoon Maconochie read the divine service himself in their room, always accompanied by several members of his own family and other friends of theirs 'always keeping distinctly in view that the men on whose account we were assembled, were doomed to die, were preparing for death, and in this light only were the objects, of our interest'. Maconochie was here applying his central tenet that convicts should use their time profitably. The stakes this time were high. 'Our mutineers looked for death, I believe, as certainly as Human Nature can look for it, they never expressed hope; and yet they were far from being intensely miserable, at times they were even cheerful.' This was his social system at work. 'Their social feelings were sedulously cultivated throughout. Their companions were admitted to see them. Mr. Naylor's children and mine, eight boys, to whom they became much attached, also frequently visited them. They were taught to consider it their duty to impress serious convictions on others, as well as entertain them themselves, and they eagerly caught at this idea, and acted on it. They became even eloquent under its influence; and though, as time advanced, they grew very pale, under the combined action of protracted confinement and emotion, their health continued good, and the expression of their countenances most strikingly improved.'

A contemporary account in *Chambers' Miscellany* explains this:

> They have long received extreme kindness from the commandant (Capt. Maconochie) and are literally bewildered at finding that even this last act has not diminished the exercise of his benevolence. That anybody should care for them, or take such pains about them, after their violent conduct, excited surprise at first almost amounting to suspicion; but this at length gave place to the warmest gratitude. They were, in fact, subdued by it. They read very much, are extremely submissive, and carefully avoid the slightest infringement of the prison regulations. At first, all this was confined to three of the men; but their steady consistency of conduct, and the strange transformation of character so evident in them, gradually arrested the attention of the others, and eventually led to a similar result.

The account tells how at the conclusion of one of the Sunday services read by Maconochie, one of the convicts, Sayers, stood up, and with his heart so full as scarcely to allow him utterance, to the surprise of every person there, he addressed most impressively the men who were present. 'Perhaps,' said he, 'the words of one of ourselves, unhappily circumstanced as I am, may have some weight with you. You all know the life I have led; it has, believe me, been a most unhappy one; and I have, I hope not too late, discovered the cause of this. I solemnly tell you that it is because I have broken God's laws. I am almost ashamed to speak, but I dare not be silent. I am going to tell you a strange thing. I never before was happy; I begin now, for the first time in my life to *hope*. I am an ignorant man, or at least I was so; but I thank God I begin to see things in their right light now. I have been *unhappily placed from my childhood, and have endured many hardships*. I do not mention this to excuse my errors; yet if *I had years since received the kindness I have done here, it might have been otherwise*. My poor fellows, do turn over a new leaf; try to serve God, and you too will be happier for it.' The effect was most thrilling; there was a death-like silence; tears rolled down many cheeks, which I verily believe never before felt them: and without a word more, all slowly withdrew.

Chambers gives a résumé of this man's history, 'a very painful one'. He had been transported for life for being an accomplice in a robbery, though later it was felt he was innocent. On arrival in New South Wales he was assigned to a master who treated him with great cruelty, and so he absconded. Once recaptured he was sent to Moreton Bay penal settlement for three years of 'horrible severity, starvation, and misery of every kind'. He absconded again and was then sentenced for life to Norfolk Island. When his companions made an attempt on the *Governor Phillip* brig, 'the love of liberty and a desire to escape from so much misery induced him to join them'. Naylor then wrote of him:

For some time past I have noticed his quiet and orderly conduct, and was really sorry when I found him concerned in this unhappy affair. His desire for freedom was, however, most ardent, and a chance of obtaining it was almost irresistible. He has since told me that *a few words kindly spoken to* himself and others by Captain Maconochie when they landed, *sounded so pleasantly to him* – such are his own words – that *he determined from that moment he would endeavour to do well*. He assures me that he was perfectly unconscious of a design to take the brig, until awoken from his sleep a few minutes before the attack commenced; that he then remonstrated with the men; but finding it useless, he considered it a point of honour not to fail them. His anxiety for instruction is intense; he listens like a child; and his *gratitude* is most touching. He, together with Jones, Woolfe, and Barry, were chosen by the commandant as a policeboat's crew; and had, up till this period, acted with great steadiness and fidelity in the discharge of the duties required from them. Nor do I think they would even now, tempting as the occasion was, have thought of seizing it, had it not been currently reported that they were shortly to be placed under a system of severity, such as they had already suffered so much from.

As Norfolk Island was not authorized for trials for capital offences, the prisoners were sent across to Sydney in October 1842. Crowds met them at the pier, anxious to catch a glimpse of these men who had dared, unarmed, to commit so bold an enterprise. Four of them were sentenced to hang, two had their death sentences commuted to transportation for life and the seventh man, John Berry, was acquitted because 'he had not taken part in the attempt to take the Brig, but had run up into the rigging of the vessel at the commencement of the fray'. The local newspaper, *The Australian*, described their last moments:

About 8 o'clock yesterday, a crowd gathered around the gates of Darlinghurst Gaol, and in the neighbouring heights, seeking a view of the gallows. Soon after eight the voices of the doomed four were heard singing a hymn with such fervour and firmness. Exactly as the clock struck nine, the prison bell began to toll, and the sad procession issued from the walls of the gaol, the Rev. Mr Elder leading the way, with his face towards the prisoners, comforting and exhorting them, followed by the Rev. Messrs Walsh and Naylor, then the Sheriff, visiting Magistrate and Gaoler. They walked to the scaffold about fifty yards, and then commenced to sing with firm voices until they reached the foot of the fatal tree. Here they knelt to receive the last ministrations. All were ghastly pale, and Jones and Sayers seemed nearly fainting: Beaver had his eyes closed, his countenance motionless, whilst Lewis was resigned and repentant. The services were read by Mr. Elder, and the prisoners responded in an audible and firm voice. They then rose, and without assistance walked up on the platform. Whilst the ropes were adjusted round their necks, and the caps fixed on their heads, they prayed audibly and fervently aided by their religious attendants, after which they shook their hands, thanking them and blessing them. The caps were then pulled over their faces, and after shaking hands with their executioner, they each joined their hands in a convulsive clasp, and with the prayer of repentance on their lips, we would trust the hope of mercy in their hearts, the fatal bolt was drawn, and they were launched into eternity.

A few seconds later, 'the man Jones, who seemed the most agitated, died whilst Sayers, Lewis and Beaver continued to struggle with convulsive twitchings of the body for some time.' The four bodies were left to hang as prescribed by law, and were then taken down and placed in their coffins. The article ended: 'We heard several of those employed about the gaol remark that they had never witnessed men come to the scaffold so firm.'

12

Gipps's Visit

GIPPS FINALLY MADE his visit to Norfolk Island in March 1843. He left Sydney on 23rd February 1843 in the sloop *Hazard* and arrived at Norfolk Island on 11th March, an unexpected visit: nobody, not even Maconochie, knew he was coming. Maconochie handed him his report for 1842 as soon as he landed. Gipps felt he 'could not have received it at a more opportune moment' and used it as the basis for his own report on the island, which he wrote for Stanley on 1st April 1843, and from which the quotations here come. He was to spend six days altogether on the island. His first impression was 'a favourable one'. He found 'good order everywhere to prevail, and the demeanour of the prisoners to be respectful and quiet'. Over his six days he visited nearly every part of the island, 'minutely inspected every establishment (almost every house), and separately questioned or examined every person having any charge or authority, however small'. He took down in writing the substance of what each individual said to him 'in his presence'.

He found 593 'new' prisoners there, 86 fewer than the 679 who had arrived in 1840-41. Of these 86, one had been sent to Sydney as insane, 6 had escaped, 4 had been removed to Van Diemen's Land for misbehaviour, and 75 had died – a higher death rate than he expected, though this was 'not chargeable on anything peculiar to Captain Maconochie's system of management'. It was due mainly to dysentery, passed on from the 'old hands' to the new prisoners before they had acclimatized to the island and its diet. Fresh meat, Gipps noted, was available only two or three times a year, and wheaten bread never (hence Maconochie's 'treat' of these items on Queen Victoria's birthday): the normal diet was maize meal and salt meat. Gipps felt that this 'deprivation of wheaten bread on their arrival' had caused dysentery. Dysentery, it is now known, is as likely to be caused by poor sanitation and impure water, as it lives on as a bacteria easily transmitted from one person to the other. The sanitation facilities on Norfolk Island when the new prisoners arrived were very primitive.

Gipps found the general appearance of the new prisoners to be 'less robust or healthy' than that of the 'old hands' but with 'less perhaps of that gloom which is to be seen in the ironed gangs of New South Wales'. There had been an epidemic of dysentery again recently, which worried many of the new prisoners, and they told Gipps they wanted to leave the island. Gipps then inspected the 509 tickets-of-leave holders on the island. There had been 549 of them, but 40 had recently forfeited their tickets for misconduct: eight for dishonesty, five for insubordination, six for boat-building, four for unnatural offences, two for strong suspicion of it, six for getting into debt, three for illicit distilling and the remainder for 'breaches of discipline, as being out at night etc'. But now seventeen had got their tickets back. 'Of the 509 Ticket of Leave holders all have acquired the number of marks fixed by Captain Maconochie as the price of their Ticket (varying from 6,000 to 8,000 each, according to their sentences), and they have acquired surplus marks to the amount, on the average, of 2,500 each.' He noted, however, that the men seemed to have made up their minds that the marks would be of little avail to them.

Gipps now tried to judge 'the degree of moral improvement' the men had made during their three years on Norfolk Island, and the way in which they could be expected to behave when returned to society. He liked much of what he saw. 'That there are many good men among them, and men who may be expected to behave well in Van Diemen's Land, cannot be doubted', but he was worried about what would happen to them once they had left and were placed in the midst of an unfriendly and hostile population in Van Diemen's Land, where public opinion had been very strongly against the system of management of Norfolk Island. Moreover, they would have considerable difficulty in finding employment as labour was less in demand in Van Diemen's Land than in any of the neighbouring colonies. 'They may not be able to obtain the wages they expect; and, under the disappointment which they are likely to meet with, and the loss of the punctual subsistence which they have been accustomed to rely on, whether they may not return to their evil ways is doubtful, to say the least.' This line of argument was consistent with Maconochie's view that they should be released somewhere new, where they could make a fresh start.

Gipps then turned to 'vices' on the island, gambling and the crime 'most repugnant to Human Nature', homosexuality.

The practice of unnatural offences is said, and probably with reason, to have been learned by them from the 'Old Hands', or doubly-convicted prisoners; but, whether this be the case or not, it seems admitted by all persons on the Island that the offence is now far more common among the 'New Hands' than the 'Old'. I endeavoured, especially from the Medical Officers and Clergymen to obtain some information tending to fix the proportion among the 'New Hands' of the tainted to that of the untainted with this crime; and though on such a point scarcely more than conjecture can be offered, I found opinions to vary from one eighth to one twentieth of the whole; that is to say, the lowest estimate supposed one man in twenty, the highest one man in eight, to be or to have been, in a greater or less degree, guilty of this crime. In every instance where the offence has been legally or satisfactorily proved it has been punished by the infliction of the lash. In the hospital one man at least died in consequence of the commission of the crime; and other instances are recorded of loathsome disease engendered by it. The crime is said to prevail almost exclusively among the prisoners of English birth; of Scotch there are very few on this Island and the

Irish are (to their honour) generally acknowledged to be untainted with it.

It is interesting to note the priority Gipps gives in his report to the subject the Victorians were obsessed with. He had started his report declaring he was going to talk about moral improvement along Maconochie's lines, but these 'vices' came first.

Gambling, he felt, was accounted for 'in a great measure, by the peculiarity of the convicts' position. So long as the idea prevailed among them that they would get their freedom as soon as they had acquired the number of marks apportioned to each by Captain Maconochie, every man had a definite object before him; his mind was fixed on the acquisition of this object, and consequently did not stand in need of other excitement; but when the acquisition of marks ceased to be an object worthy of their consideration, and at or about the same time (by the distribution of pigs, and other, means) articles of value, as well as money, began to circulate among them, the passion for gambling arose, and is now greatly prevalent.' Hence, as Maconochie would argue, the importance of giving marks a definite value.

Gipps praised the farming on the island.

When Tickets of Leave were first issued in March or April 1842, small farms were laid out, of from six to ten Acres each, and given to parties of Ticket holders, consisting generally of five or six persons; and the experiment has certainly been attended with considerable success; indeed Captain Maconochie considers the success of it to have been complete. There are now twenty-seven of these farms, but the number of men living on them is reduced to seventy-eight (50 Irish, 27 English and 1 Scotch); the reduction having been caused partly by the forfeiture by some of the men of their tickets, partly by the expulsion of some by their comrades or partners, and partly also by sickness. On each farm a hut or cottage has been erected; and of these huts many are neat and creditable. The farms were so laid out that each of them contained a portion of cleared and a portion of uncleared land.

Gipps explained the reciprocal arrangements. 'For each acre which they might cultivate of cleared land the holders were to pay a rent per annum of eleven bushels of maize, but uncleared land brought into cultivation was to be free of rent for the first year. In addition to maize, the chief article cultivated by them is the sweet potato, but common potatoes, as well as cabbages and tobacco, are raised. Sweet potatoes are the most useful article they produce, as, mixed with maize meal, they make a very palatable kind of bread; and pigs, poultry, and indeed all animals, feed and fatten on them. The maize harvest was commencing at the time of my visit; and it was expected that on the twenty-seven farms collectively about 1,500 bushels would be gathered.' Farming then seemed to be working, and giving prisoners a foretaste of life in the outside world.

Gipps now had to admit that 'having thus, to the best of my power, described the actual condition of the "New Hands" experimental prisoners at Norfolk Island, it becomes my duty to remark, that Captain Maconochie desires very anxiously that I should certify that his system has not had a fair trial; but I go further than this, and am willing to certify that his system, that is to say, the system described in his printed publications, has never been tried at all'. This was an extraordinary admission to make, since its implication was that Maconochie had never been given the full support he had needed to make his 'trial' work. Gipps quickly covered himself, however. 'Before I visited Norfolk Island doubts had frequently occurred to me of Captain Maconochie's ability to carry into effect his own theory; the indulgent portion of it seemed to him indeed to be easy and natural, but from many peculiarities of his disposition and habits of thought which fell under my notice, his sanguine and hasty conclusions, his anxiety to produce early and striking effects, his almost total disbelief in the propensity of man to crime, his great desire to avoid inflicting punishment, and his especial dislike of what he calls vindictive punishments, I was led to fear almost at the commencement of his experiments that he would not carry into effect the sterner parts of his own

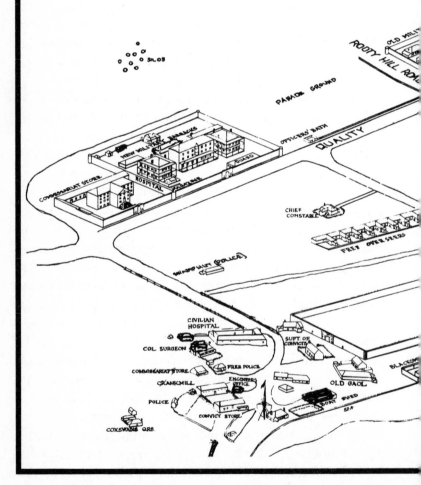

View of Kingston settlement

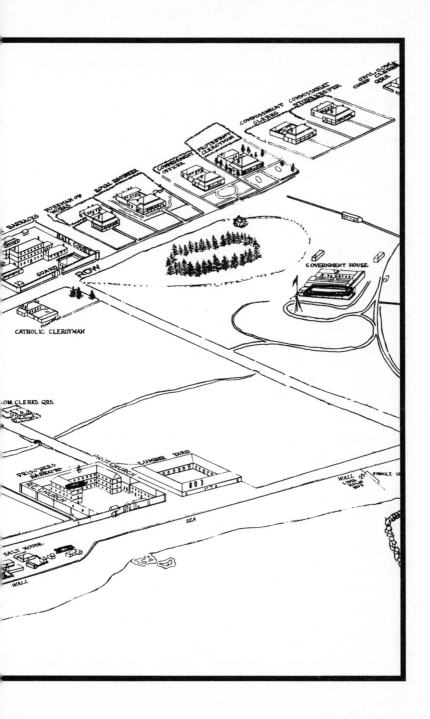

system, which are, nevertheless, the foundation of the whole.' Gipps was now agreeably surprised to find that, despite these alleged faults and his own misgivings, the system had been working well.

Gipps took up the issue of marks. 'Within a year, or very little more, after their arrival at Norfolk Island, some men had acquired the number of marks which ought to have made them free. They had up to this time worked and behaved well, as it was only natural to suppose they would, under the stimulus which the marks afforded; but when, after they had acquired their full number of marks, and they found that they nevertheless were not removed from the Island, the stimulus no longer existed, and marks gradually came, by them, to be considered as valueless.' This was where Maconochie's operation broke down. But Gipps reiterated his attachment to precedent. 'Not only had no provision been made for removing them from the Island, and placing them in an easier or comparatively in a free state, but the Law stood absolutely opposed to the making of any such provision. So long as the 2d & 3d Will. 4. c. 62 remained unrepealed it was absolutely illegal for any authority in this hemisphere to grant the men any greater indulgence than what they already enjoyed at Norfolk Island; and that Statute remains unrepealed even to the present day.' This was the nub of the argument, the double bind that had never been resolved. Gipps should have pressed for the act's repeal, or, at the very least, its amendment, so as to allow Maconochie's system to run through properly.

Gipps at least conceded one point. 'Captain Maconochie has always maintained, and maintains stronger than ever, in his latest report, dated the 10th January last, that in order to have a full trial of his experiment his marks ought to bear a definite value; and so undoubtedly they ought; but it is out of the power of the Governor, or any Colonial authority, to give them a value inconsistent with the terms of the Statute above referred to; and to affix a value to them consistently with the periods of servitude prescribed by the second clause of that Statute would be in no way satisfactory to Captain Maconochie, indeed it would be to render his system altogether nugatory.' Gipps next seemed to be endorsing Maconochie's approach. 'Of the efficacy of the system of marks, supposing them to have, as they doubtless should have, a definite value, I may not entertain so high an opinion as Captain Maconochie, but I nevertheless consider that marks may be made very useful in the management of convicts.' But he quickly added a rider. 'One objection to them, however, is that there is a strong tendency to make a lavish use of them; and doubtless (for he confesses it himself) a lavish use of them has been made by Captain Maconochie.' This was a fair comment, and one that Maconochie himself did not dispute.

Gipps liked Maconochie's other innovations. 'In respect to the principle of mutual responsibility, which is in fact the foundation of the social system, I will only say that I have found it to answer very well, as far as the distribution of rewards or earnings is concerned,' though he still felt 'there is something in punishing one man or woman (for my experience has been gained in part at the female factory at Parramatta) for the fault of another at which the sense of common justice revolts.' He went on: 'Captain Maconochie is of opinion that the principle of mutual responsibility was less objected to by the "Old Hands" than the "New Hands"'; and the officers of the old establishment that Gipps questioned agreed that the prisoners would work 'like tigers' for marks, if marks could procure their freedom. Maconochie had also found this, as he stated in his 1842 report: 'The arrangement was remarkably successful with the penal prisoners while they were subjected to it; these men knew each other better than did the home prisoners; they thus severally chose their companions better; having previously suffered hardship together, they took a deeper interest in each other's welfare; and they thus exhibited much more patience and forbearance with each other's infirmities of temper, and other occasional sources of difference.' The new prisoners had not previously 'suffered together'; they did not know each other well enough and had not formed 'friendships in adversity' and so they were less amenable to the system of mutual responsibility.

Among the 'old hands' one of the most remarkable had been Thomas Wright, known as 'Tommy the Banker', who had just died in February 1843 at the age of 105. The afternoon before his death he had been arguing with his companions on different subjects apparently in perfect health, asserting that he had never drunk anything stronger than tea in his life. A forger of counterfeit bank notes, like Magwitch in Dickens's *Great Expectations*, he had first been tried in York in 1799 and he had clearly been incorrigible, as his last court appearance for the same offence was in Sydney in 1839.

Gipps too had been impressed by the 'old hands'. 'After having animadverted as I have done on Captain Maconochie's measures in respect to the experimental prisoners, it is a relief to me to be able to say, that of his management of the "Old Hands" I can speak with almost unqualified approbation, that is to say, since they were separated from the others. These men had suffered, and suffered severely, before Captain Maconochie assumed the management of them, and their minds had consequently been brought to a state in which the manifestation of kindness on the part of their ruler was likely to make the best impression on them. Great and merciful as have been the ameliorations introduced into their condition.' This was high praise indeed. But Gipps was worried what might happen to them. 'The number of the "Old Hands" or doubly convicted is now 876; and among them are men, very many too, who have been guilty, of the highest offences that men can commit. If the mark system were applied to them without exception, the whole of them would, within a comparatively short period, return to New South Wales; and I cannot contemplate the possibility of their return without alarm; by the Colonists generally I am certain it would be viewed with terror.' Many of these 'old hands' had been convicted for cattle stealing in New South Wales, having first escaped as convicts and then become bushrangers. Their return to New South Wales was Gipps's old bugbear, prompted by his fear of the reactions of his local constituents in New South Wales. He went on, 'Whilst therefore I cannot, for these reasons, accede to the proposal so often made to me, and now repeated by Captain Maconochie, of putting, the "Old Hands" indiscriminately on the mark system, I shall make it my business seriously to consider whether it may not be introduced amongst a portion of them.'

Indeed Gipps went further:

Your Lordship is aware that shortly after Captain Maconochie arrived on the Island, indeed before he had been there a week, he abolished all distinctions between the two bodies of prisoners, or between the 'New' and the 'Old Hands' and put them all on the mark system; but that after the lapse of about three months the 'Old Hands' were, by my order, replaced upon their former footing. Of the propriety, nay, absolute necessity of the order which I then gave, I have never entertained a doubt. Indeed had I not given it, the whole of the doubly convicted would long ere the present time have been returned upon my hands, without my having the means of disposing of them either in New South Wales or elsewhere. That the disapprobation which I then expressed of Captain Maconochie's proceedings damaged him I cannot doubt, or that it tended to give colour and additional currency to the exaggerated reports which were subsequently spread abroad of the evil effects of his system of management.

Again this was an admission of harm done in the past and it looked as if, at long last, Gipps was beginning to see things from Maconochie's point of view. It needed an on-the-spot visit such as his to make this happen, as Maconochie had insisted all along. Gipps went on: 'The relaxations in the severe discipline to which the doubly convicted at Norfolk Island were formerly subjected do not consist solely in the diminished use of the lash or of irons (Captain Maconochie has, indeed, within the last six months, resumed the use of the lash to a considerable extent, as well as the occasional use of irons) but also, and perhaps more essentially, in various smaller matters, the importance of which can hardly be estimated by anyone who has not been on the Island,' and he laid out some of the advantages of this new arrangement.

Formerly, when not actually at work, and also during the whole of the Sabbath day, the prisoners were confined in a yard surrounded with high walls; now they are allowed to walk about the Settlement (or village), though not allowed to rove over the Island, also to fish and to bathe in the sea. Formerly their bread was composed entirely of maize meal; now they are allowed to mix with the maize meal, sweet potatoes of their own growth; and of this simple, and to the Government inexpensive alteration, it is impossible, without tasting the bread, to judge of the value. Formerly they had a garden only between three or four men; now every man has his garden (the sixteenth part of an acre); they have also two additional hours in the week allowed to them for working in their gardens. Formerly they were not allowed to have knives, or any sharp instruments or tools; now it is no offence to have them. Formerly no men were allowed to sleep out of barracks, except such as were in charge of sheep or cattle; now many men are allowed to sleep in huts which have been erected for their accommodation near to the places where they work.

These were clearly, in Gipps's eyes, improvements. The 'old hands' had responded well to Maconochie's presence.

I have already stated that the 'Old Hands' have suffered less during the last three years from sickness than the 'New', and that their general appearance is less sickly. It is certain that they work harder, for on this point there is no difference of opinion on the Island. The Superintendent of Agriculture stated to me deliberately that he would rather have ten 'Old Hands' to do any given piece of work than twenty of the 'New'. I have also already remarked that unnatural offences are less prevalent among the 'Old Hands' than the 'New'. In point of cleanliness there is a striking superiority in the 'Old Hands', not, indeed, so much over the 'New', as over the Generality of convicts in New South Wales, and especially those in Government service. The convict barrack in the Settlement (the one belonging to the 'Old Hands') is in every thing that regards comfort (if such a word can with propriety be used) very superior to the great convict barrack in the town of Sydney, called Hyde Park.

This seemed to prove Maconochie's argument that, having experienced harsh prison life, the 'old hands' would be keenest on co-operation and reform, once given the chance, since their desire for liberty overrode all else.

Gipps noted Maconochie's efforts with the prisoners' spiritual welfare. 'Attached to this barrack, and within the enclosure wall of it are two Chapels, one Protestant, the other Catholic, which have been erected by Captain Maconochie; and though the erection of them without authority was made a matter of charge against him, I cannot but speak in commendation of them, and bear witness to the humanizing effect which attendance in them seems to be producing on the minds of the prisoners.' The 'humanizing effect' was what Maconochie was after; he knew that spiritual well-being needed to go in hand with physical improvement.

Gipps now turned to the recent escape attempts.

What is it then which makes the life of a convict at Norfolk Island so peculiarly irksome? Or what is it which makes men ready to run any risk or endure any hardship in order to get away from it? The daring attempts which have, even of late, been made to escape, would seem to prove that the desire to get away from it is nearly as strong under the administration of Captain Maconochie as it has been under that of any of his predecessors; and it is as strong among the 'New Hands' as the 'Old'. The reason is, I believe, to be found in the extreme isolation of the place, in their being so entirely cut off from Society, or from even a view or a glimpse of society, and more especially from the Society of women. The yearning of their hearts towards Society is indescribable; it constitutes their torment; it is a punishment greater than the lash, or any other that man can inflict upon them. This torment too is also greatly increased by the state of uncertainty in which they live. The sentences of many of them are for life; in respect to many it has also been further recommended by the Judges who tried them that they should never return to the Colony; yet none of them are absolutely without the hope of returning and, according to the present system of remitting punishments, all may even expect to return.

Gipps, even during so short a visit, had clearly felt, as many visitors to the island would do, its isolation from the rest of the world, and the 'torment' and sense of longing this induced. Irish convicts felt this hopelessness and distancing from all they held dear most acutely, as they felt even further from home. It was made worse by the fact that many of them had been sent there for politically inspired crimes, trying to bring about change in what they felt was an unjust society in Ireland. Norfolk Island was only a small island, and the noise of the surf breaking was a constant reminder to the prisoners of their immense isolation. It evoked in the prisoners a yearning to reach beyond the horizon, to return to places now lost to them. Albert Camus once wrote of 'the incorrigible sorrow of all prisoners and exiles, which is to live in company with a memory that serves no purpose'. On Norfolk Island this yearning was particularly acute at night as the prisoners' barracks, where they slept, was only yards away from the breaking surf. Maconochie had always maintained that it was the prisoners' wish for liberty that motivated them to escape rather than the need to get way from an unfair regime. His system had given them a glimpse, a foretaste of freedom.

Gipps continued: 'These facts might lead to important reflections on the subject of the remission of punishments, as well as on the superiority of insular penitentiaries. An unhappy wretch shut up in a cell in the State Prison at Philadelphia, or in that new building at Pentonville, may be more completely secluded than a doubly convicted offender at Norfolk Island, but he never can be convinced that his return to the Society after which he yearns is as difficult.' He elaborated on this point: 'Transportation to Norfolk Island, notwithstanding the fertility of its soil, its genial climate, and beautiful scenery, is therefore a far greater punishment that transportation to New South Wales or Van Diemen's Land, and consequently there is the less reason to augment the hardships of transportation by supplementary punishments; a milder system of management may, *caeteris paribus* be adopted.' This was what Maconochie had realized when he first arrived there and had understood all along. Gipps was at last recognizing the special nature of Norfolk Island and that perhaps Maconochie's system had been right for it after all.

Gipps looked into how the 1,469 prisoners on the island at the time of his visit spent their day, how their labour was daily disposed of, and he concluded that a 'much larger quantity of productive labour ought to be, and must be, extracted from them'. As regards crime on the island – its alleged increase and the way it was said to go unpunished – Gipps was now 'happy to be able to express my persuasion that the reports which have reached Sydney, and which I especially alluded in my dispatch of the 15th August 1842 are much exaggerated. It is true that Captain Maconochie, during the last few months, has been more severe in his punishments than he previously had been, but the accounts which I have alluded to must, even in respect to the occurrences to which they related, have been, as far as I can judge, overcoloured.' He acknowledged that 'some crimes of magnitude have occurred, which perhaps scarcely would have been committed under the stricter rule of his predecessors; such as a robbery committed about a year ago on the Sabbath day, during the time of Divine Service, in the house of Dr. Reid (the Assistant Surgeon of the establishment). Another robbery in daylight in the house of the Superintendent of Agriculture (Mr. Pery) and an audacious robbery in Captain Maconochie's own house only a few nights before my arrival; but the perpetrators of all these offences were detected and punished.' The robbery at Government House had been carried out by four prisoners who had got out of the barracks by removing iron bars from the windows and had stolen silver plate, a loaded pistol and several bottles of spirits. After a thorough search the stolen property was later found buried under the sand on the beach. The four perpetrators were sentenced to twelve months in gaol and 300 lashes each. Overall Gipps felt that 'whatever increase of crime may have been occasioned by the additional facilities thus afforded for its commission has been, I am disposed to think, balanced by a diminution in other offences.' On balance, therefore, Gipps was voicing his approval of Maconochie's system.

As to the future of Norfolk Island, a matter of 'pressing importance', Gipps felt that 'one system of management only should be adopted on it, and not two, as has been the case for the last three years.' He went on: 'Whether Captain Maconochie's system shall further be tried or not is, of course, a question for the decision of Her Majesty's Government; and without either advocating or discouraging the further trial of it, I feel it right to say that I should regret to see the experience wholly thrown away which Captain Maconochie has, during the last three years, gained in the management of prisoners. He admits that in respect to the manner in which his principles should be applied, experience has taught him some useful lessons. He is fully aware of the necessity of a sterner and more severe application of his principles than any which he has yet attempted, and especially in the early or punitory stages of his system; and he fully also admits that in the distribution of marks (the great engine of his system) he has hitherto been too lavish.' Gipps concluded: 'He allows, however, that punishment, and punishment too of a severe nature, is a necessary part of convict discipline; and if this object be secured, as it might be, by the positive order of Government, I do not see that it matters much whether the punishment be inflicted theoretically as a terror to evil-doers, or, as Captain Maconochie would have it, as the first operation in the process of a cure, or on the principle (to use his own expression) that the amputating knife or actual cauter is used by the surgeon.' Here, at last perhaps, Gipps and Maconochie were concurring, each having moved in the other's direction. Gipps then addressed the question of whether Maconochie should continue in charge.

> From what I have stated in approbation of his management of the doubly convicted prisoners it may be gathered that I should not myself object to his continuing in charge of them, but I must submit that it should be on the express condition of his adhering implicitly to the instructions which he may from time to time receive from the Government of this Colony, so long as the prisoners under his charge are ultimately destined to return to New South Wales. This condition I consider to be (in justice to the Colony) an indispensable one. But, on the other hand, if Captain Maconochie be placed in charge of prisoners who are in no case to be sent or returned to

New South Wales, I should anxiously desire to see him relieved from any dependence on the Government of it.

This was the crux of the issue and its implied recommendation was that Maconochie should be given a free hand to run his system at a place of his choosing and with minimum government interference.

In ending his report, Gipps brought up the subject dearest to Whitehall hearts. 'It remains for me yet to say a few words respecting the expenses of the Island. I have already stated that they must be reduced; and should it be proposed to leave Captain Maconochie in charge of the Island, a reduction in the expense of it should be made an absolute condition of his remaining there. The obvious and only legitimate way in which the expenses can be lessened will be by increasing the produce of it; and this increase of produce must be looked for by the application of more labour to the soil, not by the trial of experiments founded on speculations and theories, experiments, that is to say, attended with a certain outlay, but of which the success, however sanguinely it may be counted, must be problematical.' Gipps was here on home ground. 'Captain Maconochie having been in command of the Island for three years, I have called for returns of the whole expenditure during the last six, so as to comprehend not only his own three years, but also the three last of management of his predecessors; and from the returns furnished to me by the officers of the Commissariat, the Ordnance, and the Engineer Departments, I have caused the accompanying general return to be complied. By this return it appears that the average expense of a convict at Norfolk Island during the first period of three years was £10. 18s. 4d. per annum, and during the last period of three years £13. 3s. 11d.; the increase being very nearly at the rate of twenty-one per cent.' The extra cost had been caused mainly by a recent severe drought. Expense was what Gipps concluded his report on, and expense was, as is often the case with marginal experiments, likely to be the determining factor in whether it was maintained or closed down. Imaginative

responses to intractable problems, such as Maconochie had produced on Norfolk Island, struggle to get their share of the public
purse.

Maconochie's own report for the year 1842, which he had
handed to Gipps when he arrived on the island, was extremely
long. When Gipps came to read through it in detail later on, he
commented: 'This report is as remarkable as any that have pre-
ceded it for the absence of that conciseness and compression of
thought which are usually held to be requisite in official correspondence.' This was the familiar complaint against Maconochie.
However, Gipps recognized the report contained many observations on the management of prisoners that were worthy of consideration. Maconochie had had a very difficult year in 1842: in
addition to the recent drought, which has raised expenditure, he
had had to deal with his own daughter's embarrassing behaviour.
Crime had also increased. No doubt the length and prolixity of
the report reflected these anxieties. But the second and third
years of any innovative experiment are always likely to be a
testing time, as the scheme comes under pressure from within.
This was when Maconochie needed most support, and it had not
always been forthcoming, either from the island or from Gipps
and Whitehall; hence the querulous tone of his report. His staff
often let him down, having been trained under a different
system, by which their characters, habits, and methods had been
formed. They were reluctant at their age to change. The military had always resented Maconochie's approach; they believed
in orders and uniformity and for them the idea of prisoners
learning to become individuals was anathema. Often they sought
to make life difficult for Maconochie. Whenever he wanted to
visit the prisoners' barracks at night, when they were in charge
they made sure that he had to pass through the military guard
post and sign the appropriate visitor's form before the keys were
found.

Maconochie felt vindicated by Gipps's comments in his report
on the 'old hands'. 'I am sincerely interested about these men,
many yet in the vigour of life. An effort to recover them seems

NEW SOUTH WALES.	NUMBER.	SENTENCE.	MARKS EARNED.	AMOUNT OF FINES.	PARTICULARS OF OFFENCES.
		Years.		*Marks.*	
	17 . - . . .	7	3,459	2,391	Fine.—For assault, 500 marks; careless field labour, 56 marks; share of fine for refusing to work, 10 marks; at Cascade without a pass, 100 marks; refusing to work, 200 marks; on his ward, for disorderly conduct, 25 marks; breaking out of barracks, 1,000 marks, and two months in gaol; breaking out of cells in mess-room, 500 marks, and two months in gaol.
	A scheming, troublesome Dublin tailor and thief; very bad lad.				
	18 . - . .	7	4,139	242	Fine.—For careless field labour, 68 marks; two fines for refusing to bathe, 24 marks; creating a disturbance in barrack, 50 marks; for fighting, 50 marks; on his ward, for disorderly conduct, 25 marks; refusing to work, and insolence to overseer, 25 marks, and one month in gaol.
	A violent, restless man, not so ill intentioned as conducted.				
	19 . - . .	7	3,408	2,154	Fine.—Careless field labour, 20 marks; on his ward, for stealing clothes, nine marks; on his ward, for disorderly conduct, 25 marks; for stealing a fellow prisoner's clothes, and selling them, 1,000 marks, and one month in gaol; using threatening language to Overseer Ford, 100 marks; breaking out of barracks, 1,000 marks, and two months in gaol.
	Companion to Patrick M'Loughlin (No. 17.) and much resembling him.				
	20 . - . .	7	6,537	850	Fine.—Suspicion of robbing Longridge stores, and drinking spirituous liquors, 500 marks, and one month in gaol; refusing to work, and insolence, 25 marks; stealing potatoes, 100 marks; disobedience of orders, 200 marks, and one month in gaol; on his ward, for the robbery of John Brooks, 25 marks.
	Began very well, and was policeman over the stores when they were robbed; since then has been very troublesome; at present a little better.				
	21 . - . .	7	2,201	1,418	Fine.—For careless field labour, 84 marks; on his ward, for stealing clothes, 9 marks; refusing to work, 25 marks; being absent in the bush, 300 marks, and three months in gaol; absent in bush five days, 1,000 marks, and five months in gaol.
	Has a passion for absenting himself in the bush; otherwise not bad.				
	22 . - . .	7	6,477	209	Fine.—For fighting (his own share), 100 marks; on his ward, for stealing clothes, 9 marks; breaking out of stockade, 25 marks; on his ward, for disorderly conduct, 25 marks; taking a sheaf of wheat, to make up his day's work, 50 marks; insubordination, and refusing to work, 14 days in gaol.
	Insubordinate; but recently much better.				
	23 . - . .	7	6,313	118	Fine.—For careless field labour, 84 marks; on his ward, for stealing clothes, 9 marks; on his ward, for disorderly conduct, 25 marks.
	Saucy; but also much better lately.				
	24 . - . .	7	3,546	1,000	Fine.—For unnatural crime, 1,000 marks, and twice 50 lashes inflicted.
	A poor lad, weak, and much ashamed.				

(signed)   A. MACONOCHIE.

Fines of marks

to me, in the circumstances, a public duty. From my experience
of them I am persuaded that, in the majority of cases, their
experience, hardihood of temper and constitution, greater
steadiness than is usually found among recent prisoners, and
general strong sense of kindness shown them, are all qualities

which made them receptive candidates for my system' – more so than the volatile new prisoners. This preference for reoffenders shows how deep-seated his interest in prison reform was, how much he wanted to change the way prison itself worked - the institution, as much as the individuals in it. Doubly convicted convicts were the most hardened criminals, the most institutionalized, and yet he had shown they could be reformed. The emphasis had to be on how prisoners managed their time and for that long sentences were detrimental. 'They dishearten men on their arrival in prison, and prevent their entering on their new tasks and duties with alacrity; they even give a wrong direction to their aspirations, and make them seek to accommodate themselves to bondage, and make themselves comfortable in that, instead of trying to struggle manfully through it.' Shorter sentences allowed a man to 'feel his fate always in his own hands; he has only to resolve, and keep his resolution, and he must soon be free; he is not discouraged even by partial failures; but, trying again and again, his character improving with every effort, he at length succeeds, and gets away an improved man'. This approach and his 'educational emphasis' would, he felt, convert prisons into 'theatres of preparation for the future', a contrast to the 'theatres of horror' that had been the spirit of transportation.

If his system was to be tried elsewhere, Maconochie suggested to Gipps that the Chatham Islands, east of New Zealand, could be tried. 'The principal Island, I am told, is about thirty miles long, and fifteen to twenty wide. It is well watered, fertile, and has several good harbours', and in keeping with an earlier idea of his 'a station there for building and repairing ships would greatly benefit British Trade in the Pacific, and would draw a good deal of money towards defraying the general expense. It would also strengthen British interests in New Zealand.'

Maconochie's approach showed how much he was imbued with a sense that he was on the side of progress and scientific advance and felt he was moving with the times. The age of reform, very much in the air in Britain, had not in his eyes reached Australia yet. His experience in the penal system there had convinced him that it needed to be brought up to date. The 'formerly vindictive and exemplary' penal treatment was no longer appropriate, or even necessary. 'That day is now everywhere passing away. Human Nature is becoming more studied, and with this also more respected.' This was the essence of the Associationist philosophy in which he believed: the causes of criminal behaviour could be found within the mind and heart of the offender. 'When we look at the birth and early training of most of these unhappy men, the necessary tendency of the circumstances connected with them, without much moral guilt in the several individuals, their claim consequently on our compassion as well as justice, the addition made to this claim by the undoubted fact that their unfavourable position is almost entirely caused by what constitutes otherwise our pride and glory, the wealth and advanced state of Society in our country, when all these are summed up, an active interest in their temporal and eternal welfare seems a debt rather than any less binding obligation.' This was his stance, his moral passion, and his 1842 report to Gipps reads like something of a *cri de coeur*. He must have known that matters were coming to a head and he was hoping now for a considerate audience. He had welcomed Gipps's unscheduled visit to Norfolk Island, with its favourable comments on his regime. It had come just in time, or so he thought.

13

Recall

GIPPS'S REPORT OF 1st April 1843 went back to London. While on the high seas it crossed with another ship in mid-ocean, bearing contrasting messages from Stanley in London. Stanley had decided to close Maconochie's regime down and to recall him to London. This was part of Stanley's plan to reorganize convict treatment in Australia and to turn Norfolk Island into an annexe of Van Diemen's Land. Stanley had informed Franklin of this in November 1842, but had interestingly failed to inform Gipps at the same time. The reasons are not clear – James Stephen claimed it was his fault. In fact, the ship bringing the news of Maconochie's dismissal and recall only arrived in Sydney in May 1843, more than a month after Gipps's visit to Norfolk Island.

Norfolk Island was to be returned to a harsh and disciplinarian regime. Major Childs of the Royal Marines, with a reputation for strictness gained in the Marine Corps, where men obeyed orders without question, was appointed as Maconochie's successor. Stanley's dispatch dealing with Maconochie's recall stated, 'it would be a source of the most sincere regret to me if the grounds of that decision should be misunderstood or represented in a sense unfavourable to that officer's character. For such a representation, there would not be any basis whatever in truth.' Stanley went on, 'from all the means of information within my reach I am happily able to ascribe to Captain Maconochie a most earnest solicitude for the welfare of a class of society, whose claims to compassion and benevolence have seldom been so keenly felt by persons in his station of life. From the same means of knowledge, I am able to give Captain Maconochie the fullest credit for having declined no fatigue, privation or responsibility, which was requisite for carrying into effect his views for the moral and physical improvement of the convicts at Norfolk Island.' This has clear echoes of Stephen's orotund style. 'In estimating the success of his endeavours, I do not forget that the scene of action assigned to him was not that he would himself have chosen, and was not exempt from some peculiar disadvantages which might have been avoided in a more favourable situation. Neither am I at all disposed to depreciate the results of his experiment for improving the character and the condition of the convicts under his charge. On the contrary, I gladly acknowledge that his efforts appear to have been rewarded by the decline of crimes of violence and outrage, and by the growth of humane and kindly feelings in the minds of the persons under his care.' This was seeming praise, but more likely was simply a *post hoc* rationalization for a decision already taken.

Stanley's dispatch listed some of the reasons for the change and left no room for doubt that the cumulative effect of Gipps's previous unfavourable dispatches had made their mark. Stanley referred to the absence of 'wholesome and invigorating influence of a firm and resolute discipline' on Norfolk Island, and to the extra expense, 'a minor but still a very serious evil'; he also highlighted the reported increase of 'unnatural' crime. Stanley wrote: 'Crimes, unattended with violence ... appear, unhappily, to have been on the increase ... I find no proof ... of that renovation of Religious and Moral character which was promised ... On the contrary, I find that ministers of Religion who have resorted to that place, have brought from it most unfavourable impressions on this subject.' This must have referred to McEnroe's letters, which by now had reached Stanley.

In addition, the earlier complaints of the Commissariat Officer there, Smith, must have been noted, as the Treasury was responsible for commissariat expenditure on Norfolk Island. It looked as if the sacrifice of Maconochie represented a welcome gesture by one government department to another, the Colonial Office to the Treasury. This letter of January 1843, sent by C.E. Trevelyan from the Treasury to James Stephen, seems to bear this out:

> With reference to your letter dated the 29th ultimo, I am commanded by the Lords Commissioners of Her Majesty's Treasury to transmit to you the accompanying letter and its enclosures from the Commissariat Officer in charge in New South Wales respecting certain measures adopted by Captain Maconochie at Norfolk Island, and I am to request that you will call Lord Stanley's attention to the circumstance of Captain Maconochie's having appropriated to the use of the convicts to whom he had granted Tickets of Leave a large portion of the produce of the public farm in Norfolk Island, without having previously accounted for the same to the Commissariat Officer in charge of the Military and Convict Stores. Their Lordships suggest that proper notice should be taken of this irregularity on the part of the Superintendent, and that he should be required, in accordance with the regulations which have been established for the management of the convict expenditure, to deliver into the public stores under the charge of the Commissariat the produce of every description which may be grown on the Government farms, and to obtain, by requisitions made in the usual way.

We can sense how irksome Treasury officials found Maconochie's high-handed methods. John Montagu, Maconochie's erstwhile arch-enemy, was in London at this time, advising Stanley on Van Diemen's Land; no doubt he had heard about the events on Norfolk Island and had stood out against Maconochie as well.

Gipps's favourable report on Norfolk Island arrived in London on 28th August 1843, too late to change Stanley's mind. Gipps commented: 'Although this report places Captain Maconochie's administration of his functions as Superintendent at Norfolk Island in a more favourable light than that in which I had hitherto received it, it does not alter but rather confirms my opinion of the necessity for the measures Her Majesty's Government have adopted with reference to the treatment of convicts at that settlement.' Childs's regime was told to follow 'the universal and inflexible rule that every man capable of bodily labour must be constrained to the steady performance of it. Compulsory and unrequited toil must be the rule.' The emphasis was to be on 'cleanliness, sobriety and decency', leading to 'the prevention of moral evils of another Class', the dread of homosexuality again. 'Nothing but constant vigilance and inflexible rigour in enforcing the appropriate Punishments will be sufficient to restrain the immoralities to which I refer.' As regards Gipps's report, all Stanley could say was that 'the experience derived from your recent visit to Norfolk Island will enable you to give the fullest instructions to Major Childs, who proceeds by the ship which carries this despatch'. It was an abrupt and less than generous conclusion to Maconochie's work on Norfolk Island.

Maconochie made his own dignified and closely argued rejoinder to Gipps's Norfolk Island report of 1st April 1843. Maconochie felt a 'few inaccuracies of statement' had crept into it, probably owing to the 'hurried nature of your Excellency's visit'. He explained that his first stage of punitive treatment for his 'new' prisoners had not been enforced as this would simply have meant the 'continuance of the old system' and he had been 'expressly sent' to try out a new one. As regards the vexed problem of 'unnatural offences':

> I think that the statements made to your Excellency regarding the prevalence of unnatural offences among the English prisoners are much exaggerated. I have been at some pains since receiving your letter in making exact inquiries on the subject and I find nine cases, or about one in sixty-five, of direct convictions, not of the act, but of circumstances necessarily inferring it; and nearly as many more in which the suspicion against individuals, though they have not yet been tried, is so strong as to amount perhaps to moral conviction in my own mind; the two together make almost one in thirty-three. No man died of the consequences of such bestiality but one man, otherwise very ill of Dysentery, was so affected by remorse at having

lent himself to it, that the Surgeon attributed his death, though not exclusively, yet very much to his consequent agitation.

Maconochie reviewed his stay on the island. 'When I first came on the Island I was indulgent. I interested the more sensible of the men themselves in my purpose and I had the whole benefit of their influence in turn with their companions. Even that personal character in me which your Excellency thinks opposed to my success has, in truth, aided me much in this respect, for my confidence in the capabilities of Human Nature (which, however, you somewhat overrate), inspired confidence and men long without hope of recovering themselves, and thus without making any effort to do so, became anxious and active on this head, when they saw me persuaded of the possibility of their success.' Lately he had been 'compelled progressively to revert to physical restraints, irons and the lash,' but 'still the same principle both guided and supported me' and this had retained 'the affections and co-operation of all the more manly and consequently valuable men'. His consistency had paid off, he felt, and he could see the effects of it in most of the convicts. Now he looked forward to the day when 'moral hospitals are regarded as medical ones are', anticipating that eventual combination of services brought about once psychiatry was introduced into hospital and prison treatment. He foresaw then that 'one of the most sacred moral obligations, the endeavour to recover fallen criminals will be fully and systematically discharged'. This had been his aim throughout.

With all the uncertainty surrounding Norfolk Island, morale began slipping towards the end of 1843. Escape attempts were made. A cave was found where boat-building was going on – eighteen new wattle hammocks and a quantity of pitch, nails and cordage had been stolen for this purpose and three men were apprehended and put in irons for three months. Then in December 1843, just after midnight, three soldiers on guard duty near the landing pier deserted their posts and joined six convicts, who were ready and waiting to escape from the island in a whale boat. Despite being shot at by other soldiers on shore, they all got away under cover of darkness and were seen next evening at sunset from Mount Pitt on the distant horizon, too far away to give pursuit. The escapees came from widely differing backgrounds: James Moore was an 'intelligent man formerly on board a man of war and supposed to understand navigation', Sean McBarrie, an accountant, Thomas Sullivan, a carpenter, James Hickey, another carpenter, and Cornelius O'Brien and John Cunningham were seamen. In November there had also been a convict murder on the island committed by Francis McManus, who was later found insane. This was the second convict murder during Maconochie's time: the first was that of Patrick Lynch, who had himself tried to escape in a packing case on the government brig in 1842, and was then stabbed a few months later by Stephen Brennan after what Maconochie termed a 'frivolous altercation'. Lynch's gravestone is in the cemetery on Norfolk Island. Maconochie always honoured the dead, irrespective of why they had been sent to the island, and felt every prisoner deserved his proper burial and suitable memorial. That is why the cemetery is now full of convict graves, even those of the rebellious 1842 mutineers on the *Governor Phillip*, such as that of Bartholomew Kelly, with its piratical skull and crossbones at the base.

Childs arrived on Norfolk Island on 7th February 1844 on the convict ship *Maitland*, with 194 prisoners from England (four had died on the journey and one had been put inside the lunatic asylum in Sydney). Maconochie greeted him and handed him a list of prisoners, 538 in all, who were due to be transferred to Van Diemen's Land as ticket-of-leave men. Stanley had authorized him to do this. During his four years on the island Maconochie had discharged 920 'old hands' to Sydney. They all did well, for by July 1845 not more than twenty of them had come into conflict with the law, less than two per cent. With those who went to Van Diemen's Land, a year later only three per cent were 'under punishment' – in other words, had committed offences. This was despite the hostility they met in Van

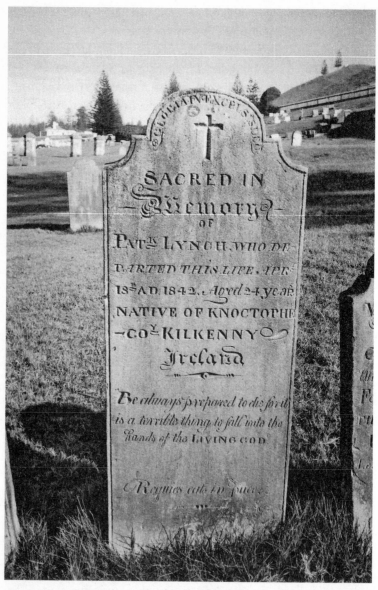

The gravestone of Patrick Lynch, stabbed to death by a fellow-convict

The gravestone of Bartholomew Kelly, transported from Ireland aged twelve and killed during the *Governor Phillip* mutiny, aged twenty-six

Diemen's Land, where serious unemployment prevailed and crimes of violence were frequent. Captain Innes, the officer in charge of the detention centre at Cockatoo Island, verified how few of his inmates were Maconochie's men. 'I have now the control of Cockatoo, every man who has been re-transported passes through my hands, and I have been quite astonished to see so few men from Norfolk Island come back who have once gone into the country.'

Maconochie accompanied this batch of ticket-of-leave men to Hobart on the *Maitland*. His family, including his daughter Catherine and her husband, Captain Hill, went with them as well. He left behind on Norfolk Island many who regretted his going. One of these was the ex-convict Principal Overseer Aaron Price.

Capt. and Mrs. Maconochie were much regretted by all. While governing the island he strove to work a reformation in the prisoner by gentle and humane treatment but it is to be regretted that many imposed upon his kindness and bid defiance to all the social and moral rules he tried to inculcate. He had remained on the island for a considerable time without inflicting corporal punishment begging and praying the men to reform but ... he is now gone and they are left to lament his loss. During his stay on the island he endeavoured to make all the free population comfortable by building houses for their residences which greatly improved the island, he created a new Protestant church, a Roman Catholic chapel and made many other improvements. To take the general character of Captain Maconochie, he was a great politician, slow to anger and merciful.

It was a fitting tribute from an ex-convict who had been on the island for twenty years.

14

Back in Britain

THE FOUNDING MYTH of Australia was one of exploitation and depredation. It created an absence of easy intercourse between opposing groups. The Aborigines suffered most from this, but even Europeans tended to live disputative relationships with each other, as Gipps found when he first arrived. The penal system became a receptacle for this and for the guilt and anxiety emanating from that founding myth.

Those at the helm of the convict system became victims as well. Maconochie stood out, in some respects, as the exception. His aim had always been to be in harmony with his surroundings, *travailler avec la nature*. He had used this phrase from Bernardin de St Pierre in his 'Observations on the Treatment of Aborigines in New Holland', written in 1837. There he had advocated using Aborigines for their native skills rather than trying to mould them into Europeans, working with nature rather than against it. By the time he left, he was still optimistic. Gipps, on the other hand, was a broken man after his eight years of office. About to leave New South Wales in 1846, two years after Maconochie, his health was ruined and he wrote 'I cannot even get up the long staircase in the house without making a halt on the way'. The constant struggle with powerful local interests and the need to placate London had drained and exhausted him. He went back to Britain, where Lady Franklin met him: 'Poor Sir Geo. Gipps. I saw him after his arrival in town – such a sad wreck – he has been a martyr to his work.' He died within a year of his return before he had any chance of taking up the easy military command that was his due.

Franklin suffered just as badly. He was sacked by Stanley in 1843, and read of his dismissal in the London *Times* some time before the official notification arrived in Hobart. In fact, it came just four days before his successor, Sir John Eardley-Wilmot, landed there by ship. John Montagu had been machinating in London behind the scenes to procure his dismissal as well. The London government's grasp of local affairs was invariably wanting. 'Except among a minority of zealots or visionaries, British imperialism was never its own cause. Parliament, always the supreme arbiter of the Empire, was seldom altogether seduced by the imperial idea, so that public money was begrudgingly spent, and every excess was questioned,' as Jan Morris has written in her book on the British empire. So far as Australia was concerned, the London government claimed a willingness to delegate but in the end always retained a controlling hand. In Maconochie's case they had wanted him to provide a quick replacement for an earlier system that had failed and had sent him across to Norfolk Island accordingly, but they got cold feet as soon as he started introducing genuine innovations. Deep down, London never let go of the view that criminals were there to be punished, that societal revenge mattered more than reform.

Maconochie's views on criminality had actually developed out of what he saw, the evidence of his own eyes when he first arrived in Van Diemen's Land. He realized that the propensity to crime came from many sources, that not all people who became convicts were irredeemable – though he always acknowledged that a small percentage were – and that, given a different approach, many could be turned round into worthwhile members of society. But for his system to work fully and properly, he needed consistent support and a relatively free hand. This was never granted. The powers in London refused to commit themselves, a reflection of how little the government sought to understand what was actually going on in Australia. They halfheartedly delegated authority to Gipps, but he never quite knew where he stood. Crime stirred then, as it still stirs today, deep emotions. For London, reform itself was a threat since too many reformed criminals might imply that there was no such thing as a criminal class, that crime itself was mostly circumstantial, and that the prevailing ideology of a justifiable hierarchical class system needed to be revised. This was much too dangerous a concept to be entertained.

Eardley-Wilmot ended just as badly as his predecessor. He was suddenly recalled – unjustly, as he thought – in October 1846 by the new Colonial Secretary, Gladstone. He died in Van Diemen's Land within a week of the arrival of his successor, another broken and disheartened man. Australia was certainly taking its toll of its leading colonial administrators.

After leaving Norfolk Island in February 1844, Maconochie was back in Britain in August that year. He went to see the Colonial Office, hoping to get official approval to continue his system elsewhere, perhaps on the Chatham Islands, as he had suggested to Gipps. James Stephen met him, but immediately spurned his efforts. He told Stanley: 'Captain Maconochie has not much that is really important to urge ... I ought to say that he does not scruple to propound the seeming paradox that the object of punishment is not only mis-stated when it is spoken of as designed to produce a wholesome terror, but that the production of terror in the minds of those who meditate crime is not even desirable, or if desirable is not practicable, so that it is to be laid out of account altogether.' Stephen went on: 'I should expect very little real aid in the practical business of life from any man who proposes to conduct it by setting at defiance what all other men consider as an elementary truth.' It shows how little Stephen had learnt of the Norfolk Island experience or appreciated its value for penal policy. Clearly Gipps's favourable view of Maconochie's regime in his April 1843 report had made no impact on him either. The same old ideas were being trotted out. Maconochie had stated all along that it was not the fear of punishment, or of its 'wholesome terror', that prevented convicts from committing crimes, but the fear of detection, and his experience on Norfolk Island had borne his ideas out.

Despite these reversals, Maconochie continued to promote his system though meeting influential people and through a series of letters and pamphlets to prominent reforming figures such as Lord Brougham and Edwin Chadwick. He tried another visit to the Colonial Office in December, but Stephen was even more acerbic this time. 'It is a great pity that so much energy should be consumed in so much ill-timed and superficial preaching – for it is little else.' The door had now been firmly closed and Maconochie's hopes of a further overseas appointment receded. On his way back by ship Maconochie had completed a valuable and thoroughly statistical study of his time on Norfolk Island, entitled 'Criminal Statistics and Movement of the Bond Population of Norfolk Island to December 1843', published in the *Journal of the Statistical Society* in March 1845. Once settled again in London, books and pamphlets began to pour forth from him. His most important work, *Crime and Punishment: The Mark System, framed to mix Persuasion with Punishment, and Make their Effect Improving, yet their Operation severe*, came out in 1846 with its detailed explanation of the mark system and its central principle that 'our penal apparatus is nearly all retrospective, framed to punish the past, not guard against the future', words that were to make it recognized in time as one of the classic reforming texts of modern penology. His own detailed personal account of *Norfolk Island* ('I sought generally by every means to recover the men's self-respect, to gain their wills towards their reform, to visit moral offences severely ...') appeared in 1847.

Maconochie's circle of friends and supporters widened. He came across Charles Dickens early in 1846, when both attended a meeting of the Ragged School Movement. Dickens then invited Maconochie to dinner a week later at 1 Devonshire Terrace – 'Can you give me the pleasure of dining here next Saturday at 6 o'clock?' The other guests were Dickens's friends Augustus Tracey, Governor of Tothill Fields Prison, and George Chesterton, Governor of the Middlesex House of Correction, described to Maconochie by Dickens as 'a very intelligent and humane gentleman, who has great experience of Criminals, and whom I have frequently consulted in reference to their condition and improvement. It happened the other evening, when I met him somewhere at dinner, that he spoke with great interest of your system (which he had been studying in your explanation of it) and shewed that he quite understood and appreciated the principles on which it was founded. As he expressed, also, a desire to know you and to have an opportunity of conversing with you about it, I said I would endeavour to give him that opportunity.' Another guest was C.E. Cottrell, to whom Dickens described Maconochie as the 'inventor of a very remarkable system indeed, of Secondary Punishment: which I have no doubt will, in some modified form or other, become as the World grows better and more compassionate, very generally received'.

Dickens had always been interested in penal issues, ever since the time of his father's stay in Marshalsea debtors' prison. In 1842 he had visited the Eastern Penitentiary at Philadelphia and written: 'I believe that very few men are capable of estimating the immense amount of torture and agony which this dreadful punishment, prolonged for years, inflicts ... There is a depth of terrible endurance in it which none but the sufferers can fathom. I hold this slow and daily tampering with the mysteries of the brain to be immeasurably worse than any torture of the body; and because its ghastly signs and tokens are not so palpable to the eye and sense of touch as scars upon the flesh; because its wounds are not upon the surface ... therefore the more I denounce it, as a secret punishment which slumbering humanity is not roused up to stay.' Like Maconochie, Dickens favoured innovation. 'Let anything with a ray of hope in it be tried', anything that would raise up 'the prostrate portion of the people of this country'. Maconochie's system appealed to him because reform came about 'through the medium of a well-arranged adversity'. People would have to work to get better.

Dickens incorporated Maconochie's mark system into the running of Urania Cottage, the 'Home for Homeless Women'

Charles Dickens

he set up in 1847 with Angela Burdett-Coutts in Lime Grove, Shepherd's Bush. It was named after Aphrodite Urania, the pure goddess of love. Its method of operation was based on Maconochie, as Dickens explained: 'I do not know of any plan, so well conceived, or so firmly grounded in a knowledge of human nature, or so judiciously addressed to it, for observance in this place, as what is called Captain Maconnochie's [*sic*] Mark System.' The girls were to be 'tempted to virtue', not 'dragged, driven, or frightened'. It would pursue, as Maconochie had done on Norfolk Island, a two-stage process. 'I would divide the interior into two portions; and into the first portion I would put all new-comers without exception, as a place of probation, whence they should pass, by their own good-conduct and self-denial alone, into what I may call the Society of the house.'

His version of the 'mark table' used at the home was to have 'as few heads as possible, in order that it may be rendered the plainer to the comprehension of the young women themselves'. Every girl was required to keep a duplicate copy of her daily mark-paper. This had a dual function. 'Besides the probability of its producing some moral effect upon her, it would be a lesson in arithmetic in which she could not fail to have a personal interest.' Girls could earn up to four marks a day under nine separate headings – for truthfulness, industry, temper, propriety of conduct and conversation, order, punctuality, economy, cleanliness and temperance (in the larger meaning of 'moderation, patience, calmness'). Dickens gave an example: 'Supposing such a case as once occurred with Emma Lea, when she called another girl by opprobrious names, and threatened her, and was otherwise violent and defiant. Such an extreme case would involve, under this table, a bad mark for "temper", a bad mark for "propriety of deportment", a bad mark for "propriety of language", and a bad mark for "improvement" – every one of which, I would certainly have entered.' Conduct of a 'particularly objectionable' kind meant a bad mark in red ink which lost the culprit forty good ones. The girls seemed to enjoy the competitive aspects of this system.

During its first six years Urania Cottage took in a variety of 'fallen women'. Dickens listed them: 'starving needlewomen of good character, poor needlewomen who have robbed their furnished lodgings, violent girls committed to prison for disturbances in ill-conducted workhouses, poor girls from Ragged Schools, destitute girls who have applied at Police Offices for relief, young women from the streets: young women of the same class taken from the prisons after undergoing punishment there as disorderly characters, or for shoplifting, or for thefts from the person, domestic servants who have been seduced, and two young women held to bail for attempting suicide.' Of the fifty-six inmates aged between fourteen and twenty-six who attended the home between 1847 and 1853, seven left of their own accord, ten were expelled for incorrigible misconduct (Dickens referred to one, Sesina, as being able to 'corrupt a Nunnery in a fortnight') and seven ran away. Those who passed through successfully emigrated to South Australia to make a fresh start, another Maconochie idea. They travelled in steerage ('less exposed to temptation', as Dickens put it) and their passage was paid for by Miss Burdett-Coutts at £12 per head. Three relapsed on the voyage out, but the rest did well and settled in Australia.

Education mattered as much to Dickens as it did to Maconochie. Dickens recognized the close connection between lack of education and crime. 'Side by side with Crime, Disease, and Misery in England, Ignorance is always brooding', as he wrote in an article in *The Examiner* in 1848. At Urania readings from Wordsworth and Crabbe were given and a piano was brought in; Dickens even persuaded his old friend John Hullah to give singing lessons. Over time Dickens's enthusiasm for penal reform went up and down, as it did in other areas. By May 1848 he was writing to Burdett-Coutts, 'Maconnochie has sent me a kind of protocol concerning such Institutions, which seems to me to be wrong from beginning to end. I will make my notes upon it, and shew it you. His head seems to be so full of the Mark System, that he has not room to turn another idea in it.' But their friendship stayed the course and the mark table remained in use at Urania Cottage throughout its existence.

From 1844 reports were beginning to come back to London of what was happening on Norfolk Island after Maconochie's departure. They were dire. Childs's regime, for all its harsh and disciplinarian intentions, had resulted in a mutiny in July 1846 that had led to twenty-two deaths. Homosexuality went on regardless. John Price, who succeeded Childs as Commandant shortly after the mutiny and ran an even more repressive regime, wrote: 'I learnt that those who pandered to their passions were paid in tobacco, extra provisions, fancy articles made for them and any indulgence they could obtain to induce them to yield to their brutal desires. That by their being deprived of their cooking utensils they would have been unable to prepare the food they might surreptitiously obtain for the objects of their lusts, and that this aroused their savage and ferocious passions to a pitch of madness.' Homosexuality had been a contributing factor to the mutiny. Revd Naylor, still on the island, witnessed these horrendous goings-on and still regretted Maconochie's departure: 'Nothing like his administration there has before or since worked so much good. As Pastor of the Island, and for two years a magistrate, I can prove that at no period was there so little crime or anything like the tone of improved feeling which characterized the period of his residence there.' Now looking back at Maconochie's time and the 'insurmountable difficulties thrown in his way', Naylor was 'astonished that he did anything' and added that he never met a prisoner 'who does not confirm my conviction of the improving tendencies of the efforts he made'.

Books appeared that endorsed Maconochie's approach. In 1847 *Settlers and Convicts*, by an 'an Emigrant Mechanic' (actually Alexander Harris), was published, dedicated 'To Captain Maconochie, R.N., K.H., in testimony of the soundness of the principles he has endeavoured to introduce into penal discipline'. The author continued: 'Captain Maconochie did more for the reformation of these unhappy wretches and in amelioration of their physical circumstances than the most sanguine practical mind could beforehand have ventured even to hope. It is greatly to be regretted that his views were not carried out to their fullest extent, in the most cordial spirit. My knowledge of the convict's character warrants my saying expressly that they offer the only approximation that has ever yet been made to a correct penal theory.' Maconochie received many letters, and manuscript offerings, from his ex-convicts (he tried to get Thomas Cook's manuscript published). A letter from an ex-convict in Australia stated that the conduct of his Norfolk Island men had been 'most exemplary' and that 'with scarcely an exception the whole are doing well, and some are in a respectable way of business, advancing fast to prosperity. They are a credit to the name they commonly bear of Captain Maconochie's men.' It was true, the phrase 'one of Maconochie's men' had begun to be known in Australia as emblematic of an ex-convict of high standing.

Maconochie himself appeared before a House of Lords select committee in March 1847 and gave a succinct summary of his system under persistent questioning from parliamentarians.

[16 March 1847]
Captain ALEXANDER MACONOCHIE, R.N., is called in, and examined as follows:
768. YOU are a Captain in the Royal Navy?
Yes.
769. Have you been employed by Government in superintending any of the penal Colonies?
I superintended Norfolk Island during Four Years.
770. When did you leave that Island?
In February 1844.
771. In the course of that Time how many Convicts had you under your Superintendence?
From Fifteen hundred to Two thousand the whole Time.
★ ★ ★
782. Were the Convicts under your Superintendence sent out for very different Offences?
Yes; I had Two Classes. I had second convicted Men from the Colonies, and first convicted Men from England.

783. Were they generally transported for the graver Offences?
Yes, chiefly so.

784. Which was the more numerous Class?

The doubly convicted were more numerous, nearly Two to One; there were from Twelve to Fourteen Hundred of those doubly convicted, and Five to Six Hundred of first convicted.

820. What was the longest Period for which any of those persons were sentenced to Banishment to Norfolk Island?
Many of them for Life.

821. What did you find to be the best Mode of dealing with those unfortunate Persons in order to reclaim them?
I found my own System worked perfectly well.

822. Will you describe that System to their Lordships?

According to the Sentence with which each Man came to the Island he was put down at 6,000, 8,000, or 10,000 Marks. Those Marks were not a Coin of any Description, but were represented by Figures in our Books. I gave to them daily Wages according to the Work they performed.

823. Before your Plan was commenced they were accustomed to work without any Wages at all?

Yes; and according to my Plan their Wages were only Marks. I consulted with the Officer of the Commissariat as to the Expense of their regular Rations, and he said it was about Eight-pence a Day. I therefore allowed them Eight Marks a Day in Commutation for their Ration, with Permission to exchange those Marks for Stores in any Manner they pleased. They were not consequently compelled to eat the regular Allowance of Salt Meat, which they disliked very much; but they got more Meal and occasionally a little Wheatenmeal. The Consequence was that they felt the Burden of their own Maintenance. A Part of my Plan as, I think unfortunately, not carried out; namely, that the Residue of the Marks which they did not expend amounting to a certain Number should purchase them their Liberation, and that they should be transferred from Norfolk Island, which was a strictly penal Settlement, to New South Wales or Van Diemen's Land, which was not so; and I am sure that if the Marks had ever had a specific Value towards their Liberation, if it had been once said to them "so soon as you have accumulated 6,000 or 8,000, or 10,000 Marks you will certainly be removed from the Island," from my Experience there I am certain that they would have done any thing for the Accomplishment of that Object. There is no Degree of Exertion they would not have made, and no Degree of Self-command which they would not have evinced for the Purpose of procuring their Liberty. The Marks never had that Value. They had an exchangable Value to the limited Extent at the Stores, but they had no prospective Value, no Value giving them any Power tending to effect their Removal from the penal Settlement to a Colony.

824. You do not consider that your System was carried completely into effect?

It was not, certainly; but still its Principles were so sound, and so much in accordance with Human Nature, that the Effect of it practically was to reduce the Number of local Offences to an extraordinary Degree.

While in London Maconochie resumed his friendship with Lady Franklin. Sir John, distraught after his experiences in Van Diemen's Land, had tried to reassert himself in the way he knew best, by taking on a new naval command. He set off in charge of another expedition to search for the North-West Passage. By now he was fifty-nine, too old perhaps to go to such remote areas. By 1847, two years later, no news had come back of his ship, the *Erebus*, and Lady Franklin was getting worried. She urged the Admiralty to mount a search party. Maconochie helped her, as she mentioned in a letter to her sister saying how grateful she was for 'the cordial assistance of Alexander Maconochie, whose continuing efforts for prison reform had inured him to struggles with officialdom, and who, despite the past, was deeply concerned for his old chief's safety'. Franklin did eventually find the North-West Passage, but his ship remained set fast in the frozen Arctic ice for two long winters and he died on board in June 1847, buried by his ship's crew in a nearby crack in the ice hewn out by crowbars. The crew all eventually perished as well. They had given out brass naval buttons to local Inuit, asking them to wear them on their sealskins in case they met anyone who would then know they knew the whereabouts of Franklin's ship.

The search for Franklin: the Arctic Council meets in 1851. Back is on the far left, Beaufort is seated in centre. Franklin and Barrow are portrayed on the wall.

Maconochie's system was tried and put into practice successfully in Ireland under Sir Walter Crofton, chairman of the Irish Convict Prisons Board. It was tried too at Birmingham's new prison between 1849 and 1851, when Maconochie became governor there through the influence of a friend, Matthew Hill, who persuaded the local authorities to appoint him. But he was up against insuperable odds this time: public opinion was against him and he was badly let down by his deputy governor, a naval officer called William Austin, who was both subversive and sadistic. Austin was subsequently prosecuted for causing the unnecessary death of a seventeen-year-old prisoner. Maconochie's stay as governor lasted for only two years.

Maconochie never lost his belief in the rightness of his views. In 1857, aged seventy, he appeared again before a further House of Lords select committee. A committee member asked him about reforming criminals and Maconochie replied: 'My experience leads me to say that there is no man utterly incorrigible. Treat him as a man, and not as a dog. You cannot recover a man except by doing justice to the manly qualities which he may have about him, and giving him an interest in developing them.' It proved to be his swan-song. A contemporary writer described his 'snowy white' hair and his 'singularly buoyant and sanguine disposition' and noted that his bearing combined 'the frank cordiality of a sailor with the refinement and courtesy of high breeding and the nobler attributes of a sincere Christian'. He went on: 'It was his genuineness of character, his entire forgetfulness of self, his gentleness of manner – the overflow of a loving heart – which, combined with great mental powers and earnest piety, gave Captain Maconochie that marvellous ascendancy over the most abandoned of men which the narratives of his residence at Norfolk Island reveal.'

Maconochie died in 1860, and his wife, Mary, followed him in 1869. Two of their children predeceased them: Francis, their youngest son, died at Balaclava in the Crimea in 1854, and Mary Ann, their eldest daughter, who had had to leave Norfolk Island so hurriedly, died in May 1855 of Bright's disease, aged thirty-two and unmarried. She had helped her father to the end with his correspondence – indeed, many of his letters are written in her elegant hand.

British penal history is mostly a chronicle of concessionary moves, usually made after the event and out of expediency. Examples of forward-looking innovation are few. Norfolk Island under Maconochie was one exception. Churchill once said you could tell how civilized a country was by the way it treated its criminals. Maconochie showed a way of doing this that addressed the core issues of re-establishing convicts' self-respect after a punitive stage and enabling them to participate in their own futures by taking charge of their lives again. It called for imagination and courage to attempt this, and Maconochie's experiment can hold important lessons for us today.

Epilogue

ONE HUNDRED AND twenty-five years after the close of Maconochie's experiment, I found myself putting similar ideas into practice at Peper Harow. We followed Maconochie's principle of using the material we had in a more constructive way. Education was a cornerstone of this and I was put in charge of it. Most of the adolescents at Peper Harow had missed out on schooling either through truanting or delinquency. Initially I halted all compulsory education to wait and see what happened. After a while a fifteen-year-old started talking to me about the myths of Greece and Rome which he had read about in a Ladybird book at a remand centre. I took him up on this and handed him a copy of Homer's *Odyssey* in translation. We began to read this out aloud as Homer intended – 'rosy-fingered dawn' was a phrase he particularly enjoyed. Word got round of his interest and others joined in, and so we formed a group to read Homer, and then plays by Sophocles and Aeschylus. These 'tragedies' presented few problems to this group as they could readily draw on their own experiences to understand them. I then put the group in for an AO-level examination on Greek Literature in Translation, their first-ever examination. They passed, and then moved on to further education.

I mention this as an example of an imaginative approach along the lines Maconochie envisaged. Yet for all this, Peper Harow was a demanding regime, which the adolescents there described as tougher than punishment. They had to be fully accountable for their actions at daily community meetings and to be aware of the effects of their behaviour on others, of the pain they caused. Maconochie, too, felt results were best achieved through the 'medium of a well-tempered adversity', and his recommendation of a combination of punishment and reform, using incentives and education as benchmarks, could still point the way ahead for penal treatment.

Sources and Acknowledgements

The most useful and influential books for me have been the Hon. Mr Justice John Vincent Barry's *Alexander Maconochie of Norfolk Island: A Study of a Pioneer in Penal Reform* (Oxford University Press, Melbourne, 1958) and Robert Hughes's *The Fatal Shore: A History of the Transportation of Convicts to Australia, 1787–1868* (Collins Harvill, London, 1987).

CHAPTER 1: VOYAGE OUT

Details of Maconochie's life have come from the article by his great-grandson Kenneth Maconochie 'Captain Alexander Maconochie, R.N. K.H.', in the *Howard Journal* (vol. IX, no. 4, 1957) and from my discussions with Kenneth's son Michael and with Anne Langlands, his cousin. Maconochie wrote an incomplete account of his life for *Our Exemplars, Poor and Rich, or Biographical Sketches of Men and Women who have, by an extraordinary use of their opportunities, Benefited their Fellow Creatures* (London, 1861), edited by his friend Matthew Davenport Hill. The quotation 'Men that emigrate' comes from W. H. Leigh, *Reconnoitering Voyages and Travels with Adventures in the new colonies of South Australia . . . during the Years 1836, 1837, 1838* (London, 1839). The account of the storm in December 1811 is taken from Terence Grocott, *Shipwrecks of the Revolutionary and Napoleonic Era* (Chatham Publishing, London, 1997). For Maconochie's time at the Royal Geographical Society see the society's library files and R.G. Ward's 'Captain A. Maconochie', in the *Geographical Journal* (London, 1960).

CHAPTER 2: TRANSPORTATION

For this chapter I have drawn on Hughes (see above), *The Australia Encyclopedia*, (10 vols., Sydney, 1958), L.L. Robson, *The Convict Settlers of Australia: An Enquiry into the Origin and Character of the Convicts transported to New South Wales and van Diemen's Land, 1787–1852* (Melbourne, 1965), A.G.L.

Shaw, *Convicts and the Colonies: A Study of Penal Transportation from Great Britain and Ireland to Australia and other parts of the British Empire* (London, 1966) and L. Evans and P. Nicholls, *Convicts and Colonial Society, 1788–1853* (Melbourne, 1976). The Mary Carpenter story comes from Jo Manton, *Mary Carpenter and the Children of the Streets* (London, 1976). For information on convict ships, the best source is Charles Bateson, *The Convict Ships, 1787-1868* (Glasgow, 1969). The Cunningham material comes from Peter Cunningham, Surgeon R.N., *Two Years in New South Wales: A Series of Letters comprising Sketches of the Actual State of Society in that colony; of its peculiar advantages to emigrants; of its topography, natural history* (2 vols., London, 1827).

CHAPTER 3: CONVICT LIFE

The Backhouse quote is from James Backhouse, *A Narrative of a Visit to the Australian Colonies* (London, 1843). The Mayhew references are from Henry Mayhew, *London Labour and the London Poor*, vol. 3 (London, 1865). For the spread of Evangelicalism and Associationism see William James Forsythe, *The Reform of Prisoners, 1830–1900* (London, 1987). Ullathorne's visit to the Molesworth Committee and other Ullathorne items are recounted in his *Autobiography* (London, 1891).

CHAPTER 4: BOUND FOR AUSTRALIA

Excerpts here and later from Lady Franklin's diary and letters and from Sir John Franklin's letters are drawn both from George Mackaness, *Some Private Correspondence of Sir John and Lady Franklin, Parts I and II* (privately printed, Sydney, 1947), and from the Lefroy Bequest at the Scott Polar Research Institute, Cambridge. Franklin's time in Van Diemen's Land is well described by Kathleen Fitzpatrick, *Sir John Franklin in Tasmania, 1837–1843* (Melbourne, 1949) and Lady Franklin's by Frances Woodward, *Portrait of Jane: A Life of Lady Franklin* (London, 1951). The young Hentys are covered in Marnie Bassett, *The Hentys: An Australian Colonial Tapestry* (London, 1954). Van Diemen's Land material comes from L.L. Robson, *A History of Tasmania*, vol. I: *Van Diemen's Land from the Earliest Times to 1855* (Melbourne, 1983), and from Revd John West, *History of Tasmania* (2 vols., Launceston, 1852). For Governor Arthur's time in Van Diemen's Land see William Douglass Forsyth, *Governor Arthur's Convict System: Van Diemen's Land, 1824–36, A Study in Colonization* (London, 1935). The Maconochies' letters to Back are mostly in the Back Papers at the Scott Polar Research Institute, Cambridge. The Boyes quotation is from his diary in the library of the Royal Society of Tasmania, Hobart. Maconochie's own papers on Van Diemen's Land were published in his *Thoughts on Convict Management and Other Subjects Connected with the Australian Penal Colonies* (Hobart, 1838).

Sources and Acknowledgements

CHAPTER 5: CHANGE OF DIRECTION

The Molesworth Committee report was printed by the House of Commons on 3rd August 1838. Maconochie's paper on Arthur, *On Colonel Arthur's General Character and Government*, was eventually published by Sullivan's Cove (Adelaide, 1989). Maconochie's letters to Captain Washington come from the Royal Geographical Society archives. For Maconochie's prison designs see James Semple Kerr, *Design for Convicts: An account of design for convict establishments in the Australian colonies during the transportation era* (Library of Australian History, Sydney, 1984).

CHAPTER 6: NORFOLK ISLAND

I am indebted to Reg Wright in Sydney and Nan Smith in Norfolk Island for their help with this chapter. Reg Wright has written a very comprehensive survey of *The Commandants of Norfolk Island* for his Ph.D. thesis at Macquarie University, and Nan Smith's informative *Convict Kingston: A Guide* (Norfolk Island, 1997) has unearthed many extra items about Norfolk Island. She also chairs the Norfolk Island Historical Society. Other books on Norfolk Island consulted are, in alphabetical order: Peter Clarke, *Hell and Paradise* (New York, 1986), Frank Clune, *The Norfolk Island Story* (Sydney, 1967), Margaret Hazzard, *Punishment Short of Death: A History of the Penal Settlement at Norfolk Island* (Melbourne, 1984), Merval Hoare, *Norfolk Island, 1774–1998* (Queensland, 1999) and Raymond Nobbs, ed., *Norfolk Island and its Second Settlement 1825–1855* (Sydney, 1991), as well as the relevant chapter in *The Fatal Shore*. The Robert Jones Norfolk Island papers on Foveaux's rule are in the Dixson Library, Sydney (MS Q168). Laurence Frayne's papers describing Morisset's time, probably written at Maconochie's instigation, are in the Mitchell Library, Sydney (MS 681/1). Other sources are the *Journal of Ensign Best, 1837–1843* (New Zealand, 1966) and Joseph Anderson's *Recollections of a Peninsular Veteran* (London, 1913).

CHAPTER 7: TOUR OF INSPECTION

Thomas Cook's memoirs are published as *The Exile's Lamentations* (Library of Australian History, Sydney, 1978). For more on 'Captain Swing' see Eric Hobsbawn and George Rudé, *Captain Swing* (London, 1969). Maconochie's own account of his stay, *Norfolk Island*, was published by Hatchards, London, in 1847.

CHAPTER 8: QUEEN VICTORIA'S BIRTHDAY

All the correspondence here cited between Maconochie, Gipps and London comes from the various Parliamentary Papers published in the 1840s, and in particular Parliamentary Papers, House of Lords, 1846, vol. 7, *Correspondence between the Secretary of State for Colonies and the Governor of New South Wales respecting convict discipline administered in Norfolk Island under the superintendence of Captain Maconochie, R.N.* Maconochie's own correspondence and reports from Norfolk Island can be found there as well. For Gipps's dealings with Maconochie see the perceptive article by S.C. McCulloch, 'Sir George Gipps and Captain Alexander Maconochie: The Attempted Reforms on Norfolk Island' in *Australian Historical Studies* (vol. 7, no. 28, 1957). The story of the Irish convict Carey comes from George Rudé, *Protest and Punishment: The Story of the Social and Political Protesters Transported to Australia, 1788–1868* (Oxford, 1978).

Chapter 9: Maconochie's First Year

Charles Anderson's experiences are recounted in *Meliora, or Better Times to Come*, vol. 4 (London, 1861).

Chapter 11: Scandalous Allegations

For information on Mary Ann and Dr Reid, I am grateful to the researches carried out by Dr Gandevia, Sydney. Extracts from Father McEnroe's letters come from 'Archdeacon McEnroe on Norfolk Island 1838–42', *Australian Catholic Record* (vol. 36, no. 4, 1959). For homosexuality in Britain at the time and its bearing on Norfolk Island see also the paper by Frank Clarke in Raymond Nobbs, ed., *Norfolk Island and its Second Settlement, 1825–1855* (Sydney, 1991). The outcome of the *Governor Phillip* prisoners is described in 'A Tale of Norfolk Island' in *Chambers Miscellany*, vol. 1 (Edinburgh, 1844).

Chapter 12: Gipps's Visit

For Gipps' report on Norfolk Island, 1st April 1843, see Parliamentary Papers, House of Lords 1846, vol. 7.

Chapter 13: Recall

For more details of the cemetery on Norfolk Island see R. Nixon Dalkin, *Colonial Era Cemetery of Norfolk Island* (Sydney, 1974). What happened to Maconochie's Norfolk Island prisoners is taken from his *Crime and Punishment: The Mark System, Framed to Mix Persuasion with Punishment, and Make their Effect Improving, yet their Operation Severe* (London, 1846). Aaron Price's account of Norfolk Island is in the Dixson Library, Sydney (MS Q247-9).

Chapter 14: Back in Britain

The Jan Morris quote is from *Stones of Empire* (London, 1983), by Jan Morris and Simon Winchester. The Dickens and Maconochie details and letters are from *The Letters of Charles Dickens*, vol. 4, *1844–1846*, ed. Kathleen Tillotson (Oxford, 1977), and vol. 5, *1847–1849*, ed. Graham Storey and K.J. Fielding (Oxford, 1981), and from Philip Collins, *Dickens and Crime* (London, 1962).

Sources and Acknowledgements

The Eastern Penitentiary quote is from Dickens's *American Notes* (London, 1891). Alexander Harris's *Settlers and Convicts, by An Emigrant Mechanic* was published in London in 1847. For life on Norfolk Island after Maconochie's departure see Marcus Clarke's harrowing account in *For the Term of his Natural Life*, book IV (Melbourne, 1874). Franklin's burial is described by Roderic Owen, *The Fate of Franklin* (London, 1978). Maconochie's system in Ireland is described in *The Prison Chaplain: A Memoir of the Rev John Clay BD, Late Chaplain of Preston Gaol*, by his son Revd Walter Clay (London, 1861). Maconochie's time as Governor of Birmingham Prison is described by Charles Reade in his *It's Never too Late to Mend* (London, 1852), where Maconochie appears as Captain O'Connor. Maconochie's 'snowy white hair' is from *Our Exemplars* (see Chapter 1 above). The full Churchill 1910 quote is: 'The mood and temper of the public with regard to the treatment of crime and criminals is one of the most unfailing tests of the civilization of any country.'

I am particularly grateful to Reg Wright and Nan Smith, as mentioned above, for their information on Norfolk Island and to Anthony and Robyn Messner for showing me round Government House there. I am indebted to the librarians of the House of Lords, the London Library, the Mitchell and Dixson Libraries, Sydney, the Royal Geographical Society, the Scott Polar Research Institute, Cambridge, and University College, London, for their help. My thanks go to Grant McIntyre for his expert editing, to Gail Pirkis for producing the book so efficiently, to Matthew Taylor for his accomplished copy-editing and to Angela Combeer for her much appreciated help in preparing the manuscript.

The author and publisher would like to thank the following for permission to reproduce illustrations: frontispiece, private collection; pp. 4, 48, 82, 194 and 258, National Portrait Gallery, London; p. 13, University College London, Library; pp. 19 and 64, Allport Library and Museum of Fine Arts, State Library of Tasmania; p. 34, National Maritime Museum, Greenwich; p. 39, Government Printing Office Collection, State Library of New South Wales; p. 51, Queen Victoria Museum and Art Gallery, Launceston, Tasmania; p. 61, Tasmaniana Library, State Library of Tasmania; pp. 93 and 177, La Trobe Picture Collection, State Library of Victoria; pp. 110, 133 and 206, Mitchell Library, State Library of New South Wales; p. 117, National Library of Australia, Canberra; p. 131, Queen's Own Regiment, West Kent Museum, Maidstone.

Index

Index

Index